BUCCANEER BOYS

BUCCANEER BOYS

True Tales by Those Who Flew
'The Last All-British Bomber'

AIR COMMODORE
GRAHAM PITCHFORK MBE, FRAeS

FOREWORD BY
AIR CHIEF MARSHAL SIR MICHAEL KNIGHT KCB, AFC, FRAeS

GRUB STREET • LONDON

Published by
Grub Street
4 Rainham Close
London
SW11 6SS

A CIP record for this title is available from the British Library

ISBN-13: 9781909166110

Cover design by Sarah Driver
Design by Sarah Driver
Edited by Sophie Campbell

Printed and bound in India by Replika Press Pvt. Ltd.

Grub Street Publishing only uses
FSC (Forest Stewardship Council) paper for its books.

————

THIS BOOK IS DEDICATED TO
ALL WHO FLEW, MAINTAINED AND
SUPPORTED THE BUCCANEER,
REMEMBERING OUR COLLEAGUES
WHO FAILED TO RETURN.

CONTENTS

FOREWORD

AIR CHIEF MARSHAL
SIR MICHAEL
KNIGHT KCB, AFC,
FRAeS

BOYS?... I ask you! But we can still remember – and dream of happy days long gone.

The Blackburn Buccaneer – the last all-British bomber – was, without doubt, one of the best. Indeed, most of those once young 'rips' featured in this book would claim it was <u>the</u> best. Certainly in terms of capability, adaptability and any number of other '-ilities' one could mention, the old 'Bucc' was up at the top.

Brilliantly designed for the job it could do so effectively – ultra low-level maritime strike/attack for the Royal Navy – it proved more than capable of adapting to the overland role with, firstly, the South African Air Force and, later, the Royal Air Force. Rugged, fast, manoeuvrable and at all times purposeful, it was a joy to fly, though beware anyone who took liberties. Like any aircraft (or, come to that, most of mankind's technological creations) the Buccaneer could bite if she felt she was being treated with less than due care and attention. But the limits were pretty generous; and it was certainly possible to stretch them a little from time to time. In this book there are one or two rather interesting illustrations of that.

All that said – and allowing for the fact that it <u>was</u> the aircraft that brought us all together – *Buccaneer Boys* is really about the people who operated and maintained her over a thirty-three-year period as a front-line combat aircraft with three air arms.

The Buccaneer first came into my own life in 1965 when, working for the, then, Deputy Controller of Aircraft (RAF) in the old Ministry of Aviation, we were heavily involved in picking up the pieces from the devastation of a new government's assault on the services' procurement programmes. Our most immediate task was to find some means of replacing the cancelled TSR2; and, among several possibilities, was a so-called 'Buccaneer 2-star' – a much developed variant of the Fleet Air Arm's prize front-line asset. As ever, cost was the decider; and its ever-present conspirator was compromise. Against a deal of opposition from many quarters, we eventually got the Buccaneer, though not the '2-star' add-ons that would have made it an even better bet but which might well have called into question the need for MRCA/Tornado.

A few years after the aircraft had entered RAF service, and an exhilarating conversion to the aircraft, I found myself much closer to the action – first as OC RAF Laarbruch (with XV and 16 Squadrons) and, later, as AOC 1 Group (with all the rest of the RAF's Buccaneer force). It proved relatively easy to exercise the 'Command' function in those jobs; but 'Control' was a much trickier business. Buccaneer aircrew tended to be – and have remained to this day – distinctly 'free spirits', up to every trick in the book while managing to stay, by and large, just the right side of the law. A wild bunch indeed, but great aviators; professional to their finger-tips and with a real passion for their jobs, but with more than their fair share of genuine 'characters' who were determined to live life to the full. I believe Graham Pitchfork to have brought all that out in his selection of those whose stories are collected here.

This is a book about an aircraft that can have few equals in the affection in which it is held by all who knew her. Witness the quite remarkable history of the Buccaneer Aircrew Association – probably the most active and best supported of all such bodies. As related here, it came into being immediately following the truly dramatic 'last hurrah' of the Bucc force at RAF Lossiemouth in March 1994. An extremely 'social' weekend had been preceded by one of the most engaging (not to say 'exciting') demonstrations of eight Buccaneers flying impeccable formation patterns before breaking away to give the airfield one of the most spectacular 'waxings' to which it had ever been subjected. At one time I was not alone among the more senior witnesses to avert my gaze, lest I be later called to give an eyewitness account to a seemingly inevitable Board of Inquiry. In the event, no untoward incident, and no B of I. Professional to the end and flown to the limits, the last of the 'Buccaneer Boys' had staged a fitting climax to an era of great flying.

In reading this well-researched and well-presented volume, the blend of the serious is laced with more than the occasional shaft of sheer good humour; and that was – and is – the very essence of life as a 'Buccaneer Boy'. Vividly presented in their own words, this is a book about military aviation by military aviators themselves. Sit back, and enjoy it.

Michael Knight

ACKNOWLEDGEMENTS

This book would never have reached publication without the contributions and great support I have been given by my colleagues, the 'Buccaneer Boys'. To those who have given away some of their trade secrets and provided the chapters that follow, I am especially grateful. Their names appear with their own chapter and I trust they will accept this as due recognition for their superb narratives.

There are others who have helped in various and valuable ways and I would not wish their contributions to go un-noticed so many thanks to Tim Cockerell, Johan Conradie, Barry Dove, Andy Evans, Ewan Fraser, Peter Gooding, John Harvey, Peter Huett, Steve Jarmain, Ben Laite, Ken Mackenzie, Tony Richardson and Norman Roberson.

Having received so much assistance from Buccaneer colleagues it is almost invidious to single out individuals but I want to thank our most senior 'Buccaneer Boy' Sir Michael Knight for his eloquent Foreword and the support he gives to the Buccaneer Aircrew Association. My old friend Tom Eeles has been a great help with ideas, support and proof reading. Jan Guyt has been tremendously helpful as the linkman in South Africa. Finally, without the support of David Herriot this book would have been a very much more difficult project. He has, in effect, been my adjutant. He has encouraged and cajoled some of the Boys, acted as a superb liaison officer with our South African colleagues, he has proof read all the chapters, corrected errors, offered suggestions and additions, provided photographs and a superb chapter, and been a constant source of enthusiastic encouragement. Any credit that may accrue from the publication of this book is due in a large measure to his efforts.

The vast majority of photographs have been provided by the authors and from my own collection. Every care has been taken to identify copyright holders of these photographs. However, if I have unwittingly transgressed, I apologise. The few photographs that have come from other sources have been acknowledged in the appropriate photograph caption. I am grateful to 24 Squadron SAAF, Denis Calvert, Malcolm Irving and Frank Mormoni for these additional photographs.

I also want to thank my son Paul who has been a great encouragement and offered some superb ideas and suggestions.

Finally, I must thank the Grub Street team. As always, the support and help given by John Davies, Sophie, Sarah and Natalie has been outstanding. It is a pleasure to work with them.

Graham Pitchfork

CHAPTER ONE

THE BUCCANEER –
A WAY OF LIFE

GRAHAM PITCHFORK

Early in 1965 I was approaching the end of a three-year tour on a Germany-based Canberra photographic reconnaissance squadron when the Boss suggested it was time to think about a choice for my next posting. "An exchange tour", was my immediate response.

Some weeks later he called me into his office. "An exchange posting has come through for you", he uttered. Visions of the Australian beaches or the Californian mountains flashed through my mind as he explained, "the Royal Navy has offered a slot for an RAF crew on their new Buccaneer aircraft, you are to be the navigator and you report to Lossiemouth in April." After a deep breath, a cursory thanks and a study of the map to discover that the exotic beaches and the mountains would be in the north of Scotland, I repaired to the bar with the thought that at least it was better than the alternative, the V-Force. Little did I know it but a life-changing experience had just started and the Buccaneer was about to play a huge role in my life.

I thought it would be prudent to find out about this new aircraft, the Buccaneer, before meeting the instructors at Lossiemouth. In tracing the history of its development, one has to go back to the early 1950s and the outbreak of the new world order of the 'Cold War' when the Soviet Union began to create a navy with a global capability. Pre-eminent in its shipbuilding programme was the development of the 17,000-ton, heavily gun-armed Sverdlov class cruiser.

To counter this threat, the Navy Board had issued Naval Air Requirement NA 39 in 1953. This specified that the primary role of the aircraft was to be the attack of ships at

A Sverdlov cruiser refuels off south-west England.

sea or large coastal targets, which would be radar-discreet and identifiable at long range. The primary weapons were listed as an anti-ship homing bomb and a tactical nuclear weapon, with an additional requirement to deliver a large range of other conventional weapons. The aircraft was also to be capable of acting as an air-to-air refuelling tanker. The operational profile envisaged a 400-mile radius of action, with a descent from high level to very low level just outside the detection range of a target's radar, followed by a high-speed low-level dash to and from the target. Stringent weight limits were imposed and the aircraft had to be capable of operating and being supported from the Royal Navy's current aircraft carriers. This imposed maximum take-off and landing weights and the aircraft size had to allow it to be lowered to the ship's hangar by the lifts.

The naval requirement set a daunting technical challenge, and in July 1955 the Blackburn and General Aircraft Company at Brough were awarded a contract to build twenty development aircraft. Just three years later, on 30 April 1958, Derek Whitehead, Blackburn's chief test pilot who had served in the Fleet Air Arm, made the maiden flight of the aircraft, soon to be christened the Buccaneer.

Development was rapid and in March 1961 the Royal Navy's Buccaneer Intensive Flying Trials Unit, 700Z Flight, was formed at HMS Fulmar (Lossiemouth). In July the following year, the first squadron, 801, was formed and in January 1963 the headquarters squadron, 809, was assembled (re-numbered 736 Squadron in April 1965). In the meantime, the second and last operational Mark 1 squadron, 800, had been commissioned and embarked in HMS **Eagle**.

It was at this time that Graham Smart and I arrived at Lossiemouth to start our training with 736 Squadron. Within days, Bill Ryce and Geoff Homan had taken us through the simulator and alerted us to the myriad of malfunctions the Buccaneer Mark 1 might throw at us, most of which we were to experience over the next three years. It was then time for my familiarisation flight (Fam 1), with Andy Alsop drawing the short straw.

On the pre-flight walk round I was surprised at the size and bulk of the aircraft, not least the amazing undercarriage that looked as if it had been cast in an iron foundry and ought to be in a ship's boiler room. Despite the two Gyron Junior engines running at full power the take-off run seemed to last forever, but the downward slope at the end of Runway 23 provided some extra momentum. The very smooth ride at low level and the view from the back seat were superb and, after the sedate Canberra, everything seemed to happen very quickly and I immediately realised that this was the aircraft for me. Over the next twenty years of active flying in the RAF, I was never to change that first opinion.

Unknown to Graham and me, our arrival at Lossiemouth as the first RAF crew on the Buccaneer was to herald an amazing, and almost certainly unique, relationship between the aircrew of the Royal Navy and the RAF which extended way beyond just operating the aircraft. In addition to the mutual respect for each other's professionalism, a dynamic, and at times hilarious, connection developed and blossomed as an increasing number of RAF aircrew joined the Buccaneer squadrons of the Fleet Air Arm (FAA).

Just before we started our brief conversion course, the first two South African Air Force (SAAF) crews had completed their conversion and were about to welcome six more of their crews to start the build-up of 24 (SAAF) Squadron and so the beginnings of another great relationship amongst the Buccaneer fraternity started to blossom.

By June, and after a mere twenty-seven flying hours on the Mark 1, it was time for us to join 800 Squadron and we were soon embarked in *Eagle* heading for the Indian Ocean and the Far East.

At this time the first of the more powerful Mark 2 aircraft, powered by the magnificent Rolls-Royce Spey engines, entered service with 700B Flight and it was soon replacing the Mark 1s of 801 Squadron. The South Africans were equipped with the Buccaneer S.50 (the overseas derivative of the Mark 2) and on 27 October 1965, eight aircraft left on the long flight back to South Africa (one was lost en route). Eight more followed by sea and 24 Squadron was formed.

After an adventurous year embarked in *Eagle,* and 154 deck landings, I returned to Lossiemouth to spend two years as an instructor with 736 Squadron where Graham Smart had arrived a few months earlier and was one of the qualified flying instructors (QFIs).

During this period, the Labour government announced a series of major defence cuts, including the cancellation of the TSR2 aircraft and CVA 01, the Royal Navy's follow-on aircraft carrier programme. The latter had resulted in the decision to run down the fixed-wing aircrew training for the FAA, which explained why on arrival back on 736 Squadron in September 1966 there was a small group of RAF pilots and navigators in the training programme.

Over the next two years, an increasing number of RAF aircrew joined us at Lossiemouth, the majority to become the foundation of the RAF squadrons that would be formed in the early 1970s. However, in 1966 that was the future. In the meantime, they were spread amongst the embarked squadrons on *Victorious, Hermes, Eagle* and *Ark Royal* and RAF aircrew would join FAA squadrons for the next eleven years.

In 1968 it was announced that the RAF would eventually take over the air support of maritime forces from land bases. The Buccaneers of the FAA would be transferred to the

RAF in addition to a new build of aircraft to be delivered direct to the RAF. In early 1969 my time with the FAA was over and I joined Wg Cdr Roy Watson at RAF Honington, the airfield designated to be the home for the RAF's Buccaneer force.

Such was the short timescale, it was decided that the FAA would train the first eight RAF courses at Lossiemouth. By this time, some of the RAF exchange crews with carrier time had joined their naval colleagues on the instructional staff of 736 Squadron. So, by the time of the formation of the RAF's first squadron, No.12, at RAF Honington on 1 October 1969, the aircrews of both services had been operating and socialising together for a number of years.

This 'special relationship' was to be further cemented in 1971 when it was no longer viable for the FAA to maintain its own training squadron and the RAF undertook the responsibility for training FAA Buccaneer crews on the recently-formed 237 Operational Conversion Unit (OCU) at Honington. The leading players on the OCU in those early days were a mix of RAF and RN crews and this would continue until the de-commissioning of 809 Squadron in November 1978. It was an arrangement that worked perfectly.

Soon after 12 Squadron became established at Honington, the first of two squadrons destined for RAF Germany, XV Squadron was formed and quickly departed for Laarbruch with 16 Squadron becoming the second Germany squadron shortly afterwards. In the meantime, 809 Squadron arrived at Honington and a Royal Navy Wing, commanded initially by Cdr Roger Dimmock RN, himself a former Buccaneer CO, was formed and remained for the next five years. And so the social extremes perfected by both services at Lossiemouth and on the aircraft carriers continued at Honington and the local hostelries of Suffolk.

During a four-year stint at Honington as the station built up it was exciting to experience all the facets of this unique period as the 'brotherhood' of Buccaneer aircrew developed and to be able to maintain close professional and social links with my chums who had served in the FAA together with the new RAF crews joining the Buccaneer world.

After a year at Staff College, I returned to Honington in 1974 to be a flight commander on the latest RAF squadron to form, No. 208, under the command of Pete Rogers. Unlike the other RAF units, the squadron was assigned to Allied Forces Northern Europe (AFNORTH) and we were to spend much time exercising over Norway. By now Honington, with three squadrons, a large OCU and with regular visits from our sister squadrons in Germany, was a lively place.

After a tour in MOD, it was a return to Honington in the spring of 1979 for a final sojourn. First there was a need for another refresher course at the OCU before taking over command of 208 Squadron from Phil Pinney. We shared 'A' Hangar with the last RAF Buccaneer squadron to form, No. 216, commanded by an old friend Peter Sturt.

Sadly, 216 was to have a short life as a Buccaneer squadron. Following the grounding of the fleet after a fatal accident during a Red Flag exercise in 1980, insufficient airframes were recovered to enable the squadron to continue and the air and ground crews joined 12 Squadron, which had just moved to RAF Lossiemouth.

After a fantastic tour in command of 208 with my outstanding pilot Eddie Wyer keeping us out of mischief (!), it was time to bid farewell to the mighty Buccaneer in December 1981. For my final sortie, Rob Wright had arranged to take an eight-ship to Lossiemouth

The author's final flight, 3 December 1981.

for an overnight stop. After a memorable evening with the team, it was a bleary-eyed and sad Pitchfork who headed for the morning briefing and a farewell from the station commander, my old friend 'Sandy' Wilson, who had been in cahoots with Rob Wright.

As we walked to the line to man our aircraft one appeared to be missing. Rob had arranged, by some brilliant intelligence gathering, to have mine parked on an adjoining dispersal, the exact spot where my love affair with the Buccaneer had begun fifteen years earlier.

After a stream take-off and a farewell bomb on Tain range, the eight of us headed south to pay a visit to our old haunts. The Phantom boys at Leuchars got a rude awakening but we were gone before they could react (not for the first time). Then it was a final salute to the Spadeadam electronic warfare range before a nostalgic flight over the factory at Brough with crowds of the brilliant British Aerospace workers out to see us. Then on to stir the other Phantom outfits at Coningsby but as we approached the Norfolk coast the weather worsened.

With no hope of a final 'airfield attack' over the base that had been my home for so many years, we had to send the other seven ahead to make singleton approaches before we joined the GCA pattern to land with a 200-foot cloud base. It was not the way to fly the last of my 2,000 flying hours on the Buccaneer but any disappointment was softened when we taxied into dispersal to be met by all the squadron air and ground crew and my flying career on the Buccaneer was over surrounded by the men I admired the most.

The Buccaneer era had many more years ahead of it and, shortly after handing over 208 to Ben Laite, the squadron left for Lossiemouth, followed not long afterwards by 237 OCU, to form a powerful and formidable maritime strike wing there under the command of 18 Group.

Meanwhile, in South Africa, 24 Squadron had been developing tactics at sea and overland and from 1978 their Buccaneers became increasingly involved in the Border Wars in Northern South West Africa (later Namibia) and Southern Angola using weapons and electronic aids developed by South African industry.

My own involvement with the aircraft was far from over. In 1984 I was working in the Directorate of Air Plans in MOD with responsibility for the Tornado GR1 and the Buccaneer and their associated weapons. It was at a time when significant financial savings had to be found and the planned update of the Buccaneer's nav/attack system was in great jeopardy and likely to be cut. Using some dubious mathematics, a smooth tongue and a little skulduggery the budget for a planned Tornado attrition buy was 'adjusted'. This released sufficient funds to allow a large proportion of the remaining Buccaneer force to be modified with the new system. After all those years sitting in the ergonomic slum of the back seat, I had finally made a worthwhile contribution to its modernisation!

The outstanding service of the RAF Germany squadrons came to an end on 29 February 1984 when 16 Squadron handed over its strike role to the new Tornado force.

The Lossiemouth Wing had another ten years to run when it introduced new weapons into the inventory and developed new tactics in support of maritime operations. Then, in January 1991 the RAF's Buccaneer force, which excelled at ultra-low level operations over the sea, went to war at medium level overland during the First Gulf War, but I will leave those involved in that epic story to relate their experiences later in this book.

As the RAF's Buccaneers went to war, the SAAF closed the chapter on their Buccaneer operations when 24 Squadron stood down on 30 June 1991. The attrition of the small force over twenty-five years had made it no longer viable to maintain the few remaining airframes.

Finally, at the end of March 1994, the mighty Buccaneer bowed out of service with the RAF – and that is a tale for later.

People often asked what made the Buccaneer fraternity such a close-knit community and one that developed such a huge affection for the aircraft. It seems to me that there are a number of reasons. The aircraft was unique in many respects, not least because it was one of the few to enter British service that met exactly a specific requirement and it continued to do so throughout its service life. Designed to operate in a very demanding environment, it enjoyed thirty-three years of distinguished service with the Royal Navy, the Royal Air Force and the South African Air Force.

The aircraft was a winner. The Royal Navy was immensely impressed by its capability to meet their requirement so successfully. The South Africans chose the aircraft as its long-range strike aircraft against international competition and took it to war where it displayed its versatility as a ground/attack aircraft. Initially, the situation for the RAF was different. With the prospect of acquiring the TSR2 and then the American-built F-111 there was no interest in taking the Buccaneer into the RAF inventory. Indeed, there was open resistance and apathy amongst some of the senior echelons of the service. Then, quite unexpectedly, the RAF was given no choice; it had to accept the aircraft.

Those of us who had flown with the FAA knew we had something special but this was far from the wider RAF view. The Phantom and the Harrier were the new breed of fast jets and the Buccaneer was looked upon as the Cinderella – some said the ugly sister. That did not bother us because we knew we could and would do the job.

A 736 Squadron Buccaneer in its element at low level.

It took some time to convince the rest of the RAF but the hard work and massive enthusiasm of those early days of 12, XV and 16 Squadrons set the tone. All this, of course, was being developed at a time when our naval chums continued to impress in the far corners of the world and our South African friends were flying the aircraft to the extreme ends of the flight envelope on long-range operations.

There is another reason. Flying very low and very fast – 100 feet and 580 knots – is, without doubt, the most exhilarating and demanding form of flying, requiring great teamwork, concentration and skill. This was a key part in shaping the attitudes and personal styles of those who flew the Buccaneer, which in turn was the bedrock of the camaraderie of the force. Time and time again we proved that we were formidable and amongst the best of the best. The reputation gained on operations and exercises on the international stage such as the Beira Patrol, the South African bush wars, tactical bombing competitions, Red and Maple Flags and the Gulf War speaks for itself.

But, behind all the magnificence of the aircraft and the thrilling environment we flew in there was the most important element; those who flew the Buccaneer and those who gave us such outstanding and loyal support on the ground. The scene had been set by the unparalleled cooperation and friendships developed between the FAA and the RAF to the extent that all that separated us was a different shade of blue uniform. It was our collective determination, our insistence on excellence (there was no mercy on the OCU for those who were unable to achieve the high standards demanded), our enthusiasm and, above all, our professionalism that were the essential ingredients for success.

Finally, there was another aspect. We were not a big force and most of us knew each other. Off duty we knew how to enjoy ourselves and have fun, often at the expense of each other. Amongst the humour and banter there was also a modest streak of irreverence and higher authority did not always condone our high spirits, not that they were aware of many of them! We left our mark on many establishments we visited and these were spread across the world. Too numerous to mention, it is unlikely that they will ever forget the 'Buccaneer Boys'.

I can do no better than allow Tony Ogilvy, one of a breed of outstanding young navy pilots in the late 1960s, to summarise the feelings of the Buccaneer fraternity:

"The spirit amongst the mixed RN/RAF crews was surely what military *esprit de corps* was meant to be. Why am I still eager to get to the Blitz [annual reunion] every year, along with all the others? Simple – we knew we were the best then, and we still think that way now."

So, let the 'Buccaneer Boys' tell you in their own words why Tony is right.

CHAPTER TWO
IN AT THE BEGINNING

BILL RYCE

It was September 1960 and I was serving in HMS *Ark Royal* in 800 Naval Air Squadron (NAS), flying Supermarine Scimitars. One evening I was enjoying a well-earned gin and tonic in the wardroom when I was called to see my boss, Lt Cdr D P (Danny) Norman, and I was expecting him to discuss with me a rather hairy event that occurred earlier in the afternoon.

Although the boss was interested in this episode, he wanted to tell me that I would be joining 700Z Flight, which was to be the IFTU (Intensive Flying Trials Unit) for the Buccaneer S1, when it formed in January 1961. This was exciting news for me.

Once I was settled into 700Z Flight at Lossiemouth, I was anxious to get my hands on the Buccaneer, but patience was required, as our first aircraft did not arrive for some months. Time was not wasted however and I managed to get a lot of flying on a variety of other aircraft, particularly the Hunter T8 and GA 11, Sea Hawk and Vampire T22. Who could ask for more?

700Z Flight was a close-knit outfit with seven pilots initially. The Boss was Alan 'Spiv' Leahy and the senior pilot was Ted Anson, a test pilot who had spent time with Blackburn Aircraft Company flying the Buccaneer. The other pilots were very experienced, most with Seahawk and Scimitar experience. Sometime later Bill Foote, an exchange pilot from the US Navy, joined us. All the observers were experienced on a range of aircraft including Sea Venom, Sea Vixen and Gannet and were led by John Coleman, the senior observer.

There was also a very hard working team of engineers, electricians and weapon specialists, led by John Dunphy and Hugh Strange. John was the airframe and engine man and Hugh was the electrical expert. Lt Cdr Bain was also attached to the flight; he was an aeronautical engineer who specialised in analysing data and producing reports on the performance of the aircraft. Also based at Lossiemouth were civilian representatives of all the main suppliers of equipment for the Buccaneer.

I finally got airborne in the Buccaneer on 22 August 1961 with the redoubtable John Coleman in the back seat. We pilots had completed a ground school course with Blackburns but there was no flight simulator available at this time, so one has to admire the observer in the back seat as his pilot took off for the first time. Having been used to the superb acceleration of the Scimitar, it was quite a shock to 'trundle' down the runway in the Buccaneer. However, once it got going it flew beautifully.

I immediately felt 'at home' in the aircraft and thought it was particularly good at low level. I had spent many hours flying low in the Scimitar and the Sea Hawk, but the Buccaneer was much better, solid as a rock especially at high speed. Until this time I had only flown single-seat combat aircraft and I soon came to appreciate the luxury of flying with another crew member. There was always someone to share problems, and the Buccaneer Mark 1 did present us with the odd problem.

During this period we received our own Hunter T8 fitted with the Buccaneer instrument panel. With just a few pilots to fly it, we used it for 'continuation' flying (keeping our hand in) and we could take it away for the weekend to visit friends and family; also on a Saturday morning it was useful in winter to check the snow conditions in the Cairngorms. We also had a Sea Prince, which we used to fetch spares from the Blackburn airfields at Holme-on-Spalding-Moor and Brough.

As the weeks passed, more aircraft arrived and we were able to accelerate the trials programme. The job of the IFTU was to fly the aircraft as hard as possible, to test the aircraft systems and to confirm the specification and performance that Blackburn had guaranteed. This required flying many profiles from sea level to max height and to test the weapons systems. The observer in the back seat did most of the latter. The engineering team also had much work to do, checking the aircraft systems after each flight, sorting out any problems and producing a servicing and maintenance schedule that would allow maximum utilisation of the aircraft when in front-line service in a carrier.

I think it was the fourth aircraft that arrived in all white livery; until then the paint scheme was the normal dark grey on top and white underneath. Apparently this new paint scheme provided some protection from a nuclear blast…a sobering thought.

One of the problems we had to deal with in the early days was malfunctioning IGVs (inlet guide vanes). Their job was to channel the air into the engine and sometimes they would slam shut, which could be quite disconcerting. I remember leading three aircraft on a low-level sortie round the Western Highlands when one of the student pilots called out in a strangled voice that the IGVs on both engines had closed. After what must have seemed an age to him, the vanes opened again and we completed the flight without further incident. Sadly the following week, this student took himself off the course and pursued other avenues. I admired him for doing this, but was sad because I think he would have made the grade.

The other troubling problem we encountered was when the BLC (boundary layer control) or 'blow' system failed. In the landing configuration this could be very tricky, as the approach and landing speed we used was dependent on the air from the blow system flowing over the wings, flaps and tail-plane. A BLC failure could result in the wing stalling. As a precaution for a short period, we did not use full flap for landing and consequently we needed a higher landing speed, but this was no good when landing on a carrier so we had no option but to sort out the BLC problems.

The operational requirement for the Buccaneer was to enable the aircraft to counter the threat from the Soviet Sverdlov cruisers by dropping a tactical nuclear bomb on the ship. This bomb was carried in the aircraft's internal bomb bay and it was released in a toss manoeuvre, which was very straightforward. I had made many similar attacks in the Scimitar, but with the bomb on a wing station and that was much more demanding and exciting.

We had to fly low level at night and this was never simple. Over land you had to know the terrain and, depending on conditions, we would regularly fly at 200 feet. Over the sea however, terrain was not a problem and we flew lower. I think the 'requirement' was to be able to fly at 200 feet but the lower you flew, the longer you kept out of the target ship's radar. We had a neat little traffic light system geared to the radio altimeter to help us maintain height. You dialled in the height you wanted to fly and the lowest I recall using was fifty feet at night. When you were steady at your selected height you had a green light; if you went below this height, you saw a red light and if you went high it was amber. On a dark night if you saw the lights of a fishing boat it was a bit off-putting, as the boat always seemed to be higher than the aircraft. Not an exercise for the faint hearted.

Certainly one of the most enjoyable experiences for me in my flying career was to fly low level through the Highlands on a clear day in the autumn, marvelling at the changing colours of the heather on the hills and mountains, to enjoy the gin clear air which gave unlimited visibility and to see the deep blue-coloured water in the lochs and sea.

On 17 July 1962 the first front-line squadron, 801, formed. I was appointed to this new outfit but sadly I had to be 'loaned' back to 700Z Flight as Bill Foote and his observer, Maurice Day, had been killed practising for the Farnborough Air Show in September.

After Bill and Maurice died I had a rather unnerving experience. I regularly visited the Steamboat Inn in Lossiemouth to down a pint or two of 'Heavy' and play darts with the locals. As I entered the pub on this particular evening, the whole place went silent. The fishermen who recovered Bill and Maurice from the sea were regulars in the pub and known to me. They thought that I was the pilot of the crashed aircraft and they had just toasted my memory. It was a very spooky feeling!

I had a couple of months to work up the routine for Farnborough. It started with a low fast run down the runway (550 knots), then a pull up with about 5g, when upside down a turn through thirty degrees to the right, then drop the undercarriage when speed permitted, and extend the flaps on the turn to final approach. The idea was to land as soon as possible by making a tight, diving circuit and to be visible to the assembled crowd, thereby demonstrating the manoeuvrability of the aircraft. It was certainly a busy few minutes. I, with Pat Cummuskey in the back seat, duly performed this at Farnborough, thankfully without incident.

The Triumph motorcycle company wanted some publicity and offered the five Buccaneer crews who were performing at Farnborough, five Triumph Tina scooters for the duration of our time at the air show. This was a very attractive proposition though Spiv had his

Members of 700Z Flight board Mike Hornblower's Bentley, NA39.

reservations...with good reason. I did not have a motorcycle licence but that did not appear to be a problem. I borrowed an RN Vespa, drove it round the squadron car park then set off to Elgin. I had been briefed on the route to take and to wear my uniform so that the examiner could spot me. A few days later my motorcycle licence arrived in the post. No real surprise that some of the Tinas were less than perfect when we handed them back.

We had publicity photographs taken before we left Lossiemouth for Farnborough. Mike Hornblower owned an old Bentley with the registration number NA39 (Blackburn's designation for the aircraft) that was rather neat, so we all piled in for the photographer.

I had been flying the Buccaneer for almost two years before returning to *Ark Royal* to carry out some deck-landing trials. Deck operations always add a little spice to any flight and it was early in 1963 that I saw the *Ark* once again, turning into wind and preparing to recover aircraft, as we let down into the circuit in Lyme Bay. I already had many deck landings under my belt, in the Sea Hawk and Scimitar, and I was looking forward to the Buccaneer challenge.

Anyone with deck-landing experience knows that it is not a good idea to regularly catch the first wire. It is the nearest to the aft end of the flight deck and the ramifications of this are obvious. To avoid this I had been in the habit, in the Scimitar, of flying the approach with the 'meatball' (the deck landing projector sight) slightly high and this ensured that I pretty well always caught three or four wire. I briefed Geoff Homan, my observer, on what I was going to do as we prepared for our landing. The approach was good and steady,

801 Squadron commissioning ceremony at Lossiemouth.

there was minimal movement of the deck so it was an 'easy' approach and I remember thinking that the visual aspect was much better than that from the Scimitar cockpit. I was mortified therefore, when we hit the deck and did not feel the comforting retardation you get when a wire is caught. With maximum power on the Gyron Juniors, we still sank a bit as we left the deck and cleaned up for another approach. I felt the flush of embarrassment for making a bolter, but the lesson was learnt – meatball right in the middle for the Buccaneer.

I enjoyed operating the Buccaneer from a carrier. The catapult launch from the flight deck was sometimes a bit critical depending on the aircraft weight, air temperature and wind speed over the deck. The Gyron Junior engines were not over powerful and if an engine failed during the launch you had a problem. The approach and landing was straightforward. Line up (there was no cross wind), fly the meatball and nail the speed. An audio signal told you when you were flying at the correct speed and a warning audio told you if you were getting below the datum speed.

We operated from the *Ark Royal* for nearly a month before returning to Lossiemouth and it was incident free for me until near the end of this period. We were operating in the Bay of Biscay and on the day in question we were going to make a four-aircraft strike on a target in France and then fly on to Yeovilton. All went well until we were approaching the airfield. It was overcast, and raining, with a 200-foot cloud base. I was concentrating on the radar controller's instructions and was about 800 foot on final approach with my gear down and selecting flap. In the Buccaneer, when the flap goes down there is a counter-balancing tail-plane flap that has to go up. If it does not, the aircraft continues to nose forward with dire consequences.

This is what happened to me. I immediately stopped the flaps extending, carried out a 360-degree turn to the right under radar control, sorted out the flap situation on the standby panel and came back on to finals. In the end the landing was no problem but for five minutes it had been quite frightening.

About three months later 801 Squadron was preparing to embark in *Victorious* and would be the first operational Buccaneer squadron to go to sea. I was looking forward to this sea time very much, but it was not to be. It had been decided that there was a requirement for a QFI, with Buccaneer experience, to help run Buccaneer pilot training and I was selected for this job. I certainly did not volunteer to become an instructor as I was enjoying life as a squadron pilot and would rather have stayed with 801 Squadron, but orders are orders.

Consequently in July 1963 I joined 219 Course at the Central Flying School (CFS), Little Rissington, back in the tender arms of the RAF, who had taught me to fly a few years earlier.

The Jet Provost was a delightful aircraft to fly and I certainly benefited from the CFS course. The instruction was excellent in both the flying and ground school and the RAF should be proud of this facility. The CFS was kind enough to give me a trophy before they packed me off back to Lossiemouth. If I had been given a choice at this stage, I would have liked to do some basic flying instruction, being newly qualified and with a new set of skills, but I was also perfectly happy to return to the Buccaneer world.

A very busy time followed. I put the trainee pilots through the simulator course, I flew with them in the Hunter T8 equipped with Buccaneer instruments and, when I felt they were ready, I sat in the back seat on their first three trips. This was overkill really and I quickly reduced this to their first trip and if this was satisfactory, an experienced observer flew with them on the remaining familiarisation sorties.

On one memorable day in August 1964 I sat in the back seat twice, both flights with first-tour student pilots. During the first flight we had a hydraulic failure and on the second an engine fire which led to a single-engine landing. The student pilots handled both emergencies very well and this gave me confidence that the conversion training we had set in place was sound. All in a day's work!

29 November 1965 was a normal working day at Lossiemouth but snow and freezing temperatures had not allowed any flying. I was 736 Squadron's duty officer so when air traffic rang, I took the call. They asked me to arrange a weather check to the north of the Moray Firth to see if any more snow was heading our way. They wanted to know if it was worth restarting snow clearance. Earlier in the day, they had tried to clear the runway but even that was stopped due to the bad weather. I went out to the runway to check the conditions and phoned back to say that in my opinion, Runway 29 was unfit for operations. The second, rather apologetic call from air traffic passed on the message that the request for a weather check was not actually a request. Such is life.

The 'landing' on Lossiemouth's icy runway.

I decided to make the flight myself and Trevor Ling, a trainee observer, joined me. The aircraft was sliding all over the place as we taxied out and with some difficulty we got lined up on R/W 29 and started a rolling take-off as the brakes would not hold the aircraft stationary when power was applied. I had briefed Trevor that if we abandoned the take-off, I would drop the hook and hopefully we would take the wire at the far end of the runway. With some relief we got airborne but then things started to go wrong.

As the Buccaneer QFI and simulator instructor I was pretty familiar with the aircraft systems and the emergency procedures that we taught the trainee crews. The multiple failures that now started to develop were well beyond any sequence of problems that I could have dreamed up.

When I selected gear up, we lost all the instrument indications in the cockpit. We had suffered a total AC failure and the back-up electrical supply also failed. We also lost most of our hydraulics (both main systems and one flying control system). However this was not obvious to me at the time, as I could still control the aircraft. There was some external noise, which I could not place, and apparently this was the nose wheel that had slewed sideways and jammed against the fuselage but obviously there was no cockpit indication.

I levelled off at about 2,000 feet and turned right, over the sea, planning to recover back on to runway 29. What worried me, when I was trying to sort things out, was that I could not find a common thread to the problems we were experiencing. I was half expecting something catastrophic to happen next. It went through my mind that shards of ice, thrown up during the take-off run may have damaged or cut the electric cables in the

A safe but unorthodox arrival.

wheel wells but I was too busy to dwell on that. I glanced over at the airfield and the icy runway did not seem very inviting but it looked considerably better than the grey Moray Firth below us.

I lowered the gear and got reassuring noises, but no undercarriage lights, so I asked air traffic to do a visual check. They replied that all three wheels appeared to be down, so I decided to land. I had no idea of my flap/droop/airbrake situation, so speed control on the approach was a bit of a problem and I was basically flying by 'feel'. I remember telling Trevor that if I called 'eject' it was not a subject for discussion!

On finals, the controls felt pretty slack, so it was with a sense of relief that I put the aircraft down on the end of the runway. I was aware of a bit of sliding, which I was expecting, but then I felt the port wing dropping, which I was not. I held the wing up as long as I could, but as we lost aerodynamic lift down it went and we started curving over the grass to the left. I was mindful all the time that Trevor was a student, but he was very helpful throughout the short flight and got rid of the canopy as we were doing our imitation of a tractor ploughing up the ground. It transpired that the port undercarriage leg was not locked down.

Pay back time. That evening when gathered in the wardroom bar, a few of the crews who had been through the simulator course with me said it could not have happened to a better person – the biter bit! I was about to leave the RN and this was almost my last flight but I was able to make one more, thankfully incident free.

By the autumn of 1965 the Buccaneer world was expanding quite rapidly and many more crews, including the first RAF crew, had been trained.

I left the RN at the beginning of 1966 after ten years as a pilot in the Fleet Air Arm and I felt very grateful for the interesting and sometimes exciting times that I had enjoyed, all the time working with some exceptional people.

My flying days however were not over and I flew for another thirty-two years, but that is another story.

———

For his outstanding flying and airmanship, the Admiralty awarded Bill a Green Endorsement, which read:

'On 29 November, 1965 at 1400Z Lieutenant W P Ryce, Royal Navy was flying Buccaneer S Mk.1 XN 967 when the aircraft suffered a complete AC power failure. Subsequently Lieutenant Ryce reacted in an extremely professional and competent manner, in dealing with a considerable number of apparently unrelated but critical failures of various systems, which resulted in the aircraft being recovered with the minimum damage.'

CHAPTER THREE

OPERATING THE MARK 1

DAVID HOWARD

Before taking up my appointment as the senior pilot of 800 Naval Air Squadron in the spring of 1965, I needed to get back into flying practice having spent the previous eighteen months as an air warfare instructor in the classrooms at Whale Island. So it was up to Lossiemouth, an old haunt from my Seahawk and Scimitar days, to spend a few weeks on a refresher course with 764 Squadron on the Hunter.

Having completed this I went across the airfield to the Buccaneer training squadron, No. 736, for my conversion to the aircraft, which was enjoyable and uneventful. It was also an eye opener for me. Flying the Buccaneer was the first time I'd had the benefit of an observer and the pilot/observer crew gave a whole new dimension to my flying. I could concentrate on flying the aircraft to its limits while the observer handled the navigation (never my forte), a lot of the weapons systems, and the variety of checks required during different phases of flight. I knew I was going to enjoy operating the Buccaneer, and was looking forward to a front-line squadron. My conversion to type complete, it was back across the airfield to join 800 Squadron.

The Buccaneer was an all-weather strike aircraft and 'all-weather' meant night as well. My boss's dislike of night flying had not gone unnoticed by the staff at Naval Air Command HQ and we were soon ordered to get each pilot forty hours on it before we embarked in a few weeks' time. This was a very tall order and there wasn't much night at that time of the year so far north. On top of that the Buccaneer Mark 1 wasn't too hot on serviceability and we had pre-embarkation checks to complete so we were always short of aircraft.

We tried. We took off from Lossiemouth late in the evening, let down to 200 feet in the Moray Firth where it was dark, headed east to Fraserburgh before turning right to fly down the North Sea to Dover and into the English Channel where it was truly pitch black.

We landed at Yeovilton and, after a quick turn round, took off and climbed to height until we had to let down to remain in the dark, landing at Lossie at dawn. This was pretty tiring stuff but was the best we could do to meet Command's orders. I did seven trips but still clocked up less than half the required hours. Even so, we had done more night flying in that short period than the squadron had achieved in the previous year.

So, off we went to sea embarked in *Eagle*. I had been looking forward to the traditional Air Group embarkation party in the wardroom and meeting up with many old buddies. I was aware that everyone was having a good time, except the aircrew of 800 Squadron. Our teetotal boss rarely visited the bar and, as the squadron's senior pilot present, I was taking a lot of stick and couldn't understand why.

Eventually I took a friend, one of the observers who had been on the previous embarked cruise, outside and asked why we were taking so much criticism. Steve explained that the previous tour had been a disaster with aircraft constantly unserviceable and regular engine changes. The amount of flying the Buccs had achieved was very limited and, worse still, the carrier appeared to have lost patience in operating them. If there was the slightest hiccup with a Buccaneer preparing to launch, and who could blame the aircrew for being cautious, the flight was cancelled and the aircraft immediately taken off the programme. Hence the opinion of the rest of the Air Group about us, and the hassle they were giving us at the party.

The boss had not warned me what to expect. I realised I had a job on my hands if I was to turn the ship's attitude around.

The loudest mouth in the wardroom, and the most unpleasant in terms of what he thought about 800, belonged to a senior pilot on the helicopter squadron. As I returned, I got the loudest jeer from him, so I grabbed him by the lapels and lifted him clear of the deck. I snarled at him, "in six months' time, I'm going to piss all over you". He stopped laughing and I put him down. 800's recovery started right then.

After an embarkation a carrier usually had three work-up periods. The first two had been in the Mediterranean then trouble in Aden escalated and we headed down the Red Sea and started the third concentrating on night flying. The more senior of us merely required a few dusk refresher deck landings (touch and goes with the arrestor hook up until the final land on in the dark) but a handful of junior pilots had to be selected with some care to make up the night-flying team. To start with they were given dusk deck-landing practice (DLP). When they were considered proficient they were launched at dusk, flew an undemanding sortie and came back when it was fully dark for some demanding touch and goes before being recovered. We had about six crews in the night-flying team.

The more we flew the better we got, the aircraft serviceability improved, as did the morale and 800 started smiling. We flew by day, by night and we flew a lot. We were now fully a part of the Air Group. Off Aden we did most of our flying overland, when we made a lot of use of the photographic pack in the bomb bay, in what is now Yemen, using RAF Khormaksar as a diversion airfield.

By the completion of the third work-up the squadron had flown more hours than it had done during the whole of the previous tour. I never actually pissed (other than

Pre-dinner drinks in David Howard's cabin aboard the Eagle, *1966.*

metaphorically) over the unpleasant senior pilot, but it would have been fully justified. He had got the message.

For some months, most of our flying was off Aden or around Malaysia, the latter whilst disembarked at RAF Changi in Singapore. On 2 March 1966, we re-embarked from Changi having been ordered to relieve **Ark Royal** on the Beira Patrol. Harold Wilson had just established this operation after Ian Smith, the prime minister of what was then Southern Rhodesia, had made a Unilateral Declaration of Independence (UDI). After unsuccessful attempts to resolve the problem politically, the Labour government had decided to blockade oil supplies to the errant colony. Since Rhodesia (now Zimbabwe) was landlocked and had no natural oil, her only access to this essential commodity was by overland supply or by sea through the port of Beira in Mozambique. Our job would be to intercept oil tankers approaching the port to try and prevent any of them carrying oil for Smith's regime entering the harbour. I never discovered how we were supposed to stop them but presumed that Lloyds would have their details and politicians would then put pressure on the ship's owners. We wouldn't have the right to stop them, just report them.

Our passage from Singapore across the Indian Ocean was to be discreet and we avoided other shipping completely, making detours as necessary to keep out of sight. *Ark* had mechanical problems and we had to make as fast a passage as possible so there was no flying en route.

We were tasked to cover as much as we could of the Mozambique Channel. With the carrier some sixty miles east of Beira, our patrols headed out north and south to our maximum range. There was no shore diversion airfield for us to use so we always had to

Keeping fit during the Beira Patrol.

be back at the carrier ('mother') with a set minimum fuel state calculated to give us some waiting time in case the deck was not available. To minimise any problems the carrier kept the deck 'open', i.e. available for landing whenever it was required by a returning aircraft. This meant that we had to calculate the fuel and time required to get back to mother no matter how far away we might be, so that we could give the ship as much notice as we could of our required recovery time (known as Charlie time). This requirement really sharpened up our attention to range and endurance flying.

Our mediocre Gyron Junior engines were heavy on fuel and therefore our range was poor. We used Scimitars modified as airborne tankers. We would rendezvous with them at height some 100 miles outbound and refuel to full before carrying on to our patrol area. The observer picked up contacts on his radar before we let down to low level to investigate them.

After a little practice we all became adept at calculating exactly how much fuel we needed for the climb back to altitude and transit back to mother with the appropriate reserve. This allowed us to work out how long we could stay at low level for any visual sightings and a photograph of any oil tankers.

Intelligence staff had been alerted that a tanker called the *Joanna V* was making for Beira from the south. A Sea Vixen from 899 Squadron found it at maximum range but then it disappeared and further efforts to locate it failed. It was thought that the ship might be trying to creep up the coast and slip into Beira un-noticed. The intelligence officer was desperate to get a photograph of her and I was keen to get it for him and to succeed in what had become fierce inter-squadron rivalry. At first light on the morning of 4 April, two of us took off and headed south. My observer was the squadron's photo recce officer

Interception of Joanna V *during the Beira Patrol, 1966.*

and he picked up a contact on his radar and we homed in and there she was. We made a couple of photo runs using the port F. 95 camera before heading back with our precious photographs.

One of the shots on the oblique overlap photographs was perfect with our wingman's Buccaneer in the foreground and there, in clear white letters on the ship's black hull, was her name, the *Joanna V.*

During our time dedicated to the Beira Patrol, from the time we'd sailed from Singapore to the time we got back there, we spent seventy-two days continuously at sea, thought to be the longest peacetime cruise by a Royal Navy carrier, and we hadn't seen land once.

After some mid-tour leave, we re-embarked in early June taking passage to the Philippines area. There we used the US air-to-ground ranges. This included dropping 1,000lb inert bombs on a shipwreck on Scarborough Sholes. We enjoyed using real, as opposed to practice, bombs albeit inert, until we noticed a few local fishing boats tied up alongside the target ship. When we had finished the bombing exercise they would scavenge for bits of scrap metal, either off the ship or from our bombs. I don't know now whether we were upset because they considered themselves safe beside the target, assuming we would never hit it, or whether they were prepared to risk themselves for the chance of a bit of scrap from the target ship. We eventually learned from the Yanks that it was the latter and our pride was restored.

In early July we started our passage home. As we left the Malacca Straits we were exercising off Butterworth, an Australian air force base on the west coast of Malaysia. My wingman, Fred Secker, was unable to get his undercarriage down in the carrier circuit. Up to this incident, the emergency checklist made it clear that it was a mandatory ejection if the undercarriage remained up but Fred agreed to try and get the aircraft down so I shepherded him to Butterworth. I had insufficient fuel to hang around and get back to the carrier so I landed first since Fred would have to make a wheels-up landing and would inevitably block the runway.

Over the radio I briefed Fred on what to do. He already knew but he was a young first tourist and I guessed it would boost his confidence if the senior pilot ran through the procedure with him. One part of the drill was to jettison the canopy, quite a chunky piece of kit, just before touch down.

Fred carried out a copybook approach and landing. His observer, Noel Rawbone, jettisoned the canopy and Fred touched down gently in the centre of the runway. He came to rest two feet off the centre-line after an immaculate piece of flying. He and Noel, a fitness fanatic who had ejected just a few weeks earlier, were out of the cockpit and away in seconds.

Later in the day, a deputation of Malayan natives arrived at the air station out of the jungle surrounding Butterworth. Their neighbouring village had found the canopy and could they have one too?

The wheels-up landing caused minimum damage to the fuselage and the engineers were able to jack the aircraft up, manually free the undercarriage and lock it down before it flew down to the Naval Air Support Unit at Changi, minus canopy.

On 14 August, in the area near Majorca, eight Buccaneers were ranged at the aft end of *Eagle* and we took off to fly direct to Yeovilton. After refuelling we headed for Lossiemouth and arrived overhead in formation, almost a year to the day since we had left. This was to be my last flight from a carrier.

The squadron had a couple of weeks much needed leave, returning in September when the first of our Marks 2s started arriving. This was quite an experience after the sluggish old Mark 1s. I hadn't known thrust like the Mark 2's Spey engines since my Scimitar days. The acceleration down the runway on my first familiarisation sortie was exhilarating to say the least and the Marks 2's range was considerably better than its predecessor.

Despite my comments on the shortcomings of the Mark 1, and they were justified, I had come to love the aircraft, knew all its characteristics, good and bad, and considered it the most stable aircraft I had taken to the deck. It sat on the approach path, constant at the correct speed, with both engines steady at their optimum setting and you simply arrived in the wires, having been steady on the meatball all the way down, day or night. And at night, this was a supreme advantage. Much as I was to come to love the Mark 2, its engines had to be throttled back on the approach to land below their optimum revs making them a little less stable. Even so, I would take the Mark 2 every time. That was really something.

At the end of December it was time to leave 800 Squadron. I had been re-appointed to take command of 736 Squadron.

Torrey Canyon *ablaze*.

A few weeks later the *Torrey Canyon* ran aground on the Seven Stones rocky shoal near the Scilly Isles. This super tanker was full of thick, black glutinous crude oil, which posed a huge threat to the nearby coasts and to wildlife. A political decision was taken to set fire to the cargo before it leaked out and spread. The navy was capable of the precision bombing necessary to do the job and the Buccaneers were the natural choice.

The two squadrons at Lossiemouth were 800, very operational with their Mark 2s, and 736 with their tired Mark 1s, lack of spares, a bunch of trainee ground crew and, except for the experience of my instructors, far from operational. We would follow.

Once we were put 'on notice' my ground crew started work and really got the bit between their teeth but there was much to do and I began to realise that we were going to be very much 'also rans' when it was all over.

I had to give a lot of thought to the flying aspects of the operation and how my Mark 1s would cope. I had major doubts about our automated dive-bombing system and the limited endurance of our aircraft. The wreck was at the extent of our range with four 1,000lb bombs on the wing stations. Any delays, always likely, and we would have to jettison the bombs and head for Brawdy – embarrassing in front of the world's press who were gathering.

Lossiemouth's captain, Doug Parker, was aware of my concerns and told me to go first. I was surprised and was unhappy that people might think that I had upstaged my old chum, Jimmy Moore, the CO of 800. So 736 was to lead the operation involving four aircraft from each squadron. A compromise was affected; I would lead and 800's senior pilot would be my wingman.

We took off at lunchtime on 28 March 1967 and headed south. In the event the operation went pretty smoothly. My initial bombs blew a hole in the side of the tanker. My wingman, Dave Mears, put his first bombs smack in the middle of her. She was on fire and the stiff breeze blew the towering, thick black smoke clear so that the six to follow could still see something to aim for on successive attacks. We then landed at Brawdy to be met by a posse of journalists, including TV crews and we were left to their mercy, which, by today's standards, was a pretty tame affair. When we got back to Lossiemouth that evening we went through much the same routine.

Over the next two days we flew back to Brawdy to re-arm with four 1,000lb high-explosive bombs, struck the tanker repeatedly to release the remaining oil, then returned directly to Lossiemouth.

When we got back to Lossiemouth for the last time, after it was all over, the impact of what we had done finally came home to me. Every newspaper in the country seemed to have covered the operation and 736 Squadron's name, and pictures of her aircrew, and 800's, were everywhere. And most important, my squadron lads were ten-feet tall. They had worked their backsides off, our second-line outfit had come up trumps, and the whole world knew about it. There was one final touching moment for me, and one that made it all worthwhile. The squadron's junior rates awarded me the 'Torrey Canyon Cross' with the gaudiest ribbon and an appropriate citation:

'In connection with your heroic exploits during the offensive action against the helpless, defenceless, stranded tanker *Torrey Canyon*, we have much pleasure in sending you the one and only "Torrey Canyon Cross".'

I still have my cross and I am very proud of it. It was my ground crew's way of saying thank you for the publicity of their endeavours.

The squadron continued with its training task punctuated occasionally with night exercises to try out my ideas for new Buccaneer tactics. What we achieved in 736 with my experienced instructors laid the groundwork for things to come.

Another 'extra to the normal task' was a flypast for the launching of the QE2 on the Clyde on 20 September 1967. We could spare only a few hours but managed a few rehearsals, flying an anchor formation with twelve Buccaneers. We had been given the job because the QE2 was the 736th ship to be built at that shipyard.

We were to fly down to the Clyde area, hopefully not have to wait too long due to the Mark 1's fuel consumption, and overfly the ship as she moved down the slipway after being launched by Her Majesty the Queen. While we were confident we could be overhead the slipway on time, we guessed there might be some delay so we had arranged to orbit if necessary. We had also put our tame Lossiemouth pongo (army officer) high up on a crane with a radio to keep us briefed.

Sure enough, come the appointed time as we were running in over the hills to the south

The 736 Squadron QE 2 flypast.

of the Clyde below a low cloud base, there was no sign of the ship moving and we went into an orbit, a large one with twelve Buccaneers, those on the inside very close to the hill tops. On the far side of the orbit our pongo screamed into the radio, "she's moving".

I called "tighten up" and I swung the formation into as tight a turn as I dared and we managed, still in perfect formation, to overfly the ship just as she slipped into the water. By this time the Mark 1s were getting very short of fuel as we headed for home, some of us joining straight into the downwind leg rather than do a circuit. We all made it safely but, yet again, working with agencies unfamiliar with our problems, we had been extended uncomfortably. It was the professionalism of the twenty-four chaps in the team that made it all work.

The time on 736 Squadron was extremely rewarding as a steady stream of very capable young aircrew converted to the Buccaneer before heading for the front line where I was to join them in December 1968 when I took command of 800 Squadron, but that is another story.

CHAPTER FOUR

SAAF AT LOSSIEMOUTH

The first SAAF course, with
Theo de Munnink back right alongside
John Murphy, Comdt Bob Rogers front left,
Major Mike Muller front right.

THEO DE MUNNINK AND ANTON DE KLERK

When the South African Air Force (SAAF) purchased the Buccaneer aircraft in order to balance their air power, it was decided to reform an ex-wartime squadron, 24 Squadron to operate the new aircraft. Eight crews were identified to man the new unit under the command of Comdt (Lt Col) Bob Rogers. Three pilots, Bob Rogers, Mike Muller and Jan van Loggerenberg, all of whom would become Chief of the Air Force, left for the UK during the middle of 1964 in order to do specialist training before the rest of the squadron arrived to convert to the Buccaneer at Lossiemouth. Six months later, two navigators joined them.

Theo de Munnink takes up the story.

John Murphy and I, accompanied by our wives, arrived at London Heathrow just after New Year's Day 1965. We were on our way to Lossiemouth to do our conversion on the Buccaneer. We departed London on a sleeper train to Elgin. I remember the train steward coming down the corridor asking travellers what they wanted to drink: "Coffee, tea or milk?" and when we said, "Coffee, please" his reply was: "Sorry, only tea!" The conductor told us that the train was actually going to Inverness and not to Elgin and we would have to get off at a siding called Craigellachie. We had no idea where this place was and asked him to repeat the name so we could try to remember it. He said not to worry. He would show us where to get off but it would be early the next morning at about 0600.

We were up bright and early and when the train stopped the conductor saw us off with our luggage and the train left immediately. Craigellachie station was isolated – not a soul in sight. It was cold and the only shelter was a structure resembling a bus stop. We waited patiently in the cold and darkness for almost an hour, without seeing anyone, until a single rail coach pulled up and stopped. This was our transport to Elgin. We were the only passengers. The coach shook so much my pregnant wife felt more comfortable standing than sitting on our journey. Finally just when I thought we might be going to experience a premature birth, we arrived. Bob Rogers and Mike Muller, our pilots, met us. Coming from mid-summer in Pretoria to mid-winter in Lossiemouth took some getting used to.

The following day Bob and Mike picked us up and took us to Elgin where we met their wives as well as Jan van Loggerenberg and his wife. Jan was still doing a weapons course with another squadron at Lossiemouth as part of his preparation for the arrival of our Buccaneers. John Murphy bought a car costing more than I could afford and I bought a 1948 Morris for fifty pounds. Then we set off to find accommodation and, using the info obtained from the local municipal office, which had a list of available places, our search began. Being mid-winter in Elgin, John and I were dressed in our SAAF issue raincoats with a thick scarf around the neck and a cap on our heads. We looked like two hoodlums. We stopped at a place in Abbey Street and knocked on the door of a large house. The owner took one look at us and informed us that all his rooms had been let.

We returned to the car knowing that he had fobbed us off. We drove round the block and then sent the girls in. The owner welcomed them and showed them what he had available. My wife selected a nice large bed-sitter with kitchenette and John's wife did the same and paid for the first week. They then called us and we moved in with the owner feeling a bit sheepish. The Murphys soon moved and we were offered a nice two-bedroomed apartment with its own entrance for five shillings per week more. We were now settled and ready for the Buccaneer conversion.

The conversion course for our two crews began with 809 NAS on 11 January 1965. We kicked off with the normal ground school, which included the technical side of the Buccaneer. We were also taken out into the bay at Lossiemouth and dumped in the North Sea. With snow lying on the land, and the temperature of the sea being about 4 degrees Celsius, I can only say it was very cold. However the immersion suit is a lifesaver and that is for sure. A chopper hoisted us up and that took care of our safety measures.

My Fam 1 was on 29 January with Lt Carl Davis as my driver in Bucc 223. This was an introduction to the best aircraft I have ever flown; it was magnificent. My second flight followed only a few hours later on the same day, my Fam 2 with Lt Cdr Willie Watson, OC of 809 Squadron at that time. During February flying progressed at a good pace despite the winter snow and short days. I flew twenty-one sorties in that month with my five Fam flights being with RN pilots and the rest with Mike Muller, my pilot.

In March I flew twenty-nine sorties and I also had my first, and only, flight in a dual Hunter. Bob Rogers and I were scheduled to do a low-level navex but there was no Bucc available at the time so we were told to take the Hunter. The fact that Bob had not flown a Hunter in months and I had never flown one made no one feel anxious – we were just told, "there is the aircraft, do it". Well with the help of the pilot's notes we got going and took off.

Soon after entering the valleys west of Tain we suddenly no longer had the V of the mountains on either side with the tops in cloud but just a white curtain of a snowfall in

NAVAL AIR STRIKE SCHOOL

ROYAL NAVY

This is to certify that
...... Captain *I.J. de Merrick*
has successfully completed Buccaneers.
S.MK.I. Conversion *on* 2nd April 1965.

WHWatson .... *A.L. Kirk.* Captain
Squadron Commanding Officer   RNAS Lossiemouth.

front of us. The only option was a pull up until we popped out of the cloud tops at about 5,000ft. We decided to fly the rest of the course on time hoping for a gap to resume the low-level exercise. When we saw enough of the ground to go down we did and found ourselves over Loch Ness, which was just outside our flying area. After cruising up to the coast we returned to Lossie having had a pleasant flight. The other flights during March included weapons system exercises, Hi-Lo strikes, 20-degree dive bombing, tactical reccе, formation flying and night flying. By the end of March we had completed our course. I had accumulated fifty-three hours on the Bucc Mark 1 and one hour on the Hunter.

Following completion of our conversion we set about preparing to run a similar one for the other six crews who would be arriving in the UK soon. We went down to the south of England to meet up with the other members of the squadron at the simulator factory in Grinstead. There was a delay in the readiness of the simulator and for a few weeks our chaps played much golf and other leisure pursuits. The hotel we stayed in near Grinstead was nicknamed 'The Prime Minister's Rest Camp for SAAF Officers'. Eventually the simulator was available and our chaps got their first feel of the Bucc.

Towards the end of May we had our first SAAF Bucc Mark 50 (413) at Lossiemouth and Mike and I did a number of flights to get to know our new aircraft. What a magnificent machine with about double the power of the Mark 1 and half the fuel consumption. I remember the very first flight we did in 413. We were at the threshold of the runway preparing for take-off, going down the checklist: Brakes on, increase to full power, check gauges. Then I felt a movement of the aircraft after which it was brakes off and away we went.

When we landed a very irate Harry Beaton, our technical officer, was on the dispersal to meet us. "Get in the car" was all he said as he took us to the threshold and showed us two black tyre stripes almost 100 yards long. "You must have gone through a number of layers of canvas on your tyres," he said. Right there and then the pilot's notes were changed. Open power to 90%, check gauges, brakes off, then open to full power for take-off. The notes had been fine for the Mark 1 Bucc but the more powerful Mark 50 would physically move the whole aircraft with locked brakes at full power.

On 2 June, Mike and I went to Brough to ferry 414 to Lossiemouth while Bob Rogers and John Murphy ferried 415. By mid June our new crews were at Lossiemouth ready for their conversion.

During the conversion course I flew with each of our pilots as they progressed through their fam flights. In between, Mike and I still got in some air time together doing test flights, ferries from Brough, formation, etc. On 26 July, Martin Jooste and I took off from Lossie on Martin's first weapons system familiarisation. During the exercise we experienced a problem with the aircraft systems and returned to the airfield. In the circuit Martin selected undercarriage down but we only got three red lights. He recycled with the same result. We were not really worried as the Bucc had three ways of lowering the undercarriage: normal, emergency and, finally, emergency override. While we were circling the airfield a flurry of support was gathering in the ATC tower including our OC, Bob Rogers, and our technical officer, Harry Beaton.

Martin then selected emergency down but that also made no difference – we still had three reds! A Royal Navy Bucc came to give us a look over informing us that the nose wheel and the port main wheel appeared down but that the door of the starboard main wheel was still closed. Martin then pressed emergency override, which sends hydraulic pressure straight to the wheel jacks bypassing all micro-switches and which we had been led to believe would break through the wheel doors. Oh Yeah? No! We got two greens – the nose wheel and the port wheel – but the starboard wheel was unchanged. So much for 'breaking through the doors'. The RN Bucc confirmed that the starboard wheel bay door was still as closed as a clam. There was nothing more we could do to lower that wheel.

We continued to circle the airfield getting advice from the boffins. We were told to lower our arrestor hook. Now the hook on the British Buccaneers is hydraulically activated and can be lowered and raised in the air as required. On our aircraft the hook was pneumatically activated and would only come down when the weight-on-ground micro-switches were made after touch down. Oh Yeah? Not so! When Martin selected the hook down it did to everyone's surprise and our delight.

The runway at Lossiemouth had one cable across the threshold. This cable was connected on either side to thick heavy chains (CHAG) laid out next to the runway. The idea is that when someone engages the cable on landing the aircraft will drag an increasing weight of chain behind it thereby bringing the aircraft to a rapid stop. With our hook down we were preparing to land. There was some concern from the tower that the aircraft may twist or bend during the landing making the canopy inoperable so we were told to jettison it on finals.

While circling, Martin told me that he would rather have become a bus driver. I replied, "yes and I would be your conductor"; but it was too late for such wishes.

We were told to burn off some more fuel and keep circling but when a generator failed for an unknown reason we decided to get on the ground before more systems packed up. On finals, Martin told me to jettison the canopy on his count of three. It went off with a terrific bang and almost every light on the standard warning panel (SWP) lit up and clanged in our ears. On crossing the threshold I saw the cable flash by below and thought, 'Oh hell Martin, we missed the cable'. The following moment though we really slowed down very fast as we dragged the chains behind us – what a relief. Martin kept the starboard wing up as long as possible and when it eventually dropped to the runway our speed was also zero. It had been a perfect landing and the aircraft came to rest just slightly right of the centreline on the runway. After switching everything off we clambered out and

Recovery of 415 at Lossiemouth, June 1965.

were met by the emergency services. All was well.

The RN lifted the Bucc with a crane and placed it on stands in our hangar. The damage to the aircraft was restricted to the canopy, the right wingtip and the right aileron. The greatest harm was caused by the ejection of the canopy as the breech block, situated on the port side of the pilot's cockpit, had blown up cutting through a thick loom of wires (causing our SWP to light up like a Christmas tree). Martin's left leg was also full of spots of cordite, which had penetrated through his flying suit.

Later when our technical chaps had connected a hydraulic rig and tried to select undercarriage down the two down wheels disappeared into the bays and would not reappear. After a bit of head scratching they realised that when 'emergency override' has been used the pistons in the gear do not return automatically to neutral. Bucc 415 was eventually repaired. The fault, which had prevented the starboard wheel from lowering, was a failure of the mechanism that releases the door locks of the wheel bay.

On 30 July Martin and I again tried to complete his weapons system Fam 1 in Bucc 416 and, by golly, we had an undercarriage problem again getting three red lights after selecting up. We recycled – down was fine but on selecting up the red lights persisted. We decided to put the wheels down and land. A few hours later we took Bucc 414 and completed the exercise successfully – third time lucky!

During this summer of 1965 we decided to have a BBQ ('braai' as we know it) on the beach at Lossiemouth for the aircrew and their wives (not all the wives had accompanied their husbands to Scotland but I was one of about half who had their mates there). The closest we could come to our traditional sausage used at our braais was the Cumberland sausage. Armed with a few kilos of Cumberlands, lamb chops and steaks and many gallons of liquid refreshment we clambered down the slopes to the beach. Soon we had a good fire going, refreshments being enjoyed and the unmistakable aroma of meat on the grill spurring us on. We had an enjoyable evening. It was starting to get dark and we were relaxing on the beach when we noticed that our space was shrinking. The tide was coming in and judging from the flotsam lying around, the tide took over the whole beach up to the dunes. Soon we realised that we were being forced back and eventually we all had to scramble up the slopes – this time in the dark. All reached the safety of the top but the BBQ was over. It had been a good evening.

By middle September all the new crews had completed their conversion course on the Bucc Mark 50 and the exercises that followed were to test the aircraft with a bomb-bay tank plus our large drop tanks. We all undertook a number of long-range navexes. No aircraft were fitted with refuelling probes as the legs en route to South Africa were all within easy range of the Buccaneer with no leg expected to take much more than four hours.

On the morning of 27 October 1965 all was set for our departure. Five SAAF C-130 Hercules would support us plus two Shackletons for search and rescue if required. One Shackleton was stationed at Ascension Island and the second one at Bissau on the west coast of Africa. Two C-130s had already deployed from Lossie to Yeovilton to receive us when we arrived. We also positioned ground staff at the staging airfields on our route. Our eight aircraft were lined up fitted with the large wing tanks and ready to go.

ANTON DE KLERK **was one of the navigators and he relates his own, unique experience.**

At the beginning of April 1965 the other eleven crew members left the RSA for the UK. After two weeks in London to 'acclimatise' we went to Grinstead, where the simulator was based. Over the next couple of weeks we learnt to fly the simulator. This introduction phase was followed with a technical course at the Blackburn factory at Brough as well as a brief stopover at the Rolls-Royce engine factory.

At this stage everybody was keen to start to fulfil a dream; to get into the cockpit of a Buccaneer. The time had come to go north and we departed for Lossiemouth during June. What a treat to see the real aircraft in a hangar.

This is where my pilot Martin Jooste and I began our Buccaneer experience. The two of us had got together when we joined 12 Squadron to fly Canberras a year earlier during July 1964. For the next eight months we flew about 100 hours together in a Canberra.

Over the next four months, Martin and I flew various sorties and accumulated about fifty flying hours. These were mostly in Scotland consisting of low-level exercises in the

Scottish Highlands, simulated attacks on targets in the North Sea and high-level navigation sorties. It was only at the end of our time at Lossiemouth that we flew south in order to undertake long-range sorties in preparation for the delivery flight to South Africa. As part of our aircrew survival training we were dropped by a naval vessel in the North Sea and recovered by helicopter. Unbeknown to me at the time, it was an experience that would become very valuable.

The move of 24 Squadron from Lossiemouth to AFB Waterkloof in South Africa was a major operation. For this purpose five C-130 Hercules joined us at Lossiemouth in order to support us technically. At this stage 24 Squadron consisted of sixteen aircrew members, five technical officers and 120 ground crew. Bucc 417 was a masterpiece, a real jewel. We flew our last eight sorties before our departure on 417 and never was there a technical problem, a 'snag', everything functioned at all times, even the 'Roller Map'.

Heading south in the eight Buccaneers were:

Bob Rogers & John Murphy
Mike Muller & Theo de Munnink
Jan van Loggerenberg & Paul van Rensburg
Martin Jooste & Anton de Klerk
Koot du Rand & Piet Oosthuizen
WAP Cronje & Johan van de Burgh
Darryl Pienaar & Anton de Beer
Ben Vorster & Mac van de Merwe

Martin Jooste and Anton de Klerk prepare to take off for South Africa.

Bon Voyage.

The First Leg: Wednesday, 27 October 1965. The final day at Lossiemouth arrived – the day we were all looking forward to. What a sight; eight Buccaneers and three C-130s on the aircraft dispersal ready to go. Two C-130s were positioned at Yeovilton in order to see us in on our arrival. The eight Buccaneers flew in two formations of four aircraft about twenty minutes apart. At last at 0940 we requested "take-off clearance" and for the last time heard: "You are clear to roll...up school". [Ed note: Gordonstoun School, close to Runway 29, is in residence.] Mike Muller and Theo de Munnink, as No.1 in our formation, started to roll and we joined them. For the last time Martin raised the nose of Bucc 417 at Lossiemouth, and selected undercarriage up – we were on our way home! Eighty minutes later we landed at Yeovilton – as usual without a snag.

The Second Leg: Thursday, 28 October 1965. We left Yeovilton repeating the take-off procedure of the previous day and were all airborne at 0920. The next stop was Las Palmas, an airfield on Gran Canaria Island about 1,500 nautical miles south, southwest, 350 nautical miles off the west coast of Africa and three-and-a-half-hours flight time. By 1315 all eight Buccs were neatly parked and we were looking forward to a day off as the next leg was scheduled for Saturday. The long stop over was intended to carry out servicing/repairs on the aircraft before the next leg to Ascension Island. Once again Bucc 417 was reliable as always.

The Third Leg: Saturday, 30 October 1965. We were ready for the longest flight of the operation. As it was outside the range of the Buccaneer, 2,400 nautical miles, the flight was divided into two legs; the first of 800 miles from Las Palmas to Sal, which forms part of the Cape Verde Island cluster, and a second leg 1,600 miles from Sal to Ascension. At this stage I started to enjoy the sorties as 417 was the perfect aircraft and just about the only one without a problem. The departure pattern was set and we were airborne by 0920 and landed safely at the small barren island of Sal at 1100. The air terminal on Sal had been developed for South African Airways as a refuelling base and had the bare essentials. It was about 35°C and we passed the time in the shadow of the Bucc wing. At last all crucial servicing had been attended to and we took once again to the skies at 1400. What a challenge, the Bucc was heavy loaded with fuel, the outside temperature had reached 40°C and these conditions were not ideal take-off parameters for this bomber. All that was in its favour was that we were at sea level. During the take-off run it felt as if the end of the runway was just too close, but we cleared the fence and turned south to Ascension, all set for a three-and-half-hour sortie. We were thankful to be back in an air-conditioned cockpit.

We levelled off at 32,000 feet and settled in for a relaxing flight to Ascension. After about forty minutes we encountered some cirrus clouds and decided to climb to 34,000 feet in order to stay in the clear, which suited the loose formation. We were barely at our new level when we encountered the same problem and we lost visual contact with No 1, Mike Muller and Theo de Munnink in Bucc 416, just to spot them again at quite a distance away. In order to get closer, before we entered clouds again, we turned left. In the process both engines flamed out, the aircraft pitched up and resulted in an uncontrolled spin.

Martin tried frantically to relight the engines and, when this was unsuccessful, he jettisoned the wing tanks, but all in vain. Only the standby instruments functioned and when I asked him what our height was, he replied: "We are through 10,000 feet and it is winding down so fast, I can't read it." He then broadcasted a Mayday, jettisoned the canopy and ejected. Realising that I was alone, I followed him.

THEO DE MUNNINK **takes up the story.**
We were approaching cloud so Mike called them to move in to close formation. Numbers 3 and 4 were quick to close in, but No.2 (Martin Jooste & Anton de Klerk in 417) did not make it in time before we entered cloud. Mike instructed Martin to execute the 'separation' drill (turn fifteen degrees to starboard for two minutes and then resume the original heading). We remained in cloud for some time when Mike decided to climb to 34,000 feet to see if we could clear the cloud and so we followed. I saw Martin at our three o'clock. He started to turn and when I looked again I saw their plane in a sharp nose-down attitude. Mike asked him what was going on and he said that he was in a spin. I lost him in the clouds and immediately plotted our position about 500 miles south of Sal Island. We had no further communication with them. Mike then told the other two in our formation to carry on flying to Ascension. We circled the area where we lost them and commenced a descent.

I radioed Dakar to send a Mayday on behalf of Buccaneer 417 and asked them to contact our Shackleton at Bissau and warn them that they must assist. I had some trouble making

Dakar understand that I was sending a Mayday message on behalf of 417 as they wanted to know our ETA for Ascension. However they soon understood what was happening and would activate Bissau. I then contacted Wideawake Tower (Ascension). Luckily when I called them Harry Gilliland, one of our C-130 commanders, answered my call. He was on the ground at Ascension in his C-130 and had just switched on the radio to contact Waterkloof when he heard my Mayday. I gave the position of our downed aircraft to him to pass to the Shackleton at Ascension.

On reaching low level we searched for almost an hour looking for Martin and Anton without success. This was probably to be expected at the speed we flew and the fact that the cockpit was also slightly misted up due to the descent. Anton and Martin saw us passing them shortly after they got into their dinghies. After the search we could no longer continue flying to Ascension and we climbed and returned to Sal Island. On the way, I also made contact with a Portuguese air force DC-6 flying from Bissau heading north. They said they would search through the area. Shortly before dark we received a message at Sal Island that the DC-6 had seen a flare in the area. Later that night we got the good news that our Shackleton picked up the signals of two SARAH beacons.

ANTON DE KLERK **relates the successful conclusion of his ordeal.**
After my parachute deployed I glanced around and saw Martin rather far away. I looked down and was stunned to see how close the sea was. The next moment I hit the drink and the real survival started, it was no longer an exercise. To my dismay my parachute time was a maximum of eight seconds.

The sea state was choppy; it was overcast with the cloud base low and the water warm. The exercise in the North Sea came in handy and very soon I was in my inflated dinghy and started to look around for Martin. Owing to the waves and sea swell I could not find him at first and only picked him up after some time. To my surprise a Buccaneer passed low and to me that meant only one thing: I am saved. This was Mike Muller, but they never saw me. Eventually I saw Martin and joined up with him just before sunset.

Shortly after we were united, we saw an aircraft at about 030 degrees and at about 5,000 feet. I shot a flare, which was sighted by the aircraft and reported. This was a Portuguese transport aircraft, which was on its way from Sal to a Portuguese airbase on the West African coast. Night set in and we settled down for a long night, concluding that rescue was somewhere in the future, but unlikely to be the next day.

By about 2130 we heard a faint sound and I switched on the SARAH location beacon, which was part of our survival kit. Shortly after this a SAAF Shackleton appeared on the horizon; what a relief and surprise. As part of the transfer operation of the Buccaneers, some of our Shackletons were deployed on the African west coast at Bissau and another at Ascension Island for possible rescue missions. For the rest of the night there were aircraft overhead at regular intervals, either a Shackleton or a C-130 Hercules.

Sunday, 31 October 1965. Unlike the previous day, the sea was calm with not a cloud in the sky. Before sunrise a Shackleton was overhead and dropped Lindholme survival gear. This included a ten-man dinghy, which was of great value as the sun became an increasing problem by the minute. Knowing that the only way out for us would have to be a ship, we passed the time by speculating what type of ship it would be. We had a wish list, with a passenger liner at the top and a Chinese fishing trawler the least favoured.

By about 1200 it became apparent that over the last hour the Shackleton was constantly approaching us from the same direction. Shortly afterwards we made out a ship on the horizon which turned out to be the *Randfontein*. It was a passenger liner, which was on its way from the Netherlands to the Far East via Cape Town and we were soon aboard.

Our wish list had worked out perfectly! Over the next nine days we were the guests of the captain and had a joyful time on the ship. Unfortunately Martin had hurt his spine during the ejection and spent the first couple of days in bed. We arrived on a glorious day in Cape Town and were reunited with our families.

The list of organisations to be thanked was very long. It had turned out to be a classic air-sea rescue operation and a very unusual and rare event in peacetime. To me the outstanding one was the South African Air Force for their foresight in their planning and execution of the operation. Lastly I would like to pay tribute to my crewmate, Martin Jooste, who passed away in March 2012. I continued to fly the best aircraft ever, the Buccaneer, until 1970 and spent 1,060 happy hours in the rear cockpit.

Above: *The moment of rescue in the Atlantic.*
Below: *Martin Jooste and Anton de Klerk welcomed home by their wives.*

Arriving in Cape Town as deck cargo.

THEO DE MUNNINK **concludes the story.**

I was very relieved that Martin and Anton had been rescued and thankful that our stay on Sal was ended; we left the island together on 1 November with Bob Rogers and Darryl Pienaar from the first formation of four to join the rest of the squadron at Ascension. They had turned back to Sal before the 417 incident took place when Darryl developed an oxygen problem. We landed at Ascension Island at about 1200 after a three-hour-fifty-minute flight. The next morning, we were airborne early for the four-hour flight to Luanda, the capital of Angola, which was then still under Portuguese rule.

The last day of our ferry from Lossiemouth to Pretoria dawned and at 1020 on 3 November we lifted off at Luanda and the last leg home. Three hours later we landed at AFB Waterkloof outside Pretoria to a large reception. We were very happy to be home, sorry that we had lost 417 but thankful that Martin and Anton had been safely rescued.

In conclusion, as the time to depart Lossiemouth had approached, we had all looked back on our few months with the Fleet Air Arm and the connections we had made. Right from the day we arrived we were made to feel at home amongst friends. Everyone welcomed us and made our stay an unforgettable experience. I recall that evening of 27 October at Yeovilton on our first stop after leaving Lossie. While we were relaxing that evening in the local pub a pilot from Lossiemouth came in, still wearing his flight suit, and handed a parcel to our CO, Bob Rogers. The parcel contained framed photographs of our departure a few hours earlier. We were all deeply touched by this lovely gesture from Lossiemouth and it confirmed the good friendships we had made during our stay. In time this bond was further cemented with our common love and admiration for the beautiful beast we flew. This link has meant that all who have had the honour to fly the Bucc have remained a close-knit group even after nearly fifty years.

CHAPTER FIVE

A FLYING LIFE ON BUCCANEERS

TOM EELES

The road from Grantown-on-Spey towards Forres crosses a desolate area known as Dava Moor. Right in the middle, half way to the Moray coastal region, there is a sharp hairpin bend and alongside it a large boulder, painted white, with the words 'Jesus Saves' written on it. Tired after the long, slow two-day drive from Laarbruch in Germany, I nearly hit it that night in July 1966, on my way to RNAS Lossiemouth and the start of my association with the Buccaneer. That connection, which so nearly never happened had I hit that boulder, ultimately lasted some twenty-three years and over 2,000 hours flying, not forgetting over 1,000 hours flying in the two-seat Hunters used as surrogate trainers for the Buccaneer.

It all started some months earlier when volunteers were sought to go on loan service with the Fleet Air Arm. The first RAF crew on the Buccaneer, the two Grahams (Smart and Pitchfork) had led the way early in 1965. Hearing of their experiences whetted my appetite and, since the initial excitement of flying Canberras in Germany had faded somewhat, I volunteered. The rest of my squadron thought I was mad to swop 9,000 feet of concrete runway that never moved, for 900 feet of rather elderly aircraft carrier that not only moved up and down but also all over the place. The Buccaneer looked a much more exciting prospect to fly than the Canberra however, and it certainly was!

The course on 736 Naval Air Squadron that summer and autumn was a brisk and no-nonsense affair. After some five trips in the primitive Buccaneer Mark 1 simulator, and a sortie with fellow RAF student Tim Cockerell in a Hunter equipped with Buccaneer flight instruments, which neither of us really understood, on 18 August I flew Buccaneer Mark 1 XN 954 on my Fam 1 with Lieutenant Nick Wilkinson, the QFI in the back seat with no control over events other than the force of his persuasive patter. The course progressed well and I flew my first Mark 2 sortie in XT 281 on 26 September.

Eventually it came time to throw this big beast of an aircraft onto the deck of an aircraft carrier and *Hermes* duly arrived in the Moray Firth and the game was on. The first day did not start well, with George Heron (a student on the course ahead) turning finals too tightly, pitching up, ejecting and being returned to Lossie by helicopter. Somewhat chastened by this event, I did not find the art of deck-landing practice at all easy and was

struggling to cope, until rescued by the excellent instructional skills of Graham Smart who had spent the previous year with 800 Squadron in *Eagle*. Having been finally declared 'proficient', it only remained for me to experience a catapult launch or two on the static steam catapult at the Royal Aircraft Establishment's airfield at Bedford.

The catapult was an impressive device, with a long ramp, which the Buccaneer taxied up, before being launched towards a disused runway. What appeared to be a sort of large tennis net was positioned at the end to catch anything that had not achieved flying speed. Without the benefit of any ship-generated head-wind component the launch tended to be much fiercer than any ship-board one; indeed, on my last launch at a fairly high fuel state for the transit back to Lossie most of the strike sight (head-up display) became detached and hit me hard in the chest. The launch itself was carried out 'hands off', a technique that actually worked very well once early problems with the Mark 2's handling at low speed and high angle of attack (AOA) were resolved.

With the conversion course now complete I was appointed (whilst the RAF posts its people, the RN appoints them, far more civilised) to 801 Naval Air Squadron, embarked in *Victorious* serving in the Far East.

After a snail-like transit by RAF Transport Command Britannia – no chance of suffering from jet lag – I joined 801, disembarked at RAF Changi whilst *Victorious* spent the Christmas break in Singapore Naval Base dockyard. After a hedonistic Christmas in the fleshpots of Singapore the squadron re-embarked in early January 1967. My first shipboard arrested landing was in Buccaneer Mark 2 XN 981 side number 234; many years later this aircraft was the subject of a die-cast Corgi model which now has pride of place in my study.

Life on board was very different from life ashore. There was an intermittent supply of old newspapers, no TV, occasional film shows, mobile phones and personal computers having not yet been invented. I had a tiny cabin deep in the bowels of the ship, and right outside it in the passageway was a big hole; you could see a propeller shaft rotating noisily at the bottom of it. There were no floors, ceilings or windows, only decks, deck-heads and portholes, and portholes were pretty rare. The inside of the ship was a labyrinth of passageways which took ages to get used to; they were regularly further restricted by watertight doors during replenishments at sea.

I recall being grabbed by the squadron commander one evening in the wardroom to take a message for him to some office in the island. Being still unsure of the route inside, I went the way I used every morning, namely, out onto the flight deck and along it. As I climbed the ladder giving access to the flight deck something made me turn and look astern. There was a Sea Vixen on short finals – and I had not realised the ship was night flying – I fled back inside, avoided the boss all evening and the message was never delivered.

The flying was exciting. Launch and recovery were always the high points of each sortie. We were restricted to day VFR flying off the ship because of the launch problems associated with the Buccaneer Mark 2 so night flying was still a distant prospect. Once safely airborne we peppered the various ranges or the towed splash target with bombs and rockets. I was one of the pilots cleared for nuclear operations as a consequence of my previous Canberra time, so had the pleasure of delivering the enormous Red Beard nuclear weapon shape in a Long Toss attack against Tabones Range in the Philippines; it hit the small target island smack in the middle. The Bullpup air-to-ground missile also featured in our armoury. It was fired at about three miles range in a shallow dive and required the pilot to steer it into the target with a small control stick whilst still flying his own aircraft, a tricky challenge.

Getting back on board was always rather a tense time. First you had to find the ship, which might not be where she was when you launched, and get back in time to make your recovery slot, or Charlie time. You then might have to hold whilst some problem was fixed on deck before being cleared in. The ship might be pitching in the swell and pushing out lots of funnel smoke, all distractions you could do without whilst trying to arrive, on speed, on time, right on the centreline of the flight deck, in a space about the size of a tennis court to pick up a wire, No.3 wire being the target. Once the rapid deceleration of the arrested landing was complete you had to get off the flight deck into the parking area (Fly1) as quickly as possible so your wire could be re-set; there would be another aircraft only some thirty seconds behind you. If you failed to pick up a wire – a bolter – you went round again amidst a shower of flares and the cry of "bolter, bolter" from Flyco (flying control). Fuel states were critical; your max hook-on weight was often so close to diversion fuel that in many ways it was better to fly non-diversion, which allowed more attempts at landing on.

It soon became apparent to me that the Buccaneer was a superb aircraft. Untouchable at low level and capable of carrying a wide range of weapons, it was way ahead of anything the RAF had at the time. It was a difficult period for both the RN and the RAF. As a consequence of the Labour administration's defence cutbacks, the RN was faced with the loss of their fixed-wing carrier capability and the RAF had seen the cancellation of its prize project, the TSR2, and its attempts to replace it with a purchase of American F-111 aircraft, which also failed. Thus it was with great delight that I learnt that the RAF was to receive a number of new-build Buccaneers in addition to the remaining naval aircraft following the phase out of the carriers.

At the time I was coming to the end of my tour on 801. We were deployed on a major exercise to RAF El Adem in Libya, pending the squadron's re-embarkation on *Hermes*, *Victorious* having been prematurely scrapped after a fire whilst in the dockyard. My return flight from El Adem to Lossie was to be non-stop, and also my last with 801, refuelled in flight by Victors.

During our detachment a local modification had been made to the aircraft's cockpit air conditioning system to prevent any hot air from entering the cockpit. Unfortunately this local modification had not been removed from my aircraft for the return flight. After about forty minutes, and before the rendezvous with the tanker, both Trevor Ling in the back and I were freezing; the canopy and windscreen were frozen over apart from a small electrically heated bit in the front and we could see little outside. The prospect of refuelling in flight like this, and enduring a bitterly cold flight of some five hours, was not attractive if not impossible, so we diverted to RAF Luqa, Malta, to raid the stores for warm clothing and carry on alone. Trevor informed Lossie by HF radio what we were doing; Lossie asked us to keep power on the aircraft on the ground and we would be instructed by HF radio how to fix the problem.

After shutting down and applying ground power, I went to the local Aircraft Servicing Flight turn-round facility and borrowed some tools, much against the better judgement of the NCO in charge. Meanwhile, a group of resident RAF aircrew had seen the Buccaneer arrive and, knowing it had just been ordered for the RAF, decided to come and have a look at it. They were somewhat dismayed and unimpressed to find an RAF flight lieutenant pulling bits of its insides out, under the direction of a naval lieutenant sitting up in the rear seat! To my mind this small incident typifies the excellent team spirit, co-operation and initiative demonstrated by Buccaneer aircrew, whatever the colour of their uniform and wherever they found themselves. We also got back in time for the end of detachment party – what else would you expect?

I left 801 for the Central Flying School course, whilst plans to introduce the Buccaneer into RAF service continued apace. Given the need to get the Buccaneer to the front line as quickly as possible after the TSR2/F-111 debacle, it was decided to form a front-line squadron first and rely on the RN's training facilities to train the first cadre of RAF crews. Thus I left Little Rissington, clutching my B2 (probationary) QFI category, via a short stint at Valley to get some instructional experience, to drive north again (this time giving the 'Jesus Saves' boulder a wide berth) to re-join 736 Naval Air Squadron as a staff QFI. I arrived late on a Saturday night to find the mother and father of all parties going on in the wardroom. *Eagle* was in the Moray Firth; most of her ship's company had come ashore that day for sport and shore time. Unfortunately bad weather prevented their return on board so the officer contingent drank the bar dry, dismantling the wardroom piano in the process. I slept in my car that night, as no beds were available. Next day, at lunchtime in the bar, the piano appeared to have been miraculously re-assembled, until an unwitting drinker placed his pint pot on it, whereupon it disintegrated. Nothing had changed and it was good to be back.

A bunch of rather tired and elderly Buccaneer Mark 1s were withdrawn from storage to supplement 736's Mark 2 fleet, specifically for the RAF courses to fly. So it was back to the dubious delights of a Gyron Junior-powered Mark 1, with its unpredictable IGVs, TCVs and lack of thrust. These Mark 1s were maintained by a bunch of RAF ground crew, commanded by John Harvey, an RAF engineering officer. Generally, the Mark 1s

L-R: Tim Cockerell, Jerry Yates, Mick Whybro, Dave Laskey,
John Harvey, Tom Eeles, Barry Dove.

were remarkably serviceable so I now became the man in the back on a student's Fam 1 with a robust line of patter but no access to flying controls. There was no single-service demarcation and I flew with just as many RN students as RAF.

Given that the RAF was taking over the Fleet Air Arm's pride and joy there might have been considerable inter-service animosity but this was not the case. All went well until the last course started in late 1970. On 1 December, during Ivor Evans's Fam 1, the port engine of XN 951 refused to respond to a full power demand on short finals, the IGVs having got stuck. Despite a gallant attempt to overshoot from 100 feet, it was obvious we were only going down by testing Martin Baker's excellent product. I left Ivor to enjoy a couple of seconds of genuine solo Buccaneer time before landing with a thump on the airfield. Desperate to deploy my SARBE in order to claim the silver tankard given by the makers to those who used it to assist their rescue, I was frustrated by the rapid arrival of the emergency services. Despite inviting them to go away to give me time to erect the SABRE, they ignored my request and I had to settle for membership of the Martin Baker Club only.

That was the end of my flying with the RN; it was also nearly the end of Mark 1 flying. One week later another Mark 1 suffered a catastrophic engine failure and exploded; the student pilot ejected safely but sadly the student navigator was killed. The Mark 1 was withdrawn from service and No. 8 RAF Course continued on the Mark 2. After three months on the ground mending my back I found myself posted to the newly-formed 237 OCU at RAF Honington in the flat fields of Suffolk, a far cry from Lossiemouth and the wild country of the north of Scotland.

The remains of XN 951.

I discovered on arrival that the OCU had just one Buccaneer, a couple of Hunters, an unfurnished hangar, a few ground crew and even fewer instructors. A very smart officer, Wg Cdr Anthony Fraser, otherwise known as Garth, after a comic strip character in the *Daily Mirror*, commanded the unit. Nevertheless we set to with a will as the first students were soon due to arrive. I well remember grubbing about in the scrap dump at the about-to-close RAF Stradishall looking for roller blackboards for our briefing rooms; the system had denied us any from normal sources. There were many familiar faces at Honington and very soon the first students arrived to sustain the pace of activity. Fam 1s started again, at least in the well-powered and reliable Mark 2. The only dramatic incident I suffered was to get caught by the arrestor cable wrapping itself around the nose-wheel leg during a night take-off and bringing the aircraft to an abrupt and unexpected halt.

However, after some three years of instructional duties on 736 and 237 the Air Secretary's posters took pity on me and sent me to the front line. It was a short trip to the next hangar to join 12 Squadron, but it made a welcome change, despite finding myself appointed as squadron training officer for a period. Life on the squadron was very busy under the leadership of Ian Henderson and then Graham Smart. As the RAF's sole maritime assigned strike/attack squadron we found ourselves almost permanently involved in exercises both at home and abroad, visiting Karup, Decimomannu, Luqa, Akrotiri, Gibraltar, Bardufoss, Stornoway and of course Lossiemouth. We developed new tactics involving large eight-aircraft formations, flying at night, hurling Lepus flares at fleeing fast patrol boats, and we introduced both the TV and anti-radar versions of the Martel missile into service and devised tactics for its use. We continued to fire two-inch rockets with great abandon and even featured on the BBC programme 'Skywatch'.

The only time I was ever recalled from leave during my RAF career occurred on 12 Squadron, when the Turks invaded Cyprus in the summer of 1974, but in the event we were not needed. We sucked thousands of gallons of fuel from Victors by day and night and regularly clocked up thirty-five to forty hours flying each month. I even got struck by lightning, twice, both times at night. Eventually, after nearly three years and the award of a Queen's Commendation for Valuable Service in the Air, I moved away from the Buccaneer world to fly Hunters at the Tactical Weapons Unit.

But not for long. I returned to 237 OCU, taking up the role of chief flying instructor in 1977. This was another very busy tour with the added responsibility of a more senior rank and appointment, but the Fam 1s still featured. The OCU was feeding four squadrons, two in Germany and two in the UK, plus a trickle of RAF and RN aircrew to the one remaining RN squadron. When *Ark Royal* decommissioned in late 1978 another RAF squadron was formed at Honington. New equipment in the shape of the Pavespike laser designator, the laser-guided bomb (LGB), an active electronic counter measure (ECM) pod and an improved radar warning receiver (RWR) were being introduced to keep us on our toes, but sadly there was no change to the 1950's vintage weapons system.

Just as the future looked really bright for the RAF's Buccaneer force, which had gained a formidable reputation through its performance on Red Flag and Maple Flag exercises, disaster struck. A wing fold retaining pin failed in a Germany-based Buccaneer and both crew were killed. The problem was quickly solved with new sets of pins being produced by the engineers at RAF St Athan in very short order, but hardly had the dust settled when another Buccaneer suffered wing failure during Red Flag, which resulted in the fleet being grounded. I experienced a four-year gap from the Buccaneer world whilst it was reorganised.

I returned in 1984 as OC 237 OCU, which was still based at Honington. The fall-out from the Red Flag accident had reduced the Buccaneer fleet considerably. A brand new fatigue test specimen had been commissioned at Brough so effectively we were flying an aircraft without a cleared fatigue life but that did not deter anyone. There were now only two front-line squadrons, both based at Lossiemouth and assigned to the maritime strike/attack role. It was with much pleasure that I took 237 OCU back to Lossie, the Buccaneer's spiritual home, in November 1984, after blowing up the officer's mess at Honington during our dining out. Some things never change!

It was a great delight to operate the OCU from the old 736 Squadron HQ building at Lossie. I also had a fascinating war role, to support RAF Germany Jaguar and Tornado squadrons with laser designation for their LGB deliveries. Considerable pressure was applied from group HQ for this role to be abandoned in favour of supporting the two Lossie-based squadrons, but I declined, and never graduated a course late or deficient in training. We had a great time there, flying and playing hard in true Buccaneer tradition, but eventually it had to come to an end. In 1987 I left the Buccaneer force for an appointment as OC Exam Wing at CFS. But, I was not finished with the aircraft as I wangled myself a

Tom Eeles (behind the piper) leads the crews of 237 OCU on their arrival at Lossiemouth.

General War Appointment Notice (GWAN) to return to the Buccaneer force in the event of the Cold War turning hot and managed one or two refresher sorties, the last one being with Gordon Robertson on 9 November 1989. We did some Pavespike work, went to Tain for some bunt retard bombing, managed a few DHs (direct hits) but that signalled the end of my time on the 'Last All-British Bomber'.

The Buccaneer was a fantastic aircraft. It generated phenomenal loyalty from those lucky enough to fly it. It was probably the best strike/attack aircraft of its day, despite the lack of development of its weapons systems. Those who flew and maintained it made it work, and made it work exceptionally well. Its operational swan-song, operating from Bahrain during the first Gulf War, designating and delivering LGBs with great accuracy, was a fitting testimony to its capability.

Those lucky enough to fly Buccaneers were an exceptional bunch. They were a team who ignored differences that might have been caused by wearing different coloured uniforms. We flew, played and drank hard, giving quarter to no-one; those of us remaining still do at every opportunity!

I am often asked what the best aircraft I flew in my RAF career was. It is not an easy question to answer. The beautiful single-seat versions of the Hunter score highly as pure flying machines, but for overall effectiveness, exhilaration, challenging handling and satisfaction it can only be Blackburn's masterpiece, the superb Buccaneer.

CHAPTER SIX

AH! THOSE WERE THE DAYS

DAVID MULINDER

Seeking inspiration after Graham Pitchfork's invitation to contribute to *Buccaneer Boys*, I repaired to my study where, among my modest collection of memorabilia, there is a photograph that quickly brought those far off days of the arrival of 12 Squadron at Honington into a somewhat sharper focus. In the photo the station commander, Gp Capt John Herrington, is welcoming the first aircraft to usher in the era of the Buccaneer into RAF service. The three crews in the picture were Wg Cdr Geoff Davies and David Edwards, Ian Henderson and Doug Wilson, and myself and Mike Thomas. On that memorable day in October 1969, I recall that Wg Cdr Roy Watson and Graham Pitchfork were also there to greet us having spent six months preparing the station for Buccaneer maritime operations. The picture does not show our two flying officers, Ken Becker and Andy Evans. We had only three aircraft and I think seniority might have played a part.

The photographer captured us when we had barely descended from the aircraft and we all appear to be looking rather introspective. Aside from the historical significance of the occasion, the fact that we had, on the run in, exceeded the aircraft's maximum speed by some measure may have contributed to a slight increase in the flow of adrenalin. Perhaps the station commander had suddenly appreciated that the locals had been alerted to the way ahead and he was pondering what neighbourly issues would inevitably hit his in-tray in the weeks and months to come.

Several years prior to my arrival at RAF Honington, while instructing at RAF Acklington, I had an unexpected opportunity to glimpse a deed of derring-do perpetrated by a naval person. I believe that an in-flight emergency had occurred, the nature of which was sufficiently dire to require a Royal Navy Buccaneer to land on the short runway that, at

3,600 feet, was highly likely to provide an interesting spectacle; and so it turned out.

When one has been a basic flying instructor for the best part of a decade, an unexpected peek at the sharp end is a reminder that, with a little imagination, the moguls in the personnel department might yet see their way clear to opening up a bright and shining future. And so it proved.

I was invited, on several occasions, for an interview at CFS. Thereafter, I maintained the lowest of profiles, reasoning that a further instructional tour would hardly enhance my suitability for a front-line appointment. At thirty-three, I had yet to make the acquaintance of an aircraft with swept wings. Eventually, the impasse was settled by way of an unseemly threat. I was directed to attend another interview the following week. Recognising that I was skating on very thin ice indeed, I reluctantly complied. While waiting to be ushered into the commandant's office, I had time to contemplate the notion that were I to be invited to serve on the 'CFS Waterfront', and were I foolish enough to demur, the long march back to Acklington would be wholly uncongenial. There followed a brief encounter during which the commandant greeted me warmly. "Well Mulinder, this is a feather in your cap", quoth he. Before he could elaborate, without invitation and with some passion, I made clear why it would be neither in the best interests of the service nor of myself to sentence me to a further stint of instructional duties.

Even now, more than forty years on, I know not whether I was deemed unsuitable for this prestigious appointment or whether the commandant was won over by the force of my argument. Suffice to say, he remained inscrutable and, slowly lighting a cigarette, brought the interview to an abrupt end with just two words, softly spoken and with no obvious menace, "Goodbye Mulinder". I do not recall him giving the slightest hint of his future plans for me. That was however the end of the matter and I heard no more about it. Shortly afterwards, I received notice of my posting to Canberras which pleased me greatly.

Where was I? Ah, yes, a spectator at the breathtaking arrival of a naval Buccaneer at Acklington. Somehow, the aircraft was stopped within the limited space available. The brakes had fulfilled their function admirably. Alas, following the early disintegration of the tyres, the locked wheels were unequal to the stress of being in direct contact with the tarmac and amidst a shower of sparks the aircraft ground to a steaming halt on what remained of the wheels. I remember gazing with awe at the hemispheres on which the aircraft now rested. Following this random brush with what I perceived to be a most impressive and intriguing aircraft, I was naturally curious to learn more about the Buccaneer which with its dark blue livery, robust construction, high tail and unique airbrakes presented a formidable, purposeful and decidedly lethal appearance.

A further year would pass before I was able to take another look at it – this time in less dramatic circumstances. The encounter took place in the autumn of 1968 while I was serving on 32 Squadron in Akrotiri. We were detached to Malta to participate in Exercise Eden Apple. An impressive row of Royal Navy Buccaneers was parked close to our elderly Canberras on the flight line at RAF Luqa. It was not long before Ian Henderson, who had recently assumed command of 32 Squadron, introduced me to Hugh Cracroft, one of several RAF pilots on an exchange tour with the Royal Navy. While I sat in the cockpit,

No. 1 RAF Course Lossiemouth.

Hugh patiently answered my questions and made clear his affection for the aircraft and its role. Was I impressed? I should say so. I little knew on that day that within a couple of months I should learn of my posting to RNAS Lossiemouth on the first RAF Buccaneer course.

I have happy memories of my year on Canberras in Akrotiri when we flitted about the Mediterranean and the adjacent countries of the Middle East. It was a pleasure to fly but its best days were in the past and for me the Buccaneer represented an exciting future with as yet unknowable challenges and opportunities.

Tuesday, 3 June 1969 was just another day in the life of Lossiemouth. I could not help but be impressed by the sheer scale and intensity of operations; and here was I, somewhat overawed, in the midst of it. As I prepared for my first take-off in the Buccaneer, I listened attentively to the pearls of wisdom emanating from the instructor in the back seat. This redoubtable personage was none other than Tom Eeles, a veteran of many such sorties. I vaguely recall that Tom had earlier divulged to me that most, if not all of the instructors on 736 Squadron had found it necessary to eject from stricken aircraft. I think the capricious nature of the Gyron Junior engines may have been a factor. Did I imagine it or did Tom sound slightly wistful? Whatever his feelings, shortly thereafter he found it necessary to abandon ship in the Lossiemouth circuit whilst engaged on an excursion similar to that

*First 12 Squadron crews greeted by Group Captain John Herrington
at Honington, October 1969.*

which occupied our attention on this day. Little did Tom and I know that in August 1984, some fifteen years later, we would again climb aboard a Buccaneer. Once more, Tom was gracing the back seat, still keeping a fatherly eye on an elderly gent on his last sortie in a Buccaneer. Three months after that first flight, I headed south to join a RAF front-line squadron with a bright future.

During the last four months of 1969 and the first half of 1970, 12 Squadron was expanding at a modest rate. Very early on, my QFI qualification came in handy; and it was my good fortune to be selected from a cast of one for QFI and IRE (instrument rating instructor) duties. After four sorties with Ian Henderson, and two hours solo on type, I was dispatched to RNAS Yeovilton to fly the required check rides with the RN Standards Flight. Conscious that my knowledge of the Hunter was somewhat sketchy, I resolved to stick to the big picture and display such knowledge as I possessed with only the broadest of brush strokes. With my logbook duly signed, I returned to Honington fully aware that my licence to practise was in urgent need of consolidation. And I kept in the forefront of my mind the perceptive observation of an earlier CFS examiner viz, 'this instructor's ability to impart knowledge is above average. Unfortunately, the knowledge imparted isn't'. One is expected to learn from such experiences and I should like to think I did. And I am ever mindful of the pitfalls inherent in, 'the older I get, the better I am' syndrome.

Very recently, I was listening to Buzz Aldrin describing his ascent from the moon. He stated plainly that he had made several mistakes during that journey but that, fortunately, they were not disastrous. "Am I going to tell you what they were?", he asked. After a suitable pause, he answered his own question, "definitely not". If that approach is good enough for an astronaut who has been to the moon, it is certainly good enough for me. Thus, I shall belay piping any revelations of past misdemeanours as yet undetected. That said, I am reminded that an undercarriage 'malfunction' in 1970 necessitated Graham Pitchfork and myself remaining close to Malta while we burned off fuel. At some stage we spotted a Soviet warship, which Graham quickly identified as a Kresta II cruiser. We were almost certainly under remit to maintain a healthy distance from such vessels but no specific distance was laid down and the intelligence-gathering community warmly welcomed our spectacular close-range photos. I know not what the Soviet captain thought about this Buccaneer circling his ship with the undercarriage down. Higher authority remained uncharacteristically silent.

As 1970 gave way to 1971, with their exchange tours complete, the RAF triumvirate of Tom Eeles, Gerry Yates and Tim Cockerell arrived at Honington together with navigators Barry Dove, Mick Whybro and Peter Bucke. Graham Pitchfork was squadron leader operations and Jock Gilroy, who had just been flying Scimitars, arrived to be the wing weapons officer. Thus, we acquired a breadth and depth of experience that enabled the RAF Buccaneer squadrons to make a highly-significant contribution to the effectiveness of our operational capability in the maritime role.

An activity that still induces a slight frisson of apprehension involved flinging Lepus flares into the stygian blackness over some remote Scottish island. As was my wont, I suggested to my navigator that he monitor with utmost care and attention the shenanigans up front. Having unleashed the flare, with the nose rising higher and higher and the speed rapidly decreasing, the proceedings were further enlivened by the eerie glow of millions of candle power emanating from the flare, which instantly assaulted the senses. Now the trick was to transfer one's gaze from the instruments and locate the target – while retaining some semblance of control.

It was essential at this stage to bring the nose down and around so that, with the aircraft in a steep descending turn with the speed going t'other way, the sight could be aligned with the target, preferably prior to weapon release. This required smooth and judicious inputs on the control column and a pretty good idea which way was up. This was very definitely a period of high concentration leavened by a modicum of excitement and a discernible increase in heart rate. Looking back, I should add that it was most exhilarating; and I for one had no doubt that this was another of those situations when, as if he did not have enough on his plate, the navigator needed to have that extra capacity and presence of mind to whisper, plead, shout or scream words of encouragement and advice as might become necessary. I am pleased to say that my navigator remained sanguine while I was performing my gyrations up front. Could be he was frozen with terror or just having a snooze. Anyway, it was just another night in the office. Phew.

Among the many attributes of the Buccaneer, I greatly appreciated the ability of the aircraft to remain in the air at low level for eons of time; and even now after the passing of so many years I can still picture the radio altimeter providing reassuring information on those dark, murky nights flying low over the North Sea. I don't know who decided that it should be located above the coaming on the starboard side (where the navigator could see it) but he surely deserves a vigorous wave of the Kudos flag, first seen at Red Flag to signal approval of any debriefing which was well delivered and therefore unlikely to delay attendance at the bar in the officers' club at Nellis AFB.

Mention of the vital importance of the radio altimeter and its location reminds me of just one of those nights. We were returning from a northern outpost at low level over the sea. I had Dave Scott on one wing and Bob Newell on the other. We encountered cloud and I offered them the chance to detach and return to Honington independently. They were made of sterner stuff than me and elected to remain in close formation for many minutes in cloud at 400 feet above the sea. To this day, I don't know how they did it. I do remember that they appeared entirely unconcerned during the debrief. I remember also the part played by the radio altimeter, which had enjoyed my very close attention throughout.

I must also doff my hat to the inventor of the airstream direction detector (ADD), which provided information on angle of attack which was vital to the safety of the aircraft. It was comforting to know that providing the audio was making harmonious noises as you turned finals you had a good chance of making beer call; and if you kept the blow pressure up you were less likely to dent the runway.

In the spring of 1971 responsibility for training Buccaneer crews passed to the RAF and I was posted to 237 OCU where I was joined by most of the outstanding aviators who had served with the Royal Navy. When I left the OCU in 1974 I was in no doubt that the final chapter of my romance with the Buccaneer had been written. I couldn't have been more wrong. Another ten years would pass before I flew the afore-mentioned last sortie with Tom Eeles.

On numerous occasions over the years I had felt Dame Fortune's hand lightly brushing my shoulder. And so it was in 1981, seven years later that I found myself arriving once more at Honington as OC 237 OCU. I am not sure what my mood was as I arrived for work on that first morning. There is, I think, a good chance that I was optimistic as usual; and I was probably elated at being allowed the chance to run what I hoped would be a tight ship and for being given the responsibility for turning out crews well prepared for the front line. I was also familiar with the observation, 'not in my wildest dreams'. More often than not such an observation was accompanied by chaos, catastrophe or something highly unusual. And so it proved.

The precise timing of the event and the ensuing phone call from the deputy commander-in-chief are a little hazy. I think, at this stage, I may have been in command (ho! ho!) for all of fifteen minutes and had not yet had time to sample my CO's chair or my PA's coffee, let alone make myself known to my team. Within the very few minutes it took the DC-in-C to make known to me his sudden interest in my welfare, I had ascertained that a student navigator had ejected from an OCU aircraft.

The student pilot quickly discovered that once it left the runway the Buccaneer was entirely unsuited to ploughing the infield. In the scheme of things, the circumstances leading to the ejection were relatively mundane. No lasting harm was done and normal operations were quickly resumed. I was not however entirely unaware of the potential for a less favourable outcome. Indeed, I already knew that an unfortunate squadron commander in the USAF had arrived to take up his post just in time to observe the depletion of his resources as a result of a wheels-up landing. His situation was not dissimilar to that which confronted me. Upon being summarily fired by the commanding general, he protested that he hadn't yet taken over. "I don't have time to differentiate between the incompetent and the unfortunate" was the response. And that was that.

Unsurprisingly, I have no great difficulty in recalling the words of wisdom emanating from the telephone that morning. The gist was that having had some part in selecting me for the job I might at least have waited until the afternoon before causing him to doubt his judgement. No, no, those were not his exact words. He was, not to put too fine a point, pithy and direct. He did however revert to his normal 'kindly' self before we were through. And I was still there three years later.

I seem to remember having a 'dream' during my time looking after the OCU in which OC Ops at Laarbruch (an ethereal Tim Cockerell – gotta use your imagination) asked if I could lend him a Buccaneer and I was happy to oblige. I think the aircraft may have resided with Tim for some months before a higher authority discovered that, 'one of our aircraft seems to be missing'. Was I really accused of consorting with the enemy (RAF Germany)? Thank goodness it was only a dream. Hmm, can't think why my knuckles are still aching after all these years.

Later still, I had another dream. In this one (yes, it was definitely a dream), tea and cucumber sandwiches were on the table. The lights were low. The overhead projector was humming. The bullet points were clear as crystal and I was briefing an eminent personage (EP) on our operations. Not wishing to bore the EP with too much detail, I turned to my hopes and expectations for the future. In the midst of my mythical peroration, I can still hear the echo, "If it would be all right with you Mulinder, I'll run my command and you can run your unit". Just a dream!

During my last year at Honington, the OCU was given the task of running a trial to establish whether it would be feasible to include crew training during the Tactical Weapons Unit (TWU) phase of pilot training by flying navigators in the empty back seat of the Hawk. A lead-in-training course was devised and, after 'an exchange of views' with higher authority, I succeeded in installing Jim Rutter at the helm. A year later, Jim (still in charge) turned sixty and I thought it would be appropriate to recognise the achievement of this milestone by joining him in a glass of 'champers' – after we had climbed out of a Hunter having enjoyed a low-level tour of the local area. We were still of sufficiently sound mind to add his sixty years to my fifty and come up with 110 which gave me much pleasure – and still does.

So after three years, the young Tom Eeles took over from my geriatric self. Now it really was time to take a firm grasp of the white stick and learn to steer that pesky zimmer. Careful now, try to exit the stage with a modicum of dignity and without tripping up. In 1989, I retired to my birthplace in Plymouth, the end of the rainbow at last. From my flat overlooking Plymouth Sound, I could watch the sunset, slurp copious gin and tonics and just occasionally reflect on the good old days.

David Mulinder hands over command of 237 OCU to Tom Eeles.

While I have no profound message to pass on, I have no hesitation in observing that flying the Buccaneer was a great privilege and a truly marvellous experience. Moreover, I learned early on that having a navigator with initiative and good air sense was the equivalent to gold dust. And it didn't take me long to realise that a good engineering team with a 'can-do' attitude was absolutely crucial to getting the job done. In this respect I was singularly fortunate and often felt that I had a surfeit of riches. Those were the days. They really were.

CHAPTER SEVEN

BUCCANEER FIRST TOUR – I DON'T BELIEVE IT!

AL BEATON

The announcement of the postings for the student pilots of No. 40 Course at RAF Valley in August 1968 was not just a huge sense of relief at having passed a gruelling flying course, it was an unbelievable moment in my life when a dream came true. Postings to Lightnings, Hunters, Canberras and CFS had been announced, but the best had been saved till last: 'Buccaneer for Al Beaton and Bill Cope'. We were the initial RAF first tourists posted to the exciting new low-level combat aircraft that was just entering service. We had timed it perfectly and were the centre of congratulations mixed with a fair measure of envy but I just remember feeling incredibly lucky.

The pre-Buccaneer weapons course on the Hunter at RAF Chivenor was a return to the reality of hard work and another test of self-confidence. We were only twenty-one years old and were now flying a single-seat thoroughbred that initially took us on the ride of our lives. Bombing and rocketing, and the precision required, became a new discipline that had to take over from the excitement of flying. Scores and results were facts none of us could argue with. Then came the low-level thrash around Wales and Devon, with a bounce aircraft to avoid, all ending up with a first-run attack (FRA) bomb or rocket on the range at Pembrey.

We were only just beginning to get to grips with the aircraft and the applied flying skills when the course came to an end. We felt lucky to have flown the Hunter, which had provided a stern test and made us confident and ready for the next important step. We had proved to ourselves, and the RAF, that we had the determination to be successful and that we possessed the fundamental skills to fly one of Her Majesty's expensive toys. Our spirits were high, and the more advanced Buccaneer was now in our sights. Failure just wasn't an option.

In February 1970 we headed for Lossiemouth and the free airspace and beautiful north-west Highlands and the Moray coastline, which were the Buccaneer's home territory. North

63

Wales and the A5 pass were supposed to be spectacular but the freedom to fly around Scotland at low level and to bomb on the excellent range at Tain provided the best facilities available. The Fleet Air Arm (FAA) approach on 736 Squadron was reassuringly relaxed after the more formal RAF style and the friendly, encouraging and competitive squadron spirit was ideal for us to make our final step to a front-line squadron. The last and most important ingredient of all, the mighty aeroplane itself, was the ultimate exhilaration.

Ground school introduced us to new navigational equipment, Blue Parrot radar and Blue Jacket doppler, a weapon-aiming system that was much more advanced than stopwatch and map. For the first time we were crewed up with our fellow first-tour navigators. Navigator training in the RAF had hardly recognised the low-level environment and their lead-in had been minimal compared to our pilot training. Throw in the avionics and the high-speed low-level tactics with a bounce, plus weapon handling and operating a radar and our first-tour navigators had their work cut out from the very beginning. Neither of our two navigators survived the course. In my mind, this was in no way a reflection on their enthusiasm and potential but highlighted the inadequate RAF pre-OCU navigator training.

With no dual-control Buccaneer, we were introduced to the aircraft's instrumentation with four or five sorties in modified two-seat Hunters. Our five simulator trips in the motionless 'box' sufficed to familiarise us with all the systems. Flap, droop and boundary layer control (BLC), or 'blow' as we called it, was a new concept to master. I soon disciplined myself to watch the cheeses [gauges] that signalled the position for flap and droop. Two engines, and therefore two throttles, was a first. I convinced myself that if I simply moved both throttles together it was effectively one power unit.

The simulator had prepared us for our first Buccaneer ride when there would be no demos. We would be on our own but after this introduction I remember thinking that I should be able to take off and land safely so my first flight in the Buccaneer was something to really look forward to.

My overriding impression of my first 'solo' was the aircraft's sheer size. The climb up the ladder into the cockpit to sit in the real thing for the first time was a moment cut all too short by the need to get on with the pre-flight checks.

Tom Eeles had the dubious honour of sitting in the back. Up until now, all of our pilot training had been geared towards single-pilot operation and we had had experience of taking off and landing in a number of aircraft. Now we had to cope with flap, droop and the blow, and they were critical additional factors in the Buccaneer. The take-off was exhilarating and having Tom talk me through cleaning up the aircraft as we accelerated away was a great comfort. To share a discussion or a decision was a pleasant change and very reassuring. Fulfilling an ambition, and in the wonderful surroundings of the Moray Firth on a fine sunny day, was a most exciting flying experience and one I, like all Buccaneer pilots, will never forget. As I savoured this first experience of the mighty Buccaneer, it had all the ingredients and excitement of another first solo. I was aware of the remarkably positive handling characteristics of the clean aeroplane at medium level. This was a comfortable aeroplane to fly. As the sortie progressed I realised that I would soon have to return this beast to earth again, and being the only one with a set of flying controls, this was going to require a serious focus of my attention. A few dummy circuits at a safe height prepared me well for the challenge ahead.

Back to the circuit, the acid test was the final approach and landing and it was reassuring to have Tom's commentary and to see the cheeses and the blow working just as advertised. The carrier landing techniques we were taught using the 'meatball' deck-landing mirror sight on the edge of Lossiemouth's generous runway was a wonderful approach aid. This aeroplane was to be set up from several hundred feet out and, with an ideally-positioned ASI and the mirror sight both displayed within the front left windscreen, it was flown as precisely as possible down to the ground with no flare. The addition of the ADD (airflow direction detector) tone was another quality item that the Buccaneer introduced us to. We could now also hear how accurately the aircraft was being flown. Visual and audio senses were tuned to achieve the steady note for a very meticulous approach. Simple really! With the almost unbreakable main undercarriage playing its vital role, I landed safely. So it was that both Tom and I survived, my pride and his relief both scoring straight tens.

The aircraft was very responsive and solid in a crisp manner. Whilst it didn't handle as lightly as a Hunter there was never any shortage of control authority to meet the demands of high speed and high rates of manoeuvre, either in the bombing pattern or in the most exhilarating low flying. In the circuit, you just had to be more precise. Crew co-operation continued into the circuit handling, particularly observing the flap and droop and blow. The talking checklist with another pair of eyes (and opinion) in the cockpit certainly lightened the load. Thus we all had a great deal of confidence and a growing affection for the airframe, although we were less sure about the performance of the avionics suite. If there was any significant cross-wind on take-off, the Gyron Junior engines might not wind up, smoothly, the inlet guide vanes (IGV) usually stalling and causing the engine to surge. The first time this happened to me I thought the aircraft was being hit by cannon shells such was the rapidity and the violence of the surging engine. Power on one engine was less than adequate on the Mark 1 and we all knew it, particularly for any single-engine overshoot.

Barry Dove next found himself on the programme to fly my Fam 2. In many ways, flying with an experienced navigator was probably more valuable than having a QFI in the back. Sorry, Tom! The senior navs had seen it all, good and bad. They had no flying controls to retrieve a situation and their focus, sense of survival and professionalism were invaluable. They were another pair of eyes on the essential instruments and certainly had strong views on where and how the aircraft should be flown. They weren't really navigators at all; they were part of a two-man team whose responsibility, through training, discussion and agreement, was to make the Buccaneer operate effectively in the low-level environment. We didn't think it was dangerous; after all, it was the best fun flying to be had in the whole of the RAF. In the low-level role, it was two guys, an aeroplane and the weather. There was no time to refer to rulebooks. Respect the regulations yes, but developing flexibility and operational effectiveness, whilst operating this large machine at low level and out of reach of any ultimate controlling authority, required an attitude of mind that the FAA had and the RAF was learning.

The all-round view from the Buccaneer was excellent and the smooth ride lent itself to low-level flying. Flying at high speed, close to the ground or over the sea was exhilarating and gave a total sense of freedom. Together with a disciplined measure of controlled hooliganism that low level brings, and which no other role can provide, it was every young pilot's dream.

On the weapons range, the modern strike sight was a great step up from the earlier generation system in the Hunter. But the Buccaneer's system really came into its own for medium toss bombing. Running in past Tarbat Ness and tossing bombs on to Tain range from three miles was very different to anything we had done before.

We only flew the Mark 2 five times on our course but I distinctly remember the awesome power of the Spey engines compared to the Mark 1's underpowered Gyron Juniors. The next first tourist course had less luck and lost two aircraft, both in the circuit on student fam sorties and, very sadly, one navigator was killed when his seat failed to operate correctly. Attending his funeral was a most moving experience for all the new Buccaneer aircrew and another new self-discipline that we would, unfortunately, have to call on several times again in our Buccaneer experience.

It was early July 1970. With only seventy-five hours on type, we finished the course with a flourish throwing Gloworms over Gralis Sgeir at night, almost just for the hell of it as they provided virtually no useful illumination. During our course we had been introduced to low-level navigation, strike progression, numerous bombing modes, including dropping our first live 1,000lb bomb, some two-inch RP, and a great deal of Lossiemouth and local Moray hospitality. We were well prepared to return to the RAF and join a squadron.

The spirit on 736 Squadron was a breath of fresh air to we first tourists. There had been too many prima-donnas in the Hunter world at Chivenor. We were operating to far greater levels of operational flexibility and achievement, the two-man principle eliminating the bullsh** and replacing it with a squadron spirit that swept us up and carried us with it throughout the course. We weren't just students, we were treated as squadron members and the sense of belonging in our formative Buccaneer days was a huge bonus which paid handsome dividends later. It certainly helped us tremendously throughout the course and flying with the navy had added another dimension and would be the foundation upon which our own personal and the RAF's Buccaneer force would build.

The early crews for the RAF's first Buccaneer squadron, No. 12, had also completed their courses at Lossiemouth. The CO, Wg Cdr Geoff Davies, had been a test pilot on the Buccaneer. His experience of the aeroplane was greater than any of us although it was primarily Mark 1 time on radar-development trials with Ferranti. Others came from a Canberra background so had experience of the all-important two-man principle. The flight commander was Ian Henderson, in my view one of the most gifted Buccaneer pilots who we all came to respect.

When we arrived at Honington it was to discover that the squadron was away in Malta on an exercise. Feeling deserted at the outset, our typical first tourist desire to keep the 736 momentum going was frustrated but we soon learned our proper place; after all, we were the junior pilots. However, that did not stop us enjoying this new phase of life, the thrill of arriving on our first squadron, fabulous flying, the team spirit, a large collection of single guys, a vibrant officers' mess, good local pubs, all were ingredients that invited us to enjoy life to the full and we did.

12 Squadron investigate a Soviet Kotlin class destroyer in the Mediterranean, 1970.

Our flying on 12 Squadron began with the standard routine of acceptance checks in both the Hunter and the Buccaneer. We now had to work up to become operational. Our role was two-fold; maritime attack and nuclear strike. The aircraft had been brought into service after the demise of both the TSR2 and the F-111. The nuclear role was a sobering thought for a young twenty-two-year old when struggling to mix the new found freedoms of squadron life with the distractions of Green King at the Four Horse Shoes at Thornham Magna and other similar hostelries of Suffolk and Norfolk.

At this early stage, maritime tactics sorties did not feature regularly and our 1 (Bomber) Group master, with its long-standing bomber mentality and years of operating the V-Force, appeared to struggle on how to include the Buccaneer in its arsenal. During my later tours I saw how the Buccaneer squadrons became a formidable maritime attack force. To my mind we weren't a conventional maritime attack squadron at all. Throwing a tactical nuke, from three or four miles away was what the aircraft was designed for and this option gave us the only chance of damaging a naval target and surviving. Delivering iron bombs against a modern well-defended naval force was, in reality, a combination of suicide and a complete waste of time. We were joining the UK nuclear strike force primarily and, with its long legs, the Buccaneer, even without using air-to-air refuelling, could strike at very long range and deep into Eastern Europe. The Cold War was in full swing and the thought that the Soviet army could be at the Rhine in three days focused our minds on overland bombing. However, with the demise of the future aircraft carrier programme, the RAF Buccaneer force had been tasked with providing land-based support of maritime operations and so we got used to enjoying the Buccaneer's multi-role capabilities.

Our early sorties on the squadron were spent bombing on the ranges close to our new

Always an excellent service from our Victor friends.

patch. We were lucky to have Holbeach, Cowden and Theddlethorpe for laydown and dive-bombing and Wainfleet for toss. The Buccaneer was a good weapons platform and I recall it was slightly less stable in yaw than it was in pitch.   Avoiding any pedalling on the rudders was important and matching the LP RPMs was essential to obtain balanced thrust from both engines. ADSL (auto depressed sight line) bombing, requiring steady tracking as the bunt increased to an automatic weapon release, was very accurate but very academic. In an operational scenario against a determined opponent, a pop-up attack was more realistic so we adapted a profile before pulling up for a low-level ADSL release.

Our use of two-inch RP was great fun, especially loosing off a full pod of them, but it was not expected that many maritime targets would be engaged with rockets. Later, when SNEB replaced the RP, we developed tactics against fast patrol boats. Just as much fun were dive attacks against a splash target towed by a ship or launch. We also introduced the Lepus flare at this early stage and it made for an exciting sortie when we flew at night, tossed a Lepus and then dived to attack beneath the illumination.

This wide variety of weapons gave us many options and we even had an excellent photo-recce capability but it was difficult at times to stay current in every mode, particularly when some flying hours had to be devoted to completing the dreaded 'basic training requirements' (BTR) of GCAs, single-engine approaches etc., etc.

I always felt that the Buccaneer was well ahead of its time. It was great to fly but just when we thought we had mastered one game, there was always something else for us to explore. It is little wonder that we enjoyed operating the aircraft and gained great respect for its capabilities. The Mark 2 Buccaneer reversed the trend of most British military aircraft designs by providing more than enough power for the majority of tasks, especially heavily laden with fuel or 1,000lb bombs. The fuel-carrying capability was another tremendous comfort, not just as a long-range strike aircraft but also allowing us to outrun most fighter adversaries who were always likely to be fuel critical before us. That ability to outperform anything at low level gained us a respect that we became very proud of and it boosted our morale.

As the squadron developed, we became a class act and the envy of many of our contemporaries in the RAF. The role and the aircraft were everything and more than we had all ever wanted. The two-man crew concept stifled any individual arrogance whilst undoubtedly increasing operational efficiency. It was the ideal world for us as first tourists. This was an aircraft that was supreme in its own environment; the opposition didn't need to know that the avionics – the weakest link in the aircraft – were frustrating the hell out of the navs. I recall reflecting that there was little point in getting through at low level if the avionics kit wasn't working. In the front seat, we gained the greatest respect for our navs, who with their heads down, whilst we flew fast and low, were trying to salvage something out of kit that was not as robust and reliable as the roles demanded. Mutual respect for each other was building and maturing the squadron all the time. When we finally added air-to-air refuelling to our bag of tricks, not only from the Victor but also using our own buddy-buddy aircraft, our operational flexibility was complete. There was now no limit to where we could go, either by day or by night.

That finally led us to the best part of squadron life, detachments to Norway, Cyprus, Italy, Malta, Stornoway and even back up to Lossiemouth exercising what we had practised from Honington. For me, the detachment to beat them all was to Tengah, Singapore, in February 1972 where, after a four-day transit with AAR, through Cyprus, Masirah and Gan to Singapore, we mixed flying over the jungle with the attractions of down-town Singapore and lots of cold Tiger beers. As I landed my Buccaneer on Malaysian tarmac, I felt a true feeling of personal achievement.

That we all have such memories of our own, of great friendships all linked to a most wonderful flying machine, is a true testament to its capability and its contribution in enriching the lives of all of us who flew the Buccaneer. This was without doubt the finest flying time of our lives. For a first tourist, I can still hardly believe my luck.

Queenie Liu, aged 20, one of the Hong Kong Tourist Association's pretty Chinese guides, welcomes navigator Flt Lt Andy Evans, son of Mr and Mrs G. Evans, of 80 Montrose Avenue, Lillington, to the colony. Andy, who has been in the RAF since 1964, was on a three day visit with Buccaneers from No 12 Squadron, RAF Honington.

Welcome to Hong Kong.

CHAPTER EIGHT
RAF GERMANY –
FIRST IN AND LAST OUT

DAVID COUSINS

It all started on a cold, gloomy winter's day.

On 6 January 1971, I was detailed off to be No.2 to the 'Boss' – Wg Cdr David Collins, OC XV Squadron. My navigator was Tom Bradley (a real coup for me as he had just completed an exchange tour on Buccaneers with the Fleet Air Arm whereas I had barely seventy-seven hours on type). We were to be the lead echelon of the first permanent Buccaneer deployment to Germany. The brief flight was from RAF Honington to RAF Laarbruch. These were heady and exciting times. David Collins said lightly to me as we walked out to the aircraft that he felt he should take an ADC (aide de camp) with him – I had just completed a tour as ADC to the then Chief of Air Staff – as we were going to be met on arrival by all the top 'brass' in RAF Germany. This was the first I had heard about it, but it began to concentrate my mind a bit more starkly when the CO had to recover to Honington shortly after take-off with an in-flight emergency.

After landing at Laarbruch, we swung rather too briskly into the dispersal area and saw a line-up of very senior officers waiting for these two lowly junior officers. Unfortunately, I had forgotten about the notorious black ice that was a feature of German airfields in winter, and the aircraft juddered sideways as we swung right towards the marshaller. Out of the corner of my eye, I could see the assembled hierarchy frantically scrabbling backwards as twenty tons of 'Blackburn's Finest' slid towards them. It was not an auspicious start. Nor did I much like the look in the station commander's eye. But we had arrived safely, and the thirteen-year tenure of the Buccaneer at Laarbruch had begun. Little did I know then that in 1984, as station commander of Laarbruch, I would fly in a Buccaneer in a 'box four' formation with a Hunter, Jaguar and Tornado, to mark the end of the Buccaneer in RAF Germany.

Buccaneers lined up at Laarbruch, 1972.

But why were we there at all? The reasoning goes back a long way.

If there ever was a visionary airman who confidently predicted at the end of the Second World War that there would be a permanent RAF presence in Germany for the next fifty-six years – there being, after all, only twenty-one years between the two Great Wars of the Twentieth Century – then I have yet to meet or even hear of him.

But that is precisely what happened. The RAF units stationed in Germany over that period were sequentially under the command of: 2nd Tactical Air Force, the British Air Forces of Occupation, RAF Germany, 2 Group, and finally 1 Group. The last RAF squadron permanently to be based in Germany finally left in 2002.

In those fifty-six years of the Cold War and its immediate aftermath, many RAF aircraft and crews have claimed Germany for their own. It is almost unimaginable now, for instance, to envisage after World War Two that there were no less than four groups, twenty wings, sixty-eight squadrons and twenty operational airfields under RAF control. So the Spitfires, Mosquitoes and Tempests of those early years can certainly lay claim to Germany; but so, too, can the Vampires, Venoms, Sabres, Hunters, Canberras, Javelins, Lightnings, Phantoms, Jaguars, Harriers, Tornados and various helicopter types that succeeded them.

What is unarguable, however, in the recorded views of a number of contemporary air force historians, is that the thirteen-year tenure of the Buccaneer in Germany – from 1971 to 1984 – coincided with a time when the reputation of 2ATAF for tactical expertise and professional competence was regarded by many as second to none. The 1970s re-equipment programme was arguably the most significant in the history of RAF Germany especially in performance and weapon-carrying capability. NATO tactical evaluation results for RAF stations were the best in the Central Region during this period. A British ambassador in Germany at the time told the RAF commander-in-chief that: "…when things are going badly with the Germans, the strongest card in my pack is the quality of your forces…I fall back on the excellence of your contribution to the defence of the Federal Republic of Germany." At a more humble level, therefore, being stationed on a Buccaneer squadron during that period certainly felt like being at the very sharp end.

The Buccaneer Wing of XV and 16 Squadrons at RAF Laarbruch, one of the four 'clutch' stations built along the German/Dutch border in the early 1950s, was intrinsic to, and very much a part of, this 'front-line' spirit. Throughout those halcyon thirteen years, it felt sometimes as if we had returned to the 'balbo and booze' era of 1946; there was a serious and demanding job to be done but with enough time left over to enjoy it all too. The emphatic emphasis and expectation was to 'work hard and play hard'.

Working Hard

What accounted for this period of exceptional professionalism that laid the foundations for all that was to follow in the Balkans, Iraq and Afghanistan?

Location helped. We were all too aware of the proximity and scale of the Warsaw Pact (WP) forces facing us. Moreover, the focus and funding in the 1970s – certainly in Great Britain – was switching from an emphasis on strategic bombing to tactical air power. The 1970s saw the advent of infrastructure hardening programmes, 'tone-down', battle damage repair, Taceval, the Tactical Leadership Programme (TLP), a close working relationship at all levels with the British Army of the Rhine and Red Flag exercises in Nevada which allowed the RAF squadrons to develop the composite tactics that were to shape the initial Gulf War air campaign and all that followed.

It seems all the more extraordinary that the Buccaneer – designed and built purely for the maritime role – felt immediately to its crews to be eminently suitable in most respects for the overland role to which it was assigned in 1971. Salvation and self-defence in those days lay in flying very low and very fast over long distances. In this respect, the Buccaneer, designed specifically for this environment with comparatively small wings and an 'area rule' design, which facilitated high cruising speeds with less thrust, simply did not have any peers.

Fortunately for us, West Germany offered unparalled low-flying opportunities. A typical training sortie of some one hour thirty minutes could be spent almost exclusively at 250 feet above ground level over terrain very similar to our operational target areas. By a series of low-flying areas linked together, it was possible to fly from the Baltic to Bavaria exclusively at low level and end up on a bombing range with a run at 100 feet and 500+ knots. The Buccaneer force took a particular pride in honing this overland low-flying skill, often passing well beneath the German air force F-104s who trained at 800 feet. The distinctive sound of their radar signature on the Buccaneer electronic warning system reminded us how crowded the low-flying environment could be.

Our assigned roles were strike (nuclear), battlefield air interdiction (essentially significant static military complexes), and close air support (attacks on armour and mobile army formations). This gave us ample scope for a wide variety of interesting and varied training.

Quick reaction alert at Laarbruch, 1972.

The challenge with all aircraft over their period of operational service is to improve their capability to match a technically improving threat. In the case of the Buccaneer, the 'heavy lifting' decisions in terms of aircraft performance had already been taken before the Buccaneer Wing formed in Germany. These amounted essentially to converting the aircraft from Gyron Junior to Spey engines, which provided a welcome total increase of some 8,000lbs of thrust, and the fitting of a conformal 425-gallon fuel tank into the outer skin of the bomb-bay door. Range was always a critical factor in the Central Region where in-flight refuelling so close to the Inner German border and a significant Warsaw Pact fighter threat would have been close to suicidal.

Over the next thirteen years, a steady flow of incremental improvements, new equipment and weapons enhanced the capability of the aircraft. This also provided a constant training stimulus for the crews as they mastered the equipment and techniques involved. Thus modifications to the Blue Parrot radar and navigation system were introduced in 1971 to give the aircraft a notional night and poor weather capability considered so essential for the strike role. Electronic counter measure pods and chaff/flare dispensers arrived; an early version of the AIM 9 air-to-air missile was fitted in the mid-1970s, and perhaps most significantly, the aircraft was fitted in 1979 with a Pavespike laser designator pod to guide Paveway bombs with precision onto designated targets.

Those early months in Germany were heady days. The aircrew were drawn from a variety of backgrounds but none could claim to be absolute master of all the disciplines we encountered. We simply had to learn on the job and discard many of the attack profiles we had been taught by the Fleet Air Arm. It became obvious early on that there was a magical mixture of characters on the squadron and so the social challenges were rapidly mastered. Morale was always high despite the tragic loss in a flying accident of Wg Cdr David Collins, OC XV Squadron, and his navigator, Paul Kelly in early 1971.

The early training emphasis was on assignment to NATO in the strike role, and this was achieved in barely five months. The paradox of the strike role was that while it was strategically so evidently vital, peacetime training for it was relatively mundane. Singleton sorties were flown to a simulated target followed by a laydown or toss attack on a range. We all knew it would be a very different kettle of fish in wartime. Moreover, there was never any tolerance allowed in making mistakes in nuclear enabling procedures and knowledge – and crews were regularly tested by specialist teams, Taceval and other routine exercises to keep us up to the mark and aware of the importance of getting everything right.

Quick reaction alert (QRA) then became the bread and butter for all Buccaneer crews after the statutory work-up, and again the paradox was very much in evidence. We knew it was essentially why we were there in Germany. But we also knew it was a chore to be borne with noble resignation. We ventured warily for the first time into the QRA area – occupied for many years previously by the Canberra squadrons armed with US nuclear weapons – to find the safe full of ageing Swedish cultural literature. The simple fact was that aircrew, fit and able to fly, do not generally welcome being locked up in a compound for twenty-four hours. And QRA duties came up on average about once a fortnight and over six weekends a year.

Having achieved strike status, we could now turn our attention to the demanding and enjoyable attack role, and full assignment in both strike and attack occurred one year after arrival following a Taceval in February 1972. My log book confirms that for months we persevered with twenty-degree dive bombing from 2,000 feet and an automatic low-level bunt attack, the former making us vulnerable to Warsaw Pact anti-aircraft defences, and the latter proving virtually unworkable and inaccurate because of wind turbulence overland. But we soon developed a shallow dive attack that involved a pull-up manoeuvre to 1,000 feet to acquire a target, and this proved an effective complement to the well-rehearsed laydown attack at 100 feet.

Rocketing is generally regarded in the world in which we operated as 'the sport of kings'. And we had 2-inch rockets and then SNEB with which to practice regularly. This was generally regarded as the weapon of choice in our close air-support role against armoured vehicles. Rocket firing on the range was always much enjoyed. But the powers that be, with little or no consultation with the front line, withdrew rockets in favour of a cluster weapon called BL 755. This was an effective 'armour buster', but as a newly-promoted weapons leader on XV Squadron, I was less than convinced that it would be my weapon of choice against armour in hilly terrain such as the Harz mountains that lay to the east of us. In that terrain, a 'line of sight' weapon seemed to me to be far more effective.

As part of our work-up training in that first year, we deployed for the first of many visits to the Air Weapons Training Installation at Decimomannu in Sardinia – a welcome break from the mists of the North German plain. Being on detachment always forges a squadron together, and we were able to observe at first-hand other NATO air forces at work, notably

David Cousins (back row centre) and his Maple Flag 1978 crews.

the Italians and Germans. Social activities centred around 'The Pig and Tapeworm', effectively a rather squalid room in a block on the Italian-owned airfield whose only redeeming feature was a well-stocked and very large refrigerator. What became clear to us early on was the very systemic way that other air forces trained, simply flying directly to the range and back. That was never going to be enough for us. We deployed along with our two Hunters, which were used to 'bounce' our formations of four aircraft during low-level sorties amongst the mountains along the Sardinian coast. This improved our tactical skills wonderfully and exhausted our reservoirs of adrenalin before we got down to the serious business of mustering a decent set of bombing and rocketing results on the nearby range at Capa Frasca.

When I returned for my second tour on Buccaneers in 1977, this time in command of 16 Squadron, I very quickly realised that the intervening years had not been wasted. The Buccaneer force had acquired a solid core of experienced air and ground crew, almost to a man devoted to the aircraft. They were more than ready to take on the extra demands of Red Flag exercises and the early work-up of laser designation, which brought about the pinpoint bombing accuracy that was so elusive from a gun sight. But this was also the era of structural defects on the aircraft, which was to claim the lives of two crews from Laarbruch in unconnected circumstances. The invincibility of the Buccaneer was undoubtedly dented by these accidents, but remedies were found and the Buccaneer remained in RAF service for another fourteen years.

My final moments with the Buccaneer could not have been better scripted. As the station commander at RAF Laarbruch in 1984, I led a detachment of Buccaneers and Jaguars on a Red Flag exercise where I flew a number of laser designator sorties on the Nellis Ranges before flying one of the aircraft back to Laarbruch via Dallas, Goose Bay and Keflavik. Life really does not get better than that.

And Playing Hard
Some twenty years later, on a quiet autumn afternoon in September 2004, I drove with my wife through the open barriers of Airport Weeze Niederrhein, pushed some temporary barriers aside, and walked down Trenchard Drive through the now-deserted officer's married quarters of RAF Laarbruch. We both swallowed hard in the stillness as grass and overgrown bushes climbed up to window level against the uninhabited houses. And the memories came flooding back.

In 1971, those quarters were smartly painted and bustling with people. The grass was cut and rows of smart duty-free cars lined the streets. The criss-cross of baby alarm wires gave lie to where the current party or barbecue was underway, even before you heard the laughter and general merriment. Later that day in 2004, standing in the deserted and forlorn bar in the officers' mess, it was not difficult to recall the welcoming sight of the three perennial barmen, Gunther, Franco and Rolf, known to generations of Buccaneer aircrew, who would slide a glass of your favourite 'tipple' towards you as you entered, even if you had only just returned after an unwelcome three-year tour in the Ministry of Defence. Somehow Laarbruch embraced you like this. Everyone was expected to play hard. The barmen knew that regular lubrication was always important to ensure smooth running engines.

Like all aircrew, the Buccaneer fraternity started their flying careers thinking of themselves as simply that: aircrew. The RAF knew better and designated us as 'general duties/pilot or general duties/navigator'. The reality of this sinister euphemism only really struck home when we came to understand that 'general duties' actually involved being posted to ground tours in the Ministry of Defence or command and group headquarters. These tours were to be endured and were seldom relished. Life began and ended for the majority of us on an operational station.

All RAF stations have a special élan and are unique to their locations. But a Germany tour brought with it a special quality of life, and the Buccaneer Wing in 1971 took to it like a duck takes to water. There were a number of reasons for this. The RAF Germany stations were large and full of operational units and the vast majority of station personnel lived on base or in married quarter complexes in nearby towns. The stations were self-contained with good schools, shops, medical support, and excellent sporting and social facilities. It was a vital and integrated community sharpened by being in a foreign country. Newcomers to the squadron would always be welcomed and cared for. Relations between the air and ground crew were also very close and based on mutual respect and trust of each other's skills and there were many joint parties to cement this special bond. There was also a sense of being better off than our contemporaries in the United Kingdom. Local overseas allowance was added to our pay principally to compensate for the extra costs of living abroad. But duty free petrol, cars, drink, cigarettes, and other items, along with easy access to European summer and winter resorts, engendered a strong feeling of *bien-être* and *wohlgefühl*.

Community relations with the long-suffering rural German community were judged to be especially important and were, for the most part, enjoyable experiences. Three, and later four flying squadrons generated a lot of noise, and every effort was made to avoid the towns and villages that surrounded us. The two Buccaneer squadrons were individually linked to local towns and took that responsibility seriously with mutual visits and social occasions.

Holland lay immediately to the west of the airfield. It offered opportunities to shop and socialise in large Dutch towns where English was universally spoken to very high standards, and where cultural traditions and informality seemed more akin to our own. In Germany, one simply needed to understand their culture and high regard for order and formality. That is until the annual *Karneval* came around. This pre-Lenten festival in our largely Roman Catholic area of Germany showed quite another aspect of the German character and at times seemed more reminiscent of the Reeperbahn in Hamburg. In their own particular way, the German community welcomed us into the week's festivities – and even occasionally crowned pillars of our RAF community with the honour of Karneval King! Of course, there was an element of hard-nosed, mutual back-scratching going on here. The sizeable Laarbruch community of over 4,000 people, after all, boosted the local economy considerably.

Significantly, there was a welcome stability (especially for the families) in the annual cycle of exercises and deployments, unlike the more frenetic but enjoyable programme of constant detachments by RAF squadrons in the United Kingdom. Apart from routine training and exercises, the year would consist of a squadron exchange with another NATO squadron, an annual armament practice camp in Sardinia and, from the mid-1970s, detachments to Goose Bay and Nevada for Red Flag exercises. Weekend 'rangers' to Cyprus or Malta provided variety and airways experience, and a welcome opportunity to fill the cavernous Buccaneer bomb bay with local delicacies; Cypriot brandy and Maltese hams and the like.

Seldom would a weekend go by at Laarbruch without the siren call to a party in a married quarter or local hostelry. Leafing back through old photo albums reveals the worrying propensity that Englishmen have to don transvestite clothes at fancy dress parties. Then there were the toe-curling 'bad taste' parties; a wheelchair-bound nun or – in one fabled case – a well-known Buccaneer navigator going as Jesus Christ on a cross so large that he had to be propped up outside the front door and spent the evening disconsolately sucking beer through an extended straw from a bottle tucked into an appalling loin cloth. And so it went on week after week.

To say that the Buccaneer Wing was boisterous socially was an understatement. There was friendly rivalry within the wing, but an easier target was to be found in bating the more precious elements within the resident recce squadron, which was equipped from 1970 with Phantoms and then Jaguars. We were a bit more circumspect, but only just, with the resident RAF regiment squadrons whose officer corps was invariably large and fit; retribution on us could thus be affected quite painfully during mess rugby following a guest night.

16 Squadron celebrate winning the Salmond Trophy, 29 May 1979.

One of the more alarming traditions of association with the Fleet Air Arm was its apparent fixation with blowing everything up at formal dinners. I had lost my eyebrows within minutes of arriving at RNAS Lossiemouth during a 'Taranto' Guest Night. A disgruntled naval observer had yelled, "bloody crab amongst us" and threw a thunder flash at me. This was a seminal moment. I had been thrilled at going onto the Buccaneer and being trained by the Fleet Air Arm, which I had always admired. To find that that sentiment was not necessarily reciprocated was a tough moment for me but blowing things up inevitably leeched into the bloodstream of the RAF Buccaneer force.

As a more responsible squadron and station commander during the late 1970s and 1980s, I would gaze fearfully and wearily during Guest Night dinners at various attachments like cabbages attached to the ceiling in the dining room; these would be linked in turn to ominous detonation wires positioned strategically above the 'top table'. Thus distracted, I would fail to notice that all my cutlery, glasses and table mat were tied by near-invisible threads to my chair, with predictable consequences when I pulled it back to sit down after grace. But long experience told me that the squadron 'junta' of junior officers needed to make their presence felt after the enforced disciplines of daily flying. And innately, I knew that Queens Regulations conferred ultimate retribution with me. The subsequent repair costs for all this frenetic activity on 'junta' mess bills was always accepted with good grace. That would pass quickly if painfully but the story, rather more regrettably, could only grow!

Envoi

The stories could only grow. It sounds prophetic now. And the memories never fade. We ensure that by telling them every year without fail at the annual Buccaneer Blitz reunion, always to tears of laughter. Of course, they were the very best of years. Flying the Buccaneer in RAF Germany, and supported by experienced and loyal ground crew, laid the foundations once again for the RAF to claim arguably that it was the best tactical air force in the world. This was certainly recognised openly by our USAF invigilators at Red Flag exercises.

Without doubt, the courage and skill shown by the Tornado force in the subsequent Gulf Wars had a lot to do with those foundations laid down by the Buccaneer force throughout the 1970s and 1980s. So, too, was the outstanding performance of the Buccaneer aircrew who themselves excelled in the first Gulf War. Performance in the air can be monitored and assessed – and it was regularly. What is more intangible, and the stuff of anecdotal evidence, was the spirit that bound the Buccaneer Wing in Germany together. The ingredients for this were a heady mixture of respect for the versatility of the aircraft, the traditions and operational skills inherited from our predecessors and the Fleet Air Arm, the belief that there was a real job to do, and the indefinable but real and sustaining camaraderie of the Buccaneer force.

The baton at Laarbruch was passed from the Buccaneer to the Tornado on 29 February 1984. I stood and saluted the last Buccaneer as it took off on that day. Then I turned, took a deep breath, and set about preparing the station, assisted by an able team, for the formal assignment of the newly-formed Tornado squadrons to NATO. Sociologists talk constantly of continuity and change. That was and always will remain the defining sense and tradition of the Royal Air Force.

The Buccaneer in Germany had played its part with distinction. And a good time – a very, very good time – was had by all.

CHAPTER NINE
THE GUY IN THE BACK

David Herriot at Nellis AFB, Red Flag 1978.

DAVID HERRIOT

By the time I was sixteen, I had decided I wanted to fly in the RAF and I applied for a sixth-form scholarship to train as a pilot. Unfortunately, Dr Lees, the rector of the High School of Glasgow, had at that stage little faith in my academic ability and had informed the RAF accordingly; I was unsuccessful. Undeterred, I applied again a year later with the same result but, as I approached the end of my school career, I bit the bullet again, was invited to Biggin Hill for assessment and passed, but with a significant caveat to my offer of acceptance. My aptitude scores for pilot were low but my aptitude for navigator training was marked as exceptionally high. There was no decision to be made. I wanted a commission in the RAF and I wanted to fly. I signed up.

133 Air Navigation Course provided a number of challenges for me. Dr Lees had not been unkind, just accurate, in the damning academic report that he had submitted to the aircrew selection board. I was no mathematician and no physicist, both skills needed by a navigator, but I did, according to my Nav School report, have a natural ability in the air, solid airmanship skills and, so the report stated, a natural aptitude for navigation when 'he is prepared to apply himself'. I am also exceedingly organised, a critical skill for any navigator who has to cope with 'fixing cycles' and maintaining an accurate air navigation log whilst airborne. Consequently, I did quite well and by the time I was half-way through the advanced stage of the course I was coasting.

During the basic course at Gaydon my course commander, an Argosy navigator by trade, and I had had a deep discussion in the bar one night as to why I wanted to fly two-seat aircraft rather than have the luxury of 'trucking' [transport flight] as my career – he didn't get it! The course commander on the advanced phase, who had served his time on Shackletons, had a much more balanced view and arranged a day trip to Scampton for a look over a Vulcan, a posting normally reserved for those who passed out in the lower half of the course.

As I climbed down the ladder that led from the black hole that was the Vulcan cockpit I vowed to myself that I was going to work much harder in the run-up to graduation. It was about this time that I decided that the aircraft for me had to be the Buccaneer. Few chaps were being sent to the Buccaneer as first tourists, not least because there were very few slots available on the nascent RAF Buccaneer force at that stage. That alone made it the challenge that I wanted plus I did not want to be a truckie and air defence seemed equally dull. Why, I imagined, would anybody want to spend their time at altitude drilling holes in the sky when they could flash around at high speed and low level dropping bombs on targets!

The day soon came when our course commander met with the 'Posters' to determine our fate. I had finished third on the course and joined my seven colleagues as we headed for the officers' mess bar at Finningley in December 1970, the chosen venue for the good/bad news announcement, which was all done in the best possible taste with the three destined for the V-Force put out of their misery pretty quickly. Those first and second got what they wanted but the best had been kept to last.

Knowing how desperately I wanted a posting to Buccaneers the course commander waited and waited, leading me on with a 'no slots' line before he capitulated with the news that 'Yes', there was a slot on Buccaneers and 'Yes', my name was marked against it! I was both ecstatic and overwhelmed by the result. Unbeknown to me, however, the challenge had been greater than I had ever imagined as I was to be the first first-tourist navigator to be trained by the recently-formed 237 Operational Conversion Unit at RAF Honington. All previous RAF navigators bound for the Buccaneer, no matter their vintage or experience, had been trained by the Royal Navy on 736 Squadron at Lossiemouth. My earlier decision to work harder had paid off and my more recent decision to get pissed that night, whatever the outcome, was soon put successfully to the test.

As I drove off the A134 between Bury St Edmunds and Thetford, and followed Green Lane round and past the threshold of Honington's 09 runway, I suddenly realised just why it was that I had been so keen to fly the Buccaneer. There, sitting at full power against their brakes, were two 12 Squadron aircraft about to launch. As my Morris 1000 eased left with the sweeping curve of the narrow road that led to the main gate, I could only stare in amazement as it dawned on me just how potent and how threatening the Buccaneer looked and wondered how in the world was I ever going to manage to navigate such an awesome piece of aviation hardware. However, there was a ground school to get through first, ten simulator missions to be completed and much, much more in terms of preparation for flying before I would get remotely close to the beast itself.

View From The Rear

Have you ever looked in a Buccaneer cockpit? It is, and has often quite rightly been described as, an ergonomic slum. However, despite the Blackburn Aircraft Company's philosophy of 'throw all the avionic boxes and cockpit switches up and screw them in where they fall' they were the only aircraft manufacturer to get one crucial aspect for a low-level fast jet bomber right. The pilot's seat in the Buccaneer is offset very slightly to the left and the nav's is positioned slightly to the right and above. This allowed the GIB (guy in the back) to see fully forward, over the GIF's right shoulder and through the right quarter-light of the windscreen. It also allowed the GIB a clear view of many of the important dials on the starboard side of the pilot's cockpit and a clear sight of the 'blow gauges', which were critical during approach and landing.

As well as navigating, the nav's role as part of the two-man crew was to:

- identify radar targets
- manage the weapons system
- manage electronic countermeasures
- manage the fuel system
- work the radio
- 'Check 6' and everything between 2 and 10 o'clock in the rear hemisphere
- mop the pilot's fevered brow (metaphorically) when things got tough!

To do all these, Ferranti provided the GIB with a multitude of navigational aids (navaids) to ease the workload. Prime amongst these was the Blue Parrot radar, designed primarily for detecting maritime targets (think Sverdlov cruiser), and the Blue Jacket doppler radar, which encompassed everything in a ground position indicator for keeping on track and on time. Well, it would have done if the ground position eastings and northings counters had not jumped up to a mile in a random direction (of their choosing) as soon as they were selected on during the take-off run. An inertial navigator they most certainly were not and the result was that they were so unreliable that many navs were unsure of their position pretty much as soon as they were airborne. They soon learnt to disregard them and use the 'mark one eyeball', the most reliant of navaids. I concede that had I ever flown 'off the deck' I might have had to become more reliant on the Blue Jacket but, never having had that privilege, I very quickly became circumspect about its utility for navigation.

In 1971, additional navaids included a 'moving roller map', which required about sixteen hours of preparation, glue, a sharp pair of scissors and lots of patience. OK, I lied about the sixteen hours but it took so much time to prepare and, given it was fed by the Blue Jacket, it was very quickly deemed 'bloody useless' and soon gave way to the radar warning receiver (RWR) control panel in the ergonomic slum. Some bright spark had also deemed it a good idea to provide the Buccaneer navigator with a fold-down table (about 18 inches square) that he could use to do his high-level chart work on; yeah that'll be right! It had to be folded away in the 'up' position at low level as it prohibited access to the bottom ejection seat handle should one have to leave in a hurry. The navigation suite was completed with a S/X-Band wide band homer system that provided directional information should it ever lock on to a Soviet maritime radar in the final stages of an attack.

During the mid-1970s, maritime Buccaneers were equipped with TV-guided and anti-radar Martel (missile anti-radar television) missiles. To allow the GIB to identify and track maritime targets in the TV mode a black and white television was fitted on a pedestal between his feet in the rear seat area. The effect of this was to splay the nav's feet outwards such that those with extra-long 'bum to kneecap' measurements would lose their toes on ejection as their feet hit the Blue Jacket as they were shot clear of the cockpit! In later years, long after I had moved on from my four tours on Buccaneers, the aircraft was equipped first with a GPI corrector unit, then an INS and, finally, a GPS.

The integrated weapons system was controlled from the rear seat through a 'box of tricks' called the control & release computer (C&RC), an eight-way bomb distributor and a clockwork pre-release timer. It is important to remember that all of these pieces of avionic wizardry were designed in the 1950s and therefore were analogue and not digital. With digital comes accuracy but with analogue you are in the lap of the gods! The rear seat also was equipped with a strip altimeter that was fixed to 1013mb, the ICAO standard pressure setting. Very useful, I hear all you aviators out there cry. Well, not really since with an analogue weapons system comes built-in lag. Take the side off the C&RC and you will find cogs, string and pulleys. Very high specification cogs, string and pulleys I grant you but, nonetheless, not renowned for their accuracy if the pilot or navigator conduct weapons attacks without paying full attention to the accuracy of their delivery parameters. So it was, therefore, that the role of the navigator during a weapons delivery was, in dive attacks, to call out the heights as the aircraft descended pointing at the target. Whilst it went some way to avoid target fixation by the pilot and prevent the aircraft becoming a 'tent peg', its prime function was to allow the pilot to hear the rate of descent and equate that to his understanding of the required rate for any given dive angle and adjust accordingly. Can you believe that?

You won't believe it further when I tell you that all this was established by conducting a pre-range 'height check' over the sea at 100 feet and at attack speed to allow the navigator to etch a chinagraph mark on his altimeter to ensure that the 1013mb was superseded for the range detail of the day by a local pressure setting mark. Accurate? Well it would have been if the chinagraph mark hadn't been about '100 feet' thick! Some bright spark came up with the notion that a simple 'angle of dangle' meter made out of a piece of string, a scale and a weight would improve accuracy during dive attacks. Great in theory but it took no account of the necessity for the GIB to focus on other aspects of the cockpit rather than on a piece of string wavering about on the side of the canopy. Needless to say, it never took off.

So the role of the navigator in the Buccaneer was not a particularly easy one but it did ensure that we were masters in the low-level world and could outfight most threats, maritime or overland, because our very lives did depend upon it.

What all this meant, of course, was that the Buccaneer was most definitely a 'crew cooperation' aircraft. The GIF could not function without the GIB and the GIB was dependent upon the GIF for getting them through successfully and back again. It became very apparent very quickly on the OCU that operating the Buccaneer was the responsibility of both crew members and that one could not, and would not, do it without the full support and agreement of the other. What this meant in reality was that there was no room for prima donnas in either seat and that mutual respect was the be all and end all of Buccaneer operations. Pilots and navigators crewed together were, generally, good mates. You had to be as life in a Buccaneer cockpit, despite its fore and aft construction, was very intimate. In fact, if you were inclined to do so, you could actually hold hands by stretching through

XV Squadron's junior crews. L-R: David Herriot, Iain Ross, Dave Symonds, John Kershaw.

a gap underneath the Blue Jacket. More importantly, however, if things did go awry with the intercom system it was possible to pass hand-written notes through the gap. Moreover, and perhaps even more importantly, if the GIF failed to act on the GIB's instructions then it was possible to give him a good clout on the side of his helmet with a MOD Store Reference 6B/349 nav ruler (a twenty-one-inch length of plastic marked with nautical miles and issued to all navs). It was a stretch but it was effective if used appropriately!

One of the highlights of the OCU course, and here I am well qualified to explain, was the social life in and around the officers' mess bar at Honington. There was a good cross-section of both RAF and FAA personnel amongst the staff of 237 OCU in the early 1970s. Some had ground their teeth on Hunters in the Gulf and many had completed more than one Buccaneer tour with the Royal Navy on more than one of Her Majesty's carriers in the 1960s. What they shared was a zest for life, a love of the Buccaneer and a capacity to drink most other people under the table. What was more important as a student, and was distinctive about the Buccaneer OCU as far as I was concerned, was that there was definitely no 'them and us' culture.

If you could fly the Bucc, drop bombs, fire rockets, behave on strike progression (Buccaneer fighter evasion) and drink your beer – and buy it too – then in Buccaneer terms and with apologies to Rudyard Kipling: 'Yours was the earth and everything that's in it, and – which is more – you were a Bucc Man, my son!' I don't mean here to give the impression that the Buccaneer force had a drink problem. It might well have done and many might accede that we were a bunch of pissheads but what it did mean was that there was an enthusiasm amongst those who flew it to share their experiences, their professionalism and their expertise, not only in and around the squadron, but also socially. We were, are and always will be a select and close-knit group of people, whether FAA, SAAF or RAF, and here I must not forget the many exchange officers from the US Air Force, Navy and Marines and also the Royal Australian Air Force who shared our company. Each one of us had the privilege of being selected to fly the last and best British bomber. In short we were highly professional but we knew how to have a good time too.

Fragment Time Contour Graphs and Other Such QWI Bluff

For many years, the RAF and the FAA had trained selected fighter pilots to specialise in air fighting and tactics. After completing a demanding post-graduate course, these demigods, for that was how they presented themselves, were entitled to the acronym PAIs (pilot attack instructors) and there were significant numbers of them, particularly on the ubiquitous Hunter squadrons that populated the RAF in the 1950s and 1960s. They were responsible for training, developing and standardising their fellow pilot's weaponry skills and the fighting capability of their squadrons.

As the Buccaneer settled into RAF service, discussion inevitably circled around creating a similar qualification for the Buccaneer force. The station commander at RAF Honington in the early 1970s was Group Captain Peter Bairsto, a former fighter pilot and PAI and he came up with a plan to create on 237 OCU a suitable course to train Buccaneer attack instructors or, more commonly, BAIs. It was an important step in the development of the Buccaneer force and placed it firmly at the forefront (maybe even slightly ahead) in terms of operational credibility amongst its peers in the RAF.

I was on my first tour at Laarbruch with XV Squadron when a squadron crew was selected for the first BAI course. The pilot was David Cousins (DC), an erstwhile Lightning pilot, who went on to become one of the great and good of the RAF, nothing to do with his Lightning days, I assure you! His accomplice, on what was colloquially known as the Bullshit And Ignorance Course was a navigator who went by the sobriquet of 'Wings', aka Barry Chown. Wings was, and remains, one of the Buccaneer force's greatest characters and probably the only man in the RAF to have flown operationally the Blackburn Aircraft Company's best two products to reach the RAF's front line; the other being the Beverley C1 on which Wings served as a sergeant signaller before being commissioned and trained as a navigator. Wings had been my mentor when I arrived on XV Squadron and he fulfilled that role admirably both professionally and socially and got me into more trouble than I care to remember although, in all honesty, I only needed his instruction for a very short time as I was a very quick learner when it came to drinking alcohol and making mischief in the officers' mess or on detachments overseas.

On their return to the fold at Laarbruch things quickly tightened up on the squadron weaponry front. Sortie debriefs were more thorough, films were analysed within a nano-metre of the 'aiming mark' and a nano-second of the 'accept'. Pure fear was set amongst the crews as they knew that the wrath of the BAI would descend on them if they screwed up on the range and failed in their attempts to maintain level flight or an accurate speed and/or dive angle.

During my time XV Squadron was commanded by Wg Cdr Roy 'Potty Watty' Watson. Potty Watty was renowned as a particularly capable pilot who had flown F-84 Thunderjets during the Korean War on exchange with the USAF. Indeed, one particular story that abounded at the time was that, as a flying officer, he had led over forty Thunderjets on one particular mission, which earned him an American DFC. I was too polite to ask the storyteller if this was for real but in all my thirty-nine years in the RAF I don't think I've ever seen a flying officer being trusted with himself, let alone forty-plus aircraft! Things were clearly much different in the early post-war years in the RAF. Anyway, Roy's experiences certainly did ensure that he was one of the original 'seat of the pants' pilots. It was he who had selected DC & Wings to become BAIs; it was he who had released them from the squadron to take the long training course back in the UK; and it was he, as I will now recount, who feared them most.

Our story takes place during a XV Squadron armament practice camp (APC) at Decimomannu in Sardinia and on a sortie to Frasca Range. Roy and his navigator, Pete Ritchie, were leading a four-ship, which was conducting SNEB rocket attacks on the ground target. DH (direct hit) followed DH without a miss on his first five attacks. Then, as he entered his ten-degree dive for his final rocket, and to the surprise of Pete, Roy declared to the range safety officer that he was "Off Dry". When challenged by Pete, "Why dry, Boss, the parameters were perfect?" Potty Watty replied: "Sorry, I've just realised that I hadn't selected the sight glass up and the BAIs (Wings and DC) will bollock me rigid at the debrief!" Such was the power of the BAI...and the skill of an old DFGA (day fighter ground attack) pilot!

I was extremely fortunate to be selected for No. 5 Course in 1976. The course had evolved significantly since the first one in 1972 and had, in line with others that had followed in the RAF, changed its name to be the Qualified Weapons Instructor Course. This fact, importantly from a career point of view, gained its graduates the significant post-nominal of QWI in the Air Force List and the right to call themselves such. Such an appellation brought with it respect amongst one's peers and fear amongst many when it came to sortie debriefs. The course was intense.

Once the basic mathematics tests had been passed in the first week and your place on the course secured 'pro tem' – the intensity of circular motion calculations; fragment time contour graphs; AMD (aiming mark depression) calculations; the understanding and calculation of gravity drop, dip, indicated release height (back to chinagraph marks on altimeters, remember); cross-trail in laydown attacks; gyro ride up; etc, etc, etc – had to be mastered. There was no time to draw breath and we hadn't even got into the swing of breaking this monotony with the occasional delight of getting airborne. Getting airborne to relax? I don't think so, chum!

Before each flying phase, which revolved around a particular weapon delivery type, one of the student body had to prepare, present and suffer the slings and arrows of a harsh debrief for their phase briefing. If successful, you could relax for the subsequent sortie as the spotlight was off you temporarily and was now focused on the poor student who hopefully had listened and was now responsible for planning, briefing, leading and

QWIs at Red Flag 1978. L-R: Graham Seward, Rip Kirby, David Herriot, Mal Prissick, Ivor Evans.

debriefing the sortie to the range.

Although technology had provided the RAF with the OHP (overhead projectors) to run sortie briefs and debriefs much of a QWI's work when under training had to be conducted using chalk and blackboard. No errors or smudges were permitted, which meant that before starting to prepare your mission briefing the night before the blackboard had to be washed, dried, washed again and, if you smudged, cleared and washed again before any progress could be made or thought of a good night's sleep could be entertained. Every QWI that I know has perfected the art of producing flat-bottom letters (drafted against a ruler to ensure straightness and linear equality) whenever they have ever produced a presentation in later life. The course was, in the main, most enjoyable even if it was hard work and the Sword of Damocles hung over one's head on regular occasions throughout its three-month duration.

On my third tour, by now an instructor on 237 OCU, I was very privileged to be selected as the staff navigator to run No. 8 QWI Course in 1978, which culminated with its involvement as a 'formed four-ship' embedded within the 208 Squadron participants on Exercise Red Flag 79-1, more of which detail you will find elsewhere in this book. For the students on the course, participating in Red Flag was highly demanding as their QWI standards had to be maintained throughout the two weeks spent at Nellis AFB in Nevada. However for Ivor Evans, the staff pilot, and me it was our first experience of Red Flag and was the icing on a very successful and enjoyable cake.

In the Cold War era, Red Flag was the ultimate operational flying experience for strike/

16 Squadron (Co Wg Cdr Peter Norriss front centre) prepare for Maple Flag 1983.

attack crews and it was a Buccaneer squadron that had the unique privilege of being the first non-American squadron to participate. Such was the success; NATO squadrons have been visiting ever since and I was able to take part twice on the two-week exercise with the Buccaneer.

My last sortie on Red Flag in the Buccaneer took place on 6 November 1982 when I was privileged as a RAF navigator to be appointed mission commander for the Blue Forces tasked with fronting a thirty-six-ship 'Gorilla' as the leader of an eight-ship of Buccaneers. I was lucky enough to participate in Maple Flag also with the Bucc and to return to Nellis twice in my Tornado GR1 career to sample Red Flag in a modern fly-by-wire aircraft with all the avionics that modern technology could provide. However, the Tornado never beat the Bucc for its enduring performance, comfort at low level and sheer manhood.

I was lucky to complete four tours on the Buccaneer: two overland in Germany; one maritime tour at Honington; and a tour as an instructor on the OCU. I even turned down a tour on Tornados when first offered because my love affair with the Buccaneer was not quite ready to be closed. From my first flight with Jerry Yates on 8 June 1971 to my last operational sortie on 8 September 1983 with the then Laarbruch station commander, Graham Smart, who had also been my boss on 12 Squadron, my infatuation with the Buccaneer had been an intense one. So, after the mammoth drunken festival at Lossiemouth in 1994 that saw the 'old lady' into military retirement, I thought it essential that we form an Aircrew Association to hold the memory of Britain's Last Bomber alive and ensure that its crews kept contact until their last breath – and found opportunities to drink in its memory too. And so I did.

CHAPTER TEN

ALPHAS IN ACTION

BRUCE CHAPPLE AND MICK WHYBRO

Maritime tactics were constantly evolving during the 1970s and two of the Buccaneer's most experienced QWIs were Bruce Chapple and Mick Whybro and here they discuss some of 12 Squadron's activities during this period.

BRUCE CHAPPLE

When 12 Squadron formed with the Buccaneer in 1969, it was the first time the RAF had had a maritime strike role since the days of the Beaufighter and Mosquito Strike Wings of Coastal Command during World War Two. They had found it essential to know exactly where targets were before mounting a co-ordinated attack. A probe aircraft was sent ahead to radio back exact positions so that the strike leader could organise and position his force of torpedo-carrying and rocket-armed aircraft to make the attack.

Little had changed since those days except our need for support was even greater as we operated at much longer range and, therefore, far larger sea areas had to be combed in order to find the target. We set about developing these World War Two tactics to suit our capabilities and over the next twenty years they were refined as new weapons were introduced into our inventory.

During an exercise in the Mediterranean in 1970 'shadow support' was developed using Victor strategic reconnaissance aircraft. The navigator/radar plotted the ship contacts over a wide area and over a period of time. He monitored sailing patterns when those contacts manoeuvring could be identified from those making steady passage along known shipping lanes. These contacts could then be carefully monitored and their position was passed in a simple code to attacking aircraft.

In due course, the Vulcans of 27 Squadron were tasked exclusively in this shadowing role. Their crews became expert at identifying targets in a cluttered sea area and new methods of passing coded dispositions were developed; the process became known as maritime radar reconnaissance (MRR). Canberras and Buccaneers flying low-level probe (LOPRO) sorties were often launched to identify the targets.

During Exercise Dawn Patrol in the Mediterranean in 1974 my nav and I were tasked to fly a LOPRO sortie as a singleton to sniff out the target, the US Sixth Fleet no less. We flew at very low level and received support from the MRR Vulcans. The task was to probe the fleet, clear the area and report back the disposition to the attacking formation via the Vulcan. We carried full fuel, anti-radar Martel missiles and were fitted with a passive radar-warning receiver (RWR).

A high-pressure weather system with a temperature inversion prevailed, an ideal situation for 'anaprop' where electronic transmissions can be bounced between the inversion and the sea surface in a sine wave which, under favourable circumstances, allows passive detection from beyond the normal radar horizon; on this occasion, flying at 100 feet, we got an RWR intercept on the Sixth Fleet search radar at 160 miles. After a thirty-degree turn onto a diverging heading held for about twenty minutes we headed back towards the fleet and got a further position line, which gave a fairly accurate fix.

As usual, the ship's 'safety cell' failed to respond to our request for a low-level fly-through but we pressed on. No fire-control radars were detected as we made a rapid exit to a safe distance to transmit a position and disposition report for the attack formation. The safety cell were called again at which point all hell broke loose as every fire-control radar fired up! (It should be noted that the safety cell were supposed to be independent of the defence cell.)

With large areas of ocean devoid of enemy activity, the standard profile adopted by a Buccaneer maritime attack formation was a Hi-Lo-Hi. This had the added advantage of extending the range to as much as 600 miles radius and this was regularly augmented by the use of air-to-air refuelling. Whenever possible, formations were made up of six or eight aircraft and during the transit to the target area in wide battle formation, all the crews listened out on the radios for the latest information on target locations. All aircraft maintained radio and radar silence to avoid giving away their approach to a target. At a range of 240 miles from the target the formation started an 'under the radar lobe' descent to sea level in order to stay outside the enemy's radar cover. During the descent the RWR was monitored for selected search radar frequencies and, if one was detected, the rate of descent was increased to remain outside the detection range. At thirty miles the leader 'popped up' and the navigator switched on his Blue Parrot radar for two or three sweeps during which time he identified and 'marked' the target before descending back to 100 feet. After choosing the radar return that was assessed to be the 'high-value target', the lead navigator then had to convey the information verbally over the radio to the rest of the formation and this created problems.

The plan sounded good in principle, but had some drawbacks, not least the ambient noise in the cockpit at high speeds, which made it difficult to understand all but the simplest messages. This was exacerbated when a senior navigator on the squadron insisted on his own solution – a lengthy dissertation over the radio describing all the contacts he could see on his radar screen. Didn't work. After a particularly 'lively' debrief, it was suggested from the floor, that perhaps the situation might be improved if the attack message was passed by someone with 'more than half a brain and without a speech impediment'.

During this period, the US Navy exchange officer, Bill Butler, suggested quietly that if the Doppler-stabilised radar track marker was used, and a suitable range ring was selected on the radar, the lead aircraft could turn to put the most likely radar return on the track marker line (the rest of the formation paralleled the leader's heading), and fly it down the track marker line until the radar return coincided with the range ring, all that was needed was a simple codeword recognisable even in poor radio conditions to convey the mark to the formation. This suggestion was taken up, tried in the air, and found to be a brilliant, simple and consistent solution.

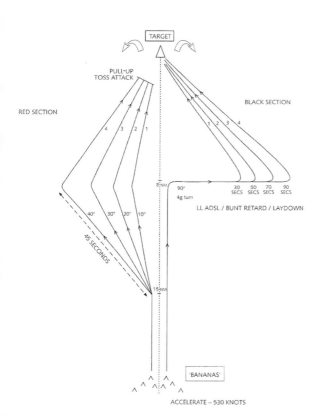

The codeword? 'Bananas!' It was never changed, and it became the trademark attack call of the Buccaneer force – usually followed by a split! And so, the Alpha attack was born.

At the pre-sortie briefing one of a number of Alpha co-ordinated attack profiles was selected as the primary option. Each was designed to provide a multi-axis co-ordinated attack depending on the defences of the planned target. The leader could change the option at short notice if weather or enemy ship dispositions dictated different tactics, and the new Alpha attack was broadcast with the Bananas call. Radio transmissions were kept to an absolute minimum. Accelerations were never called but were based on the leader's smoke emissions from the engines. All turns were with sixty degrees of bank and timing started from the beginning of the turn. In total radio silence Bananas was not called, but the leader rocked his wings and the split was executed as soon as the leader started his turn.

An Alpha Attack.

The aim of the Alpha attacks was to maintain the element of surprise for as long as possible and to confuse the target defences and delay the lock-on solutions for their radar-laid anti-aircraft defences. Once we had penetrated the target ship's weapons engagement zones, we used the exceptional low-flying performance of the Buccaneer to fly at high speed and ultra-low level and still be able to sustain high-g manoeuvres to increase the tracking problems of the enemy radars. The first attacks were delivered from a toss delivery at three miles on converging headings. Each bomb was fused to explode at sixty feet, with the aim of destroying the fire-control radars and incapacitating the missile and gun crews. In the meantime, the attack force had turned starboard through ninety degrees before rolling in to release four to six 1,000lb bombs independently from a low-level dive or laydown attack that provided the killing blow. Timing was critical if aircraft were to avoid the debris from the preceding attack. The obvious weakness of this attack was the vulnerability of the aircraft – particularly those that carried out the precision attack.

Some 'attacks' on major exercises required a degree of skulduggery if honour was to be preserved amongst our NATO allies. The American Sixth Fleet was always high on our target list for such activity. On another 'Dawn Patrol' we were tasked against a CAG (carrier air group), which included the USS *America*, which was low in the water weighed down by the admiral's staff and attendant sycophants; the group was to the west of Sicily and doubtless expected the Buccaneers to attack from the east. Unfortunately for our transatlantic cousins, who had no idea of the radius of action of the Buccaneer, the team planned to go north to Palermo along the track of the airway, but not in it, then descend to low level like a formation of cast-iron manhole covers – as only the Buccaneer could when using full airbrake – and disappear from the CAG's radar plot.

When at low level, we manoeuvred to attack from the west i.e. from 'behind' the fleet. With no reply from the safety cell (again!) the attack was carried out, the formation reformed at twenty miles followed by the normal courtesy ultra-low level flypast and climb out during which an American voice on the radio asked who we were and what were we doing. After landing it transpired that the admiral's staff had not had a good day with numbers so we sent them a chatty little signal explaining which calendar was in use and which time zone they were in. An apologetic signal followed requesting a rematch some forty-eight hours later.

The squadron obliged using the same profile, attacked the CAG and reformed without being illuminated by any defensive radar. It was not until the farewell flypast that any sign of activity became apparent; as the Buccaneers stormed past either side of the carrier marginally above the wave tops, the five-minute defensive F-4 fighter cap was being launched to intercept the attack – too late! Interestingly my directional consultant in the back seat for this sortie was Bill Butler USN whose previous tour had been on board the USS *America* and whose contribution to the squadron tactics was invaluable.

Co-ordinated attacks were also practised at night, but with formations of four aircraft operating at a minimum height of 200 feet, which required considerable concentration. The principle was similar to the day profiles, but the precision low-level bombing was avoided and the preferred delivery mode was medium toss, giving a degree of 'stand-off'. There were two periods that required particular attention. The first was the 4g recovery from the toss delivery, which required 135-degree angle of bank, until the nose passed through the horizon, when the bank was reduced to ninety degrees and the aircraft dived for the sanctuary of low level. The second was the formation re-join in the very dark conditions, which was time consuming and disorientating.

Less well-defended targets, such as fast patrol boats (FPB) were attacked in the dark using Lepus illumination flares thrown by the lead aircraft of a pair. As they approached the target, the No.2 aircraft dropped astern when the cloud base dictated the trail distance. The lower the cloud, the later the 'flare show', and so the trail distance had to be increased. The leader tossed the flares to deliver them ahead of, and beyond, the target and the second aircraft attacked with SNEB rockets or, occasionally, bombs, with the target silhouetted in the light lane created by the flares.

Whilst the No.2 attacked using a ten-degree dive profile, the leader regained control from the Lepus toss delivery and made a follow-up attack. During the toss recovery, a great amount of hands flashing round the cockpit took place – a prime situation for disorientation – in order to select switches for the next attack. During this interesting whirling dervish act, the No.2 took the lead, flew a racetrack pattern and made a second flare delivery followed by the leader firing his rockets. What made life particularly interesting during the attack was that the three flares were given different 'flare height settings', which meant that they were not in a horizontal line or in line with subsequent dive attacks. In addition, there always seemed to be one at twelve o'clock high during the 5g recoveries from the dive attacks. All very disorientating. During an exercise in the Baltic, one pair managed to get six flares burning at the same time, i.e. four attacks in four minutes. The FPBs were suitably baffled by the almost daylight conditions provided as were the innocent ships plying their sedate passage in the dark waters of the Skagerrak that night.

During 1974 the squadron deployed to the Royal Norwegian Air Force base at Bardufoss situated well inside the Arctic Circle. As part of the exercise we were tasked against the local FPBs. The Royal Norwegian Navy is particularly adept at camouflage and after about twenty minutes of fruitless cruising up and down the exercise area we had seen nothing; more in hope than anything else we pulled up and tipped in at a promising group of rocks at which point two of the 'rocks' crash started and departed at about forty knots! (The FPBs had moored up against the reef of rocks with camouflage nets deployed.)

There ensued an interesting and eye-catching engagement setting up coordinated dive attacks whilst avoiding the more vertical parts of the scenery and countering the FPB's high-speed defensive manoeuvres. Great enjoyment and we were happy to be invited back.

By the mid-1970s it had become clear that it was essential to have a stand-off capability when attacking ships with increasingly capable, and lethal, anti-aircraft defences. Mick Whybro takes up the story.

MICK WHYBRO

*Gp Capt John Herrington congratulates
Mick Whybro on being the first to achieve
1,000 hours on the Buccaneer.*

Back in 1966 I came to the end of my first tour, a brilliant three years at Akrotiri in Cyprus. I had been a member of that premier Canberra ground-attack squadron, 'Shiney 6' (opposition squadrons used a less polite name) when the world was our oyster. We flew to Singapore in the east, as far south as Salisbury (Harare nowadays), to Gibraltar in the west, north to the UK and everywhere in between. We had a ball, there was never a dull moment. I thought that any ensuing postings could not possibly live up to my first one. How wrong was I?

I was extremely fortunate to be posted to the far north of Scotland to HMS Fulmar (Lossiemouth) for loan service with the Fleet Air Arm flying the Buccaneer. Little did I know that I was to remain with the Royal Navy for five years (the highlight of my thirty-three years service) and followed by five years RAF Buccaneer flying. All in all, a really satisfying and enjoyable time, with the 'fun needle' always in the green.

By the time I was on my final Buccaneer tour, I was a steely QWI (the cream of the cream) on 12 Squadron based at Honington. The squadron was a maritime-attack outfit and the first to employ TV Martel. The missile was designed for use against a spectrum of targets, but was acquired by the RAF for the anti-shipping role. In addition to the missiles, the aircraft carried a data-link pod that provided the link between the navigator and the missile. The rear cockpit contained a TV screen and control facility.

The missile was launched from 100 feet above sea level at around 500 knots at fifteen miles from the target. On release the weapon climbed to its mid-course altitude somewhere between 1,500 to 2,000 feet. The navigator was able to side step the missile (really intended for overland use to enable the operator to do some TV map reading – not easy), and to down-step the missile in order to remain below cloud. He also had the ability to pan the camera in the nose of the missile left and right in order to facilitate early target acquisition, which was dependent on the prevailing visibility. Once visual with the target, which ideally would be when it appeared at the top of the TV screen, the navigator would wait until it reached mid-screen and select terminal phase (TP); he now had full control over the missile's flight path, up/down as well as left/right in order to fly the weapon into the target by maintaining the generated cross-wires on the aiming point.

The point at which TP was selected was fairly critical; too far out would tend to result

A 12 Squadron Buccaneer armed with one AR Martel, 2 TV Martels and the TV data link pod.

in a long shallow approach which would be difficult to control in the last few seconds to impact; too close would result in a rapid nose-down command and a very short time of controlled flight. Another problem, which the navigators usually mastered with adequate training, was the control 'stick' which positioned the cross-wires over the aiming point. It worked in the opposite sense to the hand controller we used to position the aircraft radar marker. And, it favoured right-handed operators (watch this space) – pilots would not have coped.

All the early work on the TV Martel and associated systems was carried out at Boscombe Down, culminating in a 'live' missile at Aberporth range against a warship target. The next milestone occurred in October 1974 when Trial Mistico allowed for six inert missiles to be fired from within the resources of 12 Squadron. Although the Central Trials and Tactics Organisation (CTTO) oversaw the trial, the Honington wing weapons officer managed it. Paddy O'Shea was a larger than life Irishman who was one of the leading lights in the Boscombe trials and what the burly rugby playing and hard-drinking Irishman said the navigators did their utmost to achieve! Before the trial the firing navigators were required to complete hundreds of runs in the TP simulator. This presented them with just about every possible situation they could find on selection of TP. In addition, aircraft could be fitted with a TV Airborne Trainer (TVAT), which was virtually the TV part of the actual missile.

During a routine training sortie the navigator could select a suitable 'legitimate' ship target and practise tracking. The operator would con the pilot as though he was 'flying' the missile and talk him down to a successful conclusion, with break-off in the ensuing dive at the pilot's discretion; it's fair to say that some were quite sporting! The pilots could also practise the breakaway manoeuvre required immediately after the missile launch. This was a 3-4g level turn at launch height away from the target ensuring that the data-link pod remained on the target side of the aircraft. The turn continued through 120 degrees where the aircraft was rolled out maintaining direction until impact. On an actual firing run the navigator would experience this breakaway manoeuvre with the sea streaking past his left ear at 100 feet in a 4g turn while his TV screen told him that he was straight and level at 1,500 feet. This was a discomfiting experience only stomached by extraordinary mortals.

This first Trial Mistico lost some realism for the crews when Aberporth range authorities insisted on having full control over the positioning of the launch aircraft and the actual launch point in order to fulfil the constraints of a tight safety trace. Overall, the squadron performed admirably with no major problems resulting in six direct hits on the target. (The target was a 30-foot long raft with a vertical structure towards one end with three 15-foot square sides, the centre of the facing panel being the aiming point.)

The second Trial Mistico occurred twelve months later. Although still run under the auspices of CTTO, this trial was organised by the squadron when I was detailed to run events. The plus side of this was that I got to fire a second missile. One of the basic requirements was that the 'firers' should not be the six who took part in the first trial. However, the boss, who was new, was allocated a missile and I was his navigator. The major change for this phase of the trial was that the Aberporth authorities agreed to allow crews to navigate themselves to the launch box and the firing position with no assistance (interference?) from themselves, apart from a mandatory 'STOP, STOP, STOP' – a measure they had no need to employ. As with the previous year, the trial was successful, but with only five out of six direct hits. The missile that missed was pretty spectacular nonetheless.

CTTO in their wisdom decided to run a joint trial with Mistico, which was to evaluate the RAF Phantom's radar performance in acquiring and tracking a TV Martel missile, head-on from launch to impact. Thus, they were approaching the raft target from the opposite line of attack. Apparently the Phantom navigator managed this quite successfully. However, the TV Martel on this particular day did not perform as advertised or with the same degree of success. Upon selecting TP, the navigator, in the guise of a first-class, left-handed 'dark blue' navy observer, found that he had no elevation control over the missile, which promptly went into a steep climb. The cloud over the target was a complete blanket at 2,000 feet. Our hapless observer had a clear picture on his TV screen of the missile entering cloud, emerging into clear air at 5,000 feet and then a dark blur which was a Phantom in close proximity. Needless to say, the Phantom pilot had the shock of his life when a large thirteen-foot drainpipe appeared going vertical in front of his nose. The range controller subsequently sprang into action and destroyed the missile before it left the safety trace. Poor old Ken (for that was his name) was ribbed mercilessly, particularly as he was a left-handed operator using a right-handed system! He was of course blameless – although we were slow to admit that to him.

Soon after this trial, and after some ten years flying the mighty Buccaneer, I was inevitably nobbled for a ground tour at group headquarters; at least it was a Buccaneer associated job, working with some old 'colourful' colleagues, so we could still reminisce

Top: HMS *Eagle* Air Group with 800 Squadron Buccaneers, October 1965.
Above: Fred Secker parks his 800 Squadron aircraft on the runway at Butterworth, July 1966.
Right: Buccaneer Mark 1 of 809 Squadron in 1964.

Above: Instructors of 736 Squadron enjoy a formation loop in 1966.
Left: Bombing up at Brawdy for another sortie against the *Torrey Canyon.*
Below: A 736 Squadron Mark 2 clears the snow at Karup in Denmark, 1970.

Above: An 801 Squadron Buccaneer catches a wire on *Hermes* in 1970.

Right: 12 Squadron at RAF Luqa during Exercise Lime Jug, 1970.

Below: Ian Henderson of 12 Squadron visits Holme-on-Spalding-Moor.

Above: Buccaneer and Hunter T7 of the Laa
bruch Wing.
Left: A courtesy call to Her Majesty on HMY
Britannia.
Below: A busy flight deck on *Ark Royal.*

...ve: 809 Squadron officers, 1976. (Co Lt Cdr
...h Somerville-Jones)

...ht: 809 aircraft with flight refuelling pod ap-
...aches *Ark Royal*'s deck.

...ow: HMS *Ark Royal*.

Above: Ark Royal, dressed overall with paying-off pennant, leaves Gibraltar for the final time.
Left: 208 Squadron over the Nevada desert during the first Red Flag.
Below: The RAF Germany Wing at Red Flag.

bove: 24 SAAF Squadron with a maximum load
 sixteen 250kg Mk 82 bombs.
ght: Undercarriage up! A quick get away.
low: Airborne from RAF Akrotiri.

Above: The 237 OCU aerobatic crews, 198[ ]
with Phil Wilkinson centre left.
Left: A Hunter F6 of 208 Squadron
at Honington, 1980.
Below: On dispersal at Akrotiri for Operati[ ]
Pulsator.

A TV Martel on inboard pylon with the ALQ-10 ECM pod outboard.

and tell war stories, much to the annoyance of our V-bomber 'friends'.

This was not to be the end of my association with Buccaneer flying. In 1994 I was serving with a Tornado squadron at RAF Lossiemouth (where it all started for me) at the time of the final Buccaneer squadron's disbandment (208 Squadron). The boss of that outfit happened to be a friend of mine and I managed to talk him into giving me a trip for old time's sake before it was too late. And so it was that I flew in a Buccaneer again on 15 February 1994, twenty-six years, eleven months and seven days after my first sortie. It certainly brought all those wonderful memories of the aircraft flooding back, and reinforced my belief that nothing else came close to engendering such a spirit among its aircrew – and what an aircraft.

CHAPTER ELEVEN

EMBARKED WITH THE MARK 2

TED HACKETT

During my time as a midshipman I spent a brief period in *Ark Royal* in the Red Sea, when I watched the Scimitars and Vixens thundering on and off the deck and said: "that is for me". First, however, I had to spend some time at sea to gain my ocean navigation and watch-keeping tickets and for the next year I was the navigating officer of HMS *Puncheston* in the Far East, under the command of Mike Clapp, one of the earliest and best-known Buccaneer observers. This was during the Indonesian Confrontation. *Puncheston* was acting as a gunboat in the Malacca and Singapore Straits and around and up rivers in Borneo. Then came flying training at RAF Linton-on-Ouse in September 1966 and the excitement and camaraderie of the flying community. Young's Bar springs to mind and bent pewter tankards.

RNAS Brawdy followed with a step change to the Hunter T8 in 759 NAS where lessons were soon rammed home. Two Hunters collided on the day before Christmas leave with the loss of a crew, which included a term mate and friend. This was a hard business, which could bite. People began to fall by the wayside. Next came advanced flying training in 738 NAS with the Hunter GA 11 and the Solva Inn when the airfield was clamped. More people fell by the wayside. Two-inch RP was great fun and RNAS Lossiemouth and the Buccaneer beckoned.

In 1968 the Buccaneer was still state of the art and ahead of its time; boundary layer control (blow) was a new aid. You never forget your first flight in a Buccaneer and in June, Pete de Souza drew the short straw to sit in the back of a Mark 1 when he managed to get me back on the runway in one piece. After the odd engine failure etc, at the end of December I found myself off by Comet to Singapore to join 801 NAS, disembarked from *Hermes* at RAF Changi; swimming pool, beers, Singapore night life and a great team. My 'looker' was Flt Lt Paul Kelly, sadly killed in a Buccaneer in his next appointment in Germany. Our first excitement was a complete seizure of the starboard engine, shortly after take-off. Hot and humid, it was difficult to maintain height with a barn door to starboard. Very wide

Fred de la Billière (left) leads an 801 Squadron aircrew cleaning party.
L-R: Mike Lythgoe, Nick Nicholls, Stu Leeming, Pony Moore and Steve Park.

circuit, dumping fuel all the time until overland, we managed to make a firm landing on the runway. Then came the re-embarkation of the squadron in the South China Sea and my first deck landing. The deck looked very small indeed. Mike Bickley (SOBS 801) was in the back and managed to coax me into the wires. It was exhilarating.

As many will remember, Perth and Cape Town are excellent 'runs ashore' in a wonderful climate. They were my first 'runs' from an aircraft carrier and they were very exciting. We disembarked some aircraft at Perth, but not Cape Town, to maintain 'flying practice'; it was always recognised that there was the need to be involved in these minor departures to try to get away from the watch-keeping routines on board or at least have some excuse. We did a formation flypast over Albany from Perth and it took us over two hours! The cocktail parties always went down well, particularly the excellent Royal Marine Band's 'Beating Retreat' and 'Sunset' ceremonies; many tears shed by our guests. The invitations to 'up-homers' never stopped coming; to barbecues, parties, sailing, water-skiing and 'please stay for the weekend'. And the girls were all stunning… At times these invitations were difficult to fill, but somehow we managed it.

And so it was back to Lossiemouth for the summer of 1969 and time for some sailing across the Moray Firth with David Brittain in a 13-foot Mirror dinghy, without life jackets, which was madness. In Cromarty we joined Tom Eeles in his small sailing cruiser for a dish of 'Mr Brassie's Jungle Gorge' and stayed the night.

During strike progression over the Highlands I watched my section leader's aircraft pitch up at low level and become a ballistic lump of metal before napalming the hill.

Fortunately Robin Kent and Roy Croston ejected relatively unscathed. Then it was back to sea in *Hermes* and an introduction to night flying in the Mediterranean. We were used to recovering with low fuel states, sometimes below 2,000lbs, but on one night it was very close to the bone. Gibraltar was the nominated diversion and four Buccs were up. The usual cry came up from the ship as we prepared to recover: "Conserve, we will find wind shortly!" It was a moonlit night and the sea was like glass. We could see the smoke candle going straight up into the air. We were down to 'chicken' and then started to squeeze a bit. I was the first to opt out and declined the invitation of ATC at Gibraltar to go round the Rock again to allow a civilian airliner to land. The three other aircraft quickly followed me. The first took the CHAG (chain arrestor gear) and the other two landed somewhere on the airfield. Much beer was required that evening.

Another episode at that time was on the morning of a beautiful sunny day in the Med when, having launched, I was waiting for my number two to join, to discover that Pony Moore and Mike Cunningham had ejected on the catapult after a premature breakout from the holdback. Both were recovered safely, but it certainly impressed a party of 3rd Bn. Royal Regiment of Fusiliers, the resident battalion in Gib, who were watching from the 'goofers'.

On our way to the Eastern Med we paid visits to Villefranche and Malta, disembarking the serviceable aircraft to RAF Luqa. In my haste to get to the disembarkation briefing, I slipped on a wet deck and slammed my shin into a passage door combing, slicing through my flying suit and my shin; there was blood everywhere. I did not wish to give up my seat, so declined the sickbay. That would be Luqa's problem. Paul Kelly and I were dispatched to Sicily on a TacR before recovering to Luqa at midday, to find the rest of the squadron aircrew firmly ensconced in the mess bar, led by that well-known FAA aviator and our senior pilot, Fred de la Billière. Malta was another adventure.

801 NAS disbanded at Lossiemouth in July 1970. I spent a brief interlude as Flags to FONAC and it was back to Lossiemouth in May 1972 to join 764 NAS for the final naval AWI course on Hunter GA 11s, with Mike Lucas and Mike Blissett. The only rule appeared to be 'bring the aircraft back'. Then it was goodbye to RNAS Lossiemouth and hello RAF Honington and 237 OCU, before joining 809 NAS and *Ark Royal* in October. Low-level night Lepus strikes as a three or four ship were very satisfying sorties, but the night recovery afterwards was always the major challenge.

This brings to mind a night sortie as the duty tanker with Malcolm Tennant, operating south of Decimomannu as the nominated diversion. We were to be recovered last. The last F-4 kept bolting and came up to take a couple of grand. We were told to start dumping for recovery, when the F-4 started bolting again. We were told to wait, as the F-4 was bound to get on next time. We crept below 'chicken' and decided to go for Deci, to find the airfield shut! We managed to make it to Elmas, having seen the runway lights; I am sure we taxied in on fumes.

I attended the RN Staff College at Greenwich and in June 1975 was sent back to 237 OCU at Honington to be senior pilot 809 NAS. Throughout the autumn 809 operated off *Ark Royal* in the East Atlantic conducting various NATO exercises, until disembarking to

Refuelling an 892 Squadron Phantom.

Honington for Christmas. A few of us cross-decked to the USS *Independence* and were very envious when we saw the size of her flight deck.

In February 1976 *Ark Royal* headed for Westlant (Western Atlantic region of NATO) and 800 miles off Roosevelt Roads Naval Station I had a night launch in the early hours of the morning to collect the mail, with a chief petty officer with a welfare problem in the back. Escorted by 809's American exchange crew, Dougie Hiatt and Tom Lloyd, we made it to Roosie Roads, packed the bomb bay racks with mail and put the remainder in the back seat. As I returned to *Ark*, my TACAN worked and my escorts didn't.

This was in the days of the filming of the documentary series 'Sailor' with TV cameras everywhere. We got used to them; having a camera thrust into your face as you were eating your fried egg sarnie in the aircrew refreshment bar after a sortie, was par for the course. The TV team had to be guarded constantly as they were likely to amble onto the flight deck without realising the dangers involved. They even managed to persuade the carrier-borne ground liaison officer (CBGLO), or otherwise known as 'Cballs', to get them to the Vieques Range hut to film Buccaneer action on the wide variety of targets; some were even mobile and radio controlled, which added spice to the targeting. The island of Vieques is now a nature reserve and holiday complex.

The Atlantic Fleet Weapons Range (AFWR) was a vast area of sea, fully instrumented and controlled, for a great breadth of naval warfare activity, including tracking submarines going deep with dipping sonar helicopters. 809 were able to conduct live weapons practice; from VT fused 1,000lb bombs to live Sidewinder firings at flare targets, or strike progression against the F-4s. Visibility tended to be a zillion miles and the flying conditions were perfect.

Roosie Roads Air Day will be well remembered. 809 were invited to participate, so we put on a small display with a number of aircraft. Our first pass was in a loose formation at 500 feet, plugged into our own tankers. The tankers were then detached and the remainder of the aircraft sneaked behind a ridge to the west of the airfield and dropped to low level before accelerating over the ridge and dropping down to the runway in stream, very low and at max chat, 580 knots. People standing on the fire wagons for a better view, rapidly began to realise it was almost certainly a mistake and promptly abandoned ship!

It should be remembered that it was not constant operations when we were embarked; the ship had to be replenished at sea (RAS) with food, ammunition, stores and fuel. It was good to be on the upper deck in the weather conditions we had in the Caribbean and aircrew frequently helped during a RAS in moving air ammunition down to the deep magazines, or they cleaned aircraft. There were indeed moments of levity such as that rather lethal activity called deck hockey, tugs-of-war and the more relaxed kite-flying competitions. On passage, Saturday nights at sea could include Sods Operas when 809 did a brilliant skit on The Magic Roundabout. The occasional squadron mess dinner took place, including casino nights. Horse racing would be run on the flight deck or in the hangar, if the weather happened to be inclement, the proceeds going to one of the ship's chosen charities.

Ark called into Fort Lauderdale on her way north and with 1976 being the bicentennial of the American Declaration of Independence, we could not put a foot wrong. Invitations poured into every section of the ship and we were almost overwhelmed.

Air Group aboard the Ark Royal.

The ship went into Mayport for a maintenance period covering several weeks. This of course demanded that we disembarked to NAS Cecil Field, a vast self-contained naval air base in the middle of nowhere, the sheer scale of which was mind-boggling. There was no need to go outside the base, as everything was on hand. But, being adventurous souls, we had to check. Cars were hired to explore Jacksonville allowing us to form an attachment to that hub of nightlife, Annie Tiques, amongst others; all of which I have great memories of. Flying was not too intense, although ranges were readily available. Low levels over the Everglades were fun and we even managed an overnight land-away, with the squadron air engineering officer (AEO) in the back, to NAS Pensacola and a visit to New Orleans.

Ark moved north to the US Naval Base at Norfolk, Virginia and was berthed opposite USS *Nimitz*. Seen from the air, her flight deck was four times the size of that of the *Ark*. The squadron disembarked to NAS Oceana, which seemed to be a clone of Cecil Field, but Virginia Beach was different.

Once back to UK I took part in Exercise Northern Deckslide, which entailed aircraft sliding sideways in the swell on an emulsion of oil and water, while taxiing. There were no pressure washers at that time; it was very off-putting, with only a small lip at the edge of the flight deck. Unlike the benign conditions of the Caribbean, this was where you earned your flying pay. Constant Atlantic swells caused the deck to pitch and, on occasions, the helmsman was fighting to keep the ship on the flying course, particularly if the wind was across the swell; keeping to the centreline on recovery could be difficult. Coupled with the pitching deck, the timing of one's arrival in the wires had to be judged with care. Even if you had not been waved off by the LSO, there was nothing worse than looking at the round down without being able to see the rest of the flight deck. Add a low cloud base and driving rain and you have the full gamut of flying operations in the North Atlantic.

Night flying in these conditions was very interesting and very sweaty. You just trusted that you would have a good CCA controller who would bring you in on the centreline and on sight, as it was easy to start a pendulum swing around the centreline if there was no horizon. Good fuel management was instinctive, particularly if you were the duty airborne night tanker. And to cap it all you always had to land on the first pass at max landing weight, which was dictated by the wind over deck, in order to have the maximum fuel in case there was a need to 'go around' again or divert. You had to aim to have the speed plus or minus two knots on arrival in the wires to make sure you did not over stress them or the aircraft's hook. When the deck was pitching you tended to fly a slightly high meatball and this used to cause one or two bolters. You knew, with experience, when you had missed number four wire and there was time to go to full power and close the air brake to go round again. At night this was particularly unpleasant. Far more beers were required after recovery, having finally taxied into Fly One.

All of this fun came to an end for me on 14 January 1977, when I had my final sortie out of Honington, collecting a seagull down the starboard engine to boot! It was all an incredible experience and in three carrier tours I managed to achieve 512 deck landings of which 108 were at night. I was lucky; I never had to eject.

We all know that the Buccaneer was an amazing aircraft; well ahead of its time and I am sure it could hold its own today with some modifications. It was undoubtedly the most enjoyable time of my naval career, but what really made it were the people. RN or RAF, it mattered not, fifty percent of aircrew in 809 wore light blue uniforms and the combined spirit was tremendous. This is engendered in the Buccaneer Aircrew Association (BAA) and the incredible hospitality we were given in South Africa for the fiftieth anniversary celebrations in 2008 and, of course, our annual Blitz. The BAA is a unique brotherhood and I am very glad indeed that I am one of the brethren.

CHAPTER TWELVE

RED FLAG

DAVID WILBY

Despite the fact that the USAF attained a roughly 10-to-1 kill ratio during the Korean War, when it came to the war in Vietnam the ratio had fallen to about 2-to-1 and, for a period during 1972, it dropped to 1-to-1. A paper documenting 'Lessons Learned from the Vietnam War' had also highlighted that crews who survived their first ten combat sorties were likely to survive the remainder of their tour. Thus, there was a perceived need to improve the training to better prepare crews for their operational scenarios.

Meanwhile, at Nellis AFB, a small group of relatively junior officers were promoting the idea of 'aggressor' squadrons with a plan to utilise the vast desert areas north of the air base as their 'playground'. At this stage it was very much a Fighter Weapons School (FWS) 'in-house' affair until one of the officers involved, Major Moody Suter, managed to gain access to the then commander TAC, General Robert J. Dixon. So impressed was he by the FWS plan that he instructed his operations deputy to establish Red Flag at Nellis within six months and so, on 1 March 1976, the 4440th Tactical Fighter Training Group (Red Flag) was formed to provide extremely realistic simulation of combat conditions for, at that time, the exclusive use of US forces.

The basic principle of the exercise was that visiting squadrons would be deployed to test their tactics in the desert training areas, the size of Wales, to the north of Nellis. Airfield size targets were carved into the desert and real and simulated Warsaw Pact defences and electronic warfare threats were deployed across the desert to defend the area. Suter's team at the FWS provided an 'aggressor squadron' flying F-5E single-seat aircraft chosen not only for their agility but also because they had similar characteristics to the MiG-21 operated then by the WP forces; the aircraft were camouflaged in typical WP schemes and all bore the Red Star of the Soviet Union. Aggressor pilots were selected from the top fighter pilots in the USAF and had to be FWS graduates. They were trained to fly according to the tactical doctrine of the WP, to provide participating crews with the type of

Buccaneer crews at the Tactical Fighter Meet. David Wilby seated left.

threat they would encounter in real combat should the Cold War ever turn hot. The F-5E Tigers became the mainstay of Red Flag until they were replaced by the F-16 in 1988.

During bilateral talks with his UK counterpart in 1976, General Dixon offered Air Chief Marshal Sir David Evans, C-in-C Strike Command, an invitation to send RAF aircraft to participate in Red Flag. An opportunity not to be missed was eagerly grasped and Honington-based 208 Squadron was selected as the first RAF squadron to participate. During the first half of the exercise 208's Buccaneers were joined by two Vulcans and for the second half, the UK-based aircraft were flown by a detachment drawn from the Laarbruch Wing in Germany. As a flight commander on 208 at the time, I was delighted to be selected by the boss, Wg Cdr Phil Pinney, as the project officer.

To meet the demands of flying on Red Flag it was essential that we carried out some dedicated work-up training. In August 1976, Mike Bush, Alfie Ferguson, Dave Symonds and I had been fortunate to participate in the Tactical Fighter Meet (TFM) at Leuchars. There, against the best of the RAF's air defence and offensive forces, we gained much in evolving and refining the squadron's overland tactics that had been developed for our primary conventional role in support of NATO's northern flank. Our normal day-to-day minimum height over land was 250 feet but, for Red Flag, we would be flying at 100 feet above ground level (AGL), so it was valuable on TFM to be cleared down to that height over the specifically-designated ultra-low level (ULL) flying areas in the Scottish Borders. Some two months later, the lessons learned on TFM were put into practice when the squadron took part in Exercise Strand, designed to test the RAF's Rapier air defence systems at a location in Northumberland. All this ULL flying was an excellent lead-in for the crews selected to participate in Red Flag and its prelude, the official work-up, which required the squadron to deploy across the Atlantic to Canadian Forces Base, Goose Bay,

Flying low level over Labrador, 1979.

in Labrador. Goose is in a remote location just south of the tundra and an ideal base from which to practise and develop low-level operations.

We deployed half the squadron at a time with a changeover after two weeks with each crew programmed for around nine sorties. The terrain was perfect, difficult navigation over featureless tracts, no built-up areas (though we still raised the odd complaint from a disgruntled trapper) and some dodgy weather to keep us alert. The squadron worked hard and individual low flying was honed to fly safely at 100 feet over and through varied terrain. Similarly, low-level formation penetration tactics were attempted and tested using our own aggressor 'bounce' aircraft. We even tried a grey and white camouflage scheme on some aircraft, which became very useful when employed as the bounce. The detachment was a great sharpener for what was to come.

Back in the UK and readying for our deployment we were familiar with the first part of our route, which would take us to Nellis via a night stop back at Goose Bay. However, as we approached our Victor tanker off north-west Scotland on 2 August 1977, its captain declared a navigation kit malfunction and handed over the task of getting us to Goose to the lead Buccaneer. Now, at low level over the sea, this would not be a problem to solve for any experienced Buccaneer navigator. However, at 34,000 feet over the Atlantic with all the vagaries of high-level winds and with only the ergonomic slum of the Buccaneer's back cockpit to assist, prospects were not great as we could only rely on dead reckoning for the majority of the route and the occasional turn onto north to take a peek at the maximum range of the Blue Parrot radar to ensure that first Iceland and then Greenland were still on the right hand side.

En route there were some interesting lunges, in cloud, into a refuelling basket being

208 Squadron air and ground crew ready for Red Flag, October 1977.

whipped by a snaking rubber hose. We attempted to feed the bite-sized sandwiches under our oxygen masks, as we listened to music on the aircraft's HF radio, but we drank very little. Nobody wanted to try and find the shriven member hiding deep inside his rubberised immersion suit and use the pee-tube provided for our convenience. Eventually, after some five-and-a-half hours, the Goose Bay TACAN beacon began to twitch and twenty minutes later we landed in the barren wastes of Labrador.

After a night in the bar with our tanker buddies and many 'war stories' of the outward journey, and just a few beers, we continued the next morning in pairs across the sterile wastes of Canada and across the US, still in our immersion suits and with our tankers who remained with us until we were in reach of Nellis. By dint of some nifty speed control, our second pair was able to join us in the descent and, much to Nellis's displeasure, we joined the circuit for a four-ship run-in and break. As we taxied in past aircraft pans the size of our airfields, and crammed tight with the latest modern high-speed pursuit ships, we gazed in awe and listened to the mirth of air traffic noting the dated look of our noble coke-bottle shaped steeds; even more laughter when we folded the wings. After six hours and forty minutes in our rubber suits, Stu Ager and I were glad to step on to the concrete, which was baking in the ninety-degree heat of a Nellis summer's day. A welcome ice-cold Coors was thrust in our hands but quickly hidden to avoid the prying eyes of the TV cameras that had turned up to film the 'Limeys' arrival. We had arrived as the first non-US participants in Red Flag.

In the summer before we deployed, two wonderful 'cowboys' visited us from the Red Flag staff at Nellis. Unfortunately these laconic fighter pilot gods, whilst also melting a red crimpoline suit that got rather too close to a bar side candle in the officers' mess at Honington, let slip to our awestruck wives that Nellis was not a lonely outpost in the middle of the desert, as we had hitherto described, but was actually just ten miles as the crow flies from Las Vegas. Our cover was well and truly blown!

The Nellis officers' 'O Club' had all the delights that one could imagine being just those ten miles north-east of the 'Desert Jewel': slot machines; burgers; cheap beer; fries and large screen TVs were just a few of its attractions. It was a very, very entertaining establishment and nothing like a traditional RAF officers' mess to which we were accustomed. It was crammed to the gunnels with overloaded egos, vibrant aircrew banter and some very decorous scenery that 'sure loved our English accents' – it was a great place to be after a hard day's work over the desert. Particularly so at a Wednesday and Friday night happy hour when strippers performed in a ring in the centre of the bar. This was no 'Tailhook' but it did have all the makings! Between this hallowed ground and the glitzy entertainment of downtown Las Vegas, we were afforded some essential recreational diversion from the pressure of our training. On a more serious note, it was also a unique opportunity to discuss operational tactics with our American counterparts in relaxed surroundings. Oh well – I tried!

As this deployment was planned to be a one-off, our allowances were virtually non-existent but crews soon discovered where to enjoy the best deals in town and how to spend an evening taking in the extraordinary sights of Vegas whilst keeping body and soul in reasonable shape. Careful operations on the gaming tables not only gave access to complimentary drinks but, if you were lucky, also furnished a small supplementary income to bring home all the latest Fisher Price toys you could carry for our young families (now still used by grandchildren some thirty-five years later). The local golf courses were also very generous and offered us excellent discounts and some freebies. Playing on US courses was a revelation; it appeared that it was beneath the dignity of rich Americans to look for any errant balls. However, not so the Brits. We had many excursions off the fairways and it was a common sight to see our folks wading into pools or the undergrowth to gather the very obvious treasure trove. It is rumoured that Ken Evans is still playing with some of them today.

We soaked up the ambience of Vegas and Nellis and looked forward to the opportunity to train in such a comprehensive operational arena with our doughty comrades. The base was huge by any standard and just brimming with modern aircraft and the latest technology; before they met us in the air we were without doubt seen and humoured as the country bumpkins over from the UK.

After a few days acclimatisation to both the heat and the complexities of this very large military installation, we started to earn our stripes. I had constructed a flying programme using our Goose Bay training as a template. Each formation was planned for eight sorties during the exercise, all by day and with plenty of time for preparation and de-brief. With the participants' 'In Brief' completed and our workplace and planning area established, and having individually found time to read, digest and sign the incredibly long but essential Red Flag SPINS (special instructions) we were fully indoctrinated into Red Flag and its ethos and were ready to participate. After a familiarisation sortie at 100 feet over the Nellis and Tonopah Ranges we felt ready to mix it with the aggressors and the rest of Red Air. And so, with the Red Flag operations building boasting an entrance somewhat humbly inscribed, 'Through This Portal Pass the World's Best Fighter Pilots', we were ready to prove that so did 'The World's Best Bomber Crews' and we were there not only to prove it but also to win against our foe.

Initial sorties were flown equipped with practice bombs in order to test and ensure that our safe separation distances and time splits over the target were achievable in the sparse terrain where navigation was done by flying from massive ridge line to massive ridge line that grew out of the desert floor. That achieved, we soon moved on to carrying and releasing our normal Red Flag conventional weapon load of both live and inert 1,000lb bombs as well as BL755 cluster bomb units (CBU). We flew in large coordinated missions with our US colleagues who were flying an impressive array of aircraft. Briefings were comprehensive and, yes, we were always given the callsign 'Limey'.

Perhaps the most complicated part of the mission was the taxi and take-off with many participants, lots of instructions and 'last chance' weapons' safety checks before being given our departure clearance, which was difficult to understand (do we really speak the same language?) before being read back in a cool, laconic John Wayne voice that befitted the moment. However, once headed at medium altitude to our start point of Student Gap, the game was most definitely on.

As this was our first participation we were a relatively unknown quantity on the continental United States. We needed to get to the target on time without being 'killed' by either the aggressors or by the ground defences in the target areas and then exit quickly and unscathed. Importantly, we also wanted no mistakes, incidents or accidents.

We flew to our limits and employed the tactics that we had evolved during the lead-in training. The skills that all our crews had developed over the difficult terrain and weather of Labrador worked even better in the desert where the more favourable environment gave a little more individual scope for thinking time and action. It was hot and the battlefield was relatively high and both factors dictated that we needed to watch our thrust and energy levels whilst operating near the ground. We also needed to consider the sun, glare and perspective.

We were cleared to fly down to 100 feet minimum separation distance (MSD), in other words a clearance bubble of 100 feet around the aircraft. In truth, and despite legislation and our rather dated instrumentation suite, at ultra-low level the height you fly becomes more of an individual comfort feel, which will vary, depending on terrain, speed, manoeuvre and individual skill. In the Buccaneer the pilot, particularly when very low and very fast, was responsible for avoiding the ground and obstacles and trying to spot any threat aircraft in the frontal sector. Navigators looked after the navigation, aircraft systems, most weapon inputs and tended to loosen straps in order to monitor the visual threat envelope from high to low and, with considerable effort, the rear sector from two o'clock through to ten o'clock. Excellent lookout was imperative in such a clear air mass with few places to hide. If the pilot had to look into the cockpit, he warned the navigator to look ahead. At no time could you afford both heads to be diverted from the forward sector. This lesson was very quickly learned by one of our experienced crews who discovered this when they had a momentary lapse of concentration as they cleared the target area and were decelerating to re-join formation. Striking the telegraph wire at thirty-seven feet was a very welcome attention getter to pull-up from their induced gentle descent towards the desert floor; they were very lucky – it could have been a lot worse.

Speed was essential to aid manoeuvre, to pass through the threats quickly and to make enemy defence engagement solutions more difficult. Speeds were kept high as fuel was not in short supply and we were carrying representative weapon war loads. We planned to fly at 480 knots as we entered hostile territory and increased this to 540 (nine nautical miles per minute) as we moved into the target area. We could still generate further knots in extremis and for running out of the target area.

We always flew as constituted crews so that we were totally familiar with each other's *modus operandi* and, for the same reason, we were teamed up with another crew to make a constituted pair and, further, joined with another pair as a constituted four-ship unit. Participation in Red Flag was mandated for experienced pilots with no less than 500 flying hours, who were CR (combat ready) and had completed a structured and appropriate work-up period. Accordingly, and in order to facilitate ease of programming but, more importantly, to ensure familiarity of action within formations, 208 Squadron nominated particular formation leaders who would retain that role on every mission flown. Those selected were particularly experienced crews both in terms of the role flown and hours on the Buccaneer. The task was given to Pete Jones, Mike Bush and myself with Stu Ager as my pilot. Wing men, each excellent low-level operators, developed supreme flexibility and skills in keeping formation integrity in all terrains and weather conditions, which allowed a little more thinking time for navigation checks and threat perception. Formation shapes varied to suit conditions and aircraft over the flat desert areas could be several miles apart which provided a compromise between ease of passage and, importantly, made it difficult for an intercepting aircraft to identify all members. As experience developed, it was not always necessary to see a wingman to know where he was and where he would appear as he emerged from behind ground features.

At Goose Bay, we had learned to avoid wing flash when flying over the middle of plain ground features like lakes, dry or full, and to keep away from the valley floor by hugging the sides of large valleys. We also developed our own techniques for crossing ridges without undue exposure to a following threat, either by turning sharply to parallel it before pulling over the ridge, inverting to regain terrain masking as soon as possible or to just bunt over. Ideally, we would find a small gap and scrape through. Standing waves, inflamed by the heat and terrain, could also cause severe turbulence even for the Buccaneer and our crews were careful to ease a tad at high speed to prevent undue fatigue on the airframe.

Every crew had a comprehensive route map with regular real times, the 'timeline', to achieve the tasked time on target (TOT). Achieving one's TOT was crucial to maintain deconfliction from other aircraft and weapons' fragmentation zones during live drops. Often the formation would be split after an air engagement on the run to the target but it was common to see wingmen sliding back into place as they regained the timeline. Getting through the target first time maximised the elements of surprise and confusion and was always preferable to going round and coming in to a stirred threat with a single focus: you. We employed a strict EMCON (emission control) policy, which included radio silence, and we kept our radars off. As we were flying nap (near as possible) to the earth, most threats came from above and an evasive manoeuvre by any member of the formation gave a fairly pointed clue to the rest of the team without the need for a radio call. Each

Airborne from Nellis AFB for a Red Flag mission (Frank Mormillo).

aircraft would make its own appropriate counter and re-join the timeline in due course. In the clear air of the desert, a puff of exhaust generated by an increase in speed to aid manoeuvre became the silent clue.

At the time, the Buccaneer was relatively well equipped for operations in the electronic warfare mode. Flying low kept us in a quiet and fairly uncluttered radar environment and gave our RWR (radar-warning receiver) a good chance of picking up an early threat signal. A long-range early-warning radar indication told us to fly lower to mask the aircraft and a high pitch quadrant indication, or pulsed Doppler warning light of a hostile defence threat, enabled us to take the appropriate evasive action. Not least, we had a one-shot load of chaff bundles taped in the very effective clam-shaped airbrake. These customised strips of tinfoil were designed to confuse radars but they also could be a little disturbing to a visual fighter closing at high speed. Because in 1977 the Buccaneer had no forward-firing weapons, as a last resort, we had developed a tactic that would destroy the aim of any fighter pilot closing in for a guns kill. It was simple and, although never tested for real, effective, as our enemy confessed and credited us with a kill against them if used. It was nothing more than a 1,000lb HE 'bomb in the face' (BIF) tactic, released from 100 feet. The very sight of which, we were assured, would ruin the hardiest of fighter pilot's day. The code word? KNICKERS! We also put a few aircraft in desert camouflage but, on the desert floor, we found that, as well as wing flash, ground shadow was what aggressor pilots looked for; our camouflage efforts were for nought. Moreover, we also discovered, to our chagrin, that when we really got down to very low levels we could create a dust storm trail on the desert floor that announced our presence.

After every sortie, and a few marching paces to get the story straight, all mission participants gathered for a comprehensive debrief led by the Red Flag directing staff, which included reports by each lead element involved and by the aggressors and ground-defence operators. In those early days, before the current plethora of very comprehensive electronic tracking and scoring systems, claims could be quite droll if well argued, and stories became quite entertaining, particularly when air-to-air or ground engagement films were available. There was little room for exaggeration. It was amusing whilst instructive and was an excellent training vehicle in which each unit's pedigree soon became apparent.

Our contribution went down extremely well. Our radio silence procedure caused doubt in some quarters as to whether we had actually been in the target area. We had very few air kills against us and the ground defenders on the EW (electronic warfare) ranges took great delight at leaving their control cabins to see some spectacular runs against their positions; they even produced video at the daily mass debrief of Buccaneers screaming past their radar heads to prove it. Our crews used map, stopwatch and some major 'mark one eyeball' activity to navigate in the difficult desert terrain, which lacked pinpoint navigational fixes and gave little cover to our aircraft on fairly predictable target routes. Early spots, high speed and, when necessary, counter manoeuvring at ULL made us difficult targets for the aggressors to substantiate kills with their then weapons load.

Our coordinated weapons attacks were also highly successful. The Buccaneer weapons system, which had been designed to toss a nuclear bomb against a Sverdlov cruiser, lacked much sophistication compared to modern digital computer-generated displays. Nevertheless, most squadron pilots had developed a seaman's eye appreciation – 'that looks about right' – which worked pretty well at low level and close range. Many of our attacks were aimed at suppressing airfield defences and runways using sticks of 1,000lb bombs tossed from around three miles out. I remember feeling quite elated as my four-aircraft formation were tossing from our planned direction and there, from another quadrant, was Pete Jones's four in a simultaneous attack tossing from their planned point; all followed by an impressive inverted 'Red Arrows' bomb-burst'. The CBU attacks at close range against convoy targets were also great fun. By the standards of the late 1970s era we produced excellent results.

The F-5 fighters of the aggressors were small, highly manoeuvrable and if we were spotted from their high observation perch, the pilots were quickly able to convert height to speed for rapid intercepts at low level. On most occasions, we were able to counter these attacks by an early spot, a formation split and an even more concentrated dive for the dirt. In this manner, though one of our aircraft might be claimed as a kill, the rest escaped unscathed and would regain track on the timeline. Similarly, against ground defences, our RWRs gave us an early warning of a threat and we were able to change direction to avoid the engagement envelope. When unavoidable we would fly lower and randomly jink to make the tracking operator's task more difficult. This made good video material particularly when accompanied by the tracker's commentary, which tended to be quite base and emotional.

Some of the Red Air opposition, flying in support of the aggressors, were flying the F-15, which had only been in service three years and many of its pilots had only a few hours on its very capable radar system. On our penultimate sortie, Stu Ager and I led a six-aircraft strike on a Hi-Lo-Hi mission to the Utah ranges. We were loaded with 1,000lb bombs and had the assistance of a US Navy EA-6B Prowler who flew with us for EW suppression. Unfortunately, our naval aviators enjoyed the run at low level so much that they had to 'bingo out' (short of fuel) well before the target. After attacking the target, and much against our doctrine, we tangled with a bunch of these F-15s and enjoyed a wonderful engagement before returning home at high level.

As the exercise progressed we added some embellishments to our sorties. On our sixth mission after a live CBU attack, we cleared the exercise areas, joined up and flew an eight-ship down Death Valley – all below sea level. After our last mission, with all our Buccaneers airborne, we joined in diamond-nine formation and took photos from the airborne spare.

As we finished our two-week stint, we welcomed our chums, XV and 16 Squadrons from RAF Germany, who took over our aircraft and completed the second part of the Red Flag with similar distinction and results. We later returned to Nellis to collect our aircraft and retrace the route home via Goose Bay.

As I close, I must pay much deserved homage to our engineering and logistics experts, and experts they were, led by our squadron engineering officer Arun Patel. The squadron always had a busy flying and detachment schedule but that year, with all our training demands and the rigours of operations in the barren wastes of Goose Bay and the heat of the Nevada Desert, it had been particularly difficult. That we did not drop a sortie at either Goose or Nellis was an amazing feat, and to finish our final Red Flag sortie with all ten aircraft airborne after such a demanding operational exercise was truly exceptional. Long hours of preparation and rectification, excellent leadership and teamwork and a great sense of pride combined to great effect. Not least, our logisticians had also worked miracles to move our heavy weapons and critical aircraft spares to the right place when needed. We could not have asked for better.

Once back in the UK, news of our results had spread and we were tasked to brief every conceivable senior staff headquarters including the Chiefs of Staff Committee at the MOD. Our briefs were honest and to the point and with factual reports to enforce the lessons learned, we also showed some quite good film that left no doubt as to the parameters to which we had flown. Having worked on the premise that this Red Flag was to be a one-off event, we were surprised to receive another invitation for the following year. Our success had set a trend for the RAF with repeat invitations in the coming years for many other RAF, and NATO, squadrons.

On subsequent Flag exercises, (Green, Maple, Blue etc.), which all had slightly different emphasis and complexity, we developed the work-up and tactics to give us comprehensive training across the whole operational environment. Nevertheless ours, and the RAF's, very first Red Flag still remains a very special and pleasing memory and it has shaped the standard and format for RAF operational training for many years since.

CHAPTER THIRTEEN

OPERATIONS IN SWA/ANGOLA 1975-1981

Gert Havenga displays his 500 Buccaneer hours badge whilst gently fondling a 400kg bomb.

GERT HAVENGA

Although the conflict in Angola and the problem of insurgency into northern South West Africa were escalating at a steady pace, it was to be several years before the Buccaneers of 24 Squadron were committed to battle. On 4 May 1978, combined elements of the SAAF and army attacked insurgent training bases near Cassinga and Cheteguera in southern Angola. This operation, dubbed Reindeer, marked the Buccaneer's introduction to the conflict and was the first of twenty-six operations in which Buccaneers were involved. However, detachments had been flying to the area for some years before the conflict escalated for what was, in effect, a 'hearts and minds' operation. On one such occasion we certainly arrived with a 'bang'.

24 Squadron was tasked to fly from AFB Waterkloof to Grootfontein with four Buccs and, on our arrival, to fly around over Ovamboland in a show of force. The aim of the exercise was to show the inhabitants that the Republic of South Africa (RSA) Government was able to protect them, and would.

So, on 15 May 1975 at 1000, we took off from Waterkloof under the leadership of the squadron commander, Cmdt Dan Zeeman. Sandy Allison was No.2 with me as No.3 with my navigator, Ken Snowball. Matthew Morton (a former Fleet Air Arm Buccaneer pilot) and his navigator Phillip Rosseau were the No.4. The briefing was to fly in a loose battle formation and, once over the airfield, to break from initial onto a right hand downwind leg at thirty-second intervals for the runway at Grootfontein which, at that time, was

24 Squadron crews, May 1975. Gert Havenga centre below SAAF marking.

relatively short for the Buccaneer.

What we didn't know was that the ATC tower frequency had changed the previous day but we had not received the NOTAM with the new details. Approaching the airfield Dan called for landing instructions without result. As we came overhead at 420 knots, Dan called us into 'box' formation as we started to turn onto a downwind leg.

Unfortunately in that turn, Matthew's aircraft (Bucc 426), hit the underside of mine (Bucc 412) with its tail plane, breaking it off. 426 went out of control and the pitot tube on the port wing of my aircraft was broken off giving me no airspeed indication.

The crew of 426 ejected safely but Matthew experienced serious injury with Phillip just hurting an ankle. I saw their Buccaneer burst into flames as it hit the ground. Adrenaline was now flowing. Ken immediately called SAAF HQ on the HF radio and informed them of the accident.

After I had determined the extent of damage to my aircraft, I called Dan to lead me in onto the runway. We came in hot and, according to the SOP (standard operating procedure), Dan was supposed to overshoot on short finals and leave me to land on my own. Unfortunately, he landed in front of me leaving me to fight the slipstream with a slightly bent aircraft with no airspeed indication. A very jittery pilot and nav eventually passed him on the runway without further damage. After stabilising Matthew and Phillip, they were taken to 1 Military Hospital in Pretoria where they both made a full recovery. The next two days we 'entertained' the locals by screaming over them at treetop heights before departing back to Waterkloof. The Buccs had now really arrived in South West Africa!

During the following four years from 1975 to 1979 it was just force preparation for 24 Squadron. Night flying with night attacks under NATAK flares, medium toss bombing by day and night, night formation and even night in-flight refuelling were practised and fine tuned in preparation for the long awaited operations in the war zone. The NATAK flares were tossed by the lead Buccaneer in a medium toss profile from 1,000 feet above ground level. They deployed with a parachute at about 3,000 feet above release height, giving ten-million candle power light over an identified target and allowing the rest of the formation to attack in a thirty-degree dive-bombing profile under virtually daylight conditions.

The most demanding of all was the night formation and night in-flight refuelling from another Buccaneer where you must fly into something that you cannot see, often under vertigo conditions. But the satisfaction after such a sortie was tremendous.

Although I was posted to 24 Squadron on 1 January 1975, I was only appointed as officer commanding on 1 November 1978. Eventually a dream came true. I had motivated, dedicated and well-trained air and ground crew men available to support me in my task. With only six aircraft available at that stage, we strived to have at least five of them operationally available at all times.

On 28 December 1978 I was tasked for an electronic warfare surveillance flight over (the then) Rhodesia with Phillip Rousseau as navigator. It was the first taste of operations for the Buccs under my command. Due to the political situation and denial of activities in Angola, it took another three months to convince the powers that 24 Squadron was ready for serious operations in SWA.

On 6 March 1979 at 0630 we departed with four aircraft, each loaded with 8 x 450kg bombs and full fuel, from Waterkloof to launch our first attack on a target called Base 52, somewhere on the border between Angola and Zambia. I was in the lead with Koos Botha as nav. The take-off with that heavy load at high altitude of 3,600 feet ASL was in itself a nightmare. The books recommend that you must have at least a one knot per second acceleration after take-off but we settled for half that during operations. So you were on the ADD steady and on the wrong side of the curve up to about Hartbeespoort dam, which is fifty miles away.

The attack was planned to be from a pitch-up into a thirty-degree dive. As the target was very difficult to recognise, my No.2 and I did not release our bombs. No.3 – no names no pack drill – inadvertently dropped his bombs during the roll-in. Confusion reigned and No.4 in the formation followed him, releasing his bombs. Accepting that No.3 and 4 must have recognised the target, myself and No.2 also bombed on their bomb bursts. As a result, 32 x 450kgs were dropped on an unidentified target. The feedback later from the recces was that the target had been cleared about a week before our attack but that we killed at least six elephants. All aircraft landed safely back at Grootfontein. Not a good result for the first attempt.

That same afternoon at 1230 we took off to attack identified SWAPO bases named Franca 3 and 4. This was repeated the following morning. Regular sorties were now flown from Grootfontein between the period 6 to 14 March on identified SWAPO bases at Efitu, Senanga, Cahama, and Nova Catenque all in the southern area of Angola.

Our first night attack was launched on 8 March 1979. In preparation for this I had to fly to Ondangwa in the nose of a Canberra for the planning session. There we planned with the radar controller, the late Tom Engela, that he would guide us in to a turn-in point. The four Buccs, in thirty-second radar trail, were to roll in for a blind thirty-degree

Refuelling a Cheetah D.

dive-bombing attack. This was, to say the least, terrifying, as it was a pitch-black night. However, everything worked exactly as planned and the feedback that we got was that twenty-six, of the thirty-two bombs dropped, hit the target area.

The next attack on 6 July was a dawn strike during Operation Rekstok. Four aircraft took off from Grootfontein to attack a THTC training camp that was deep into Angola in a medium toss attack. A 'very' low-level approach was required from the IP thirty miles away with an automatic release of the bombs during the toss manoeuvre. As soon as the bombs released at about 4,000 feet AGL we started the escape manoeuvre when all eyes were looking for possible missiles launched. The feeling that you were now exposed to enemy fire was just incredible because you must be on full alert. After this attack the Buccs were withdrawn from the scene until 5 November when the same attack was repeated. For this attack we operated directly from Waterkloof and landed back at Grootfontein, something that the fighter aircraft could not do. They had to deploy to Ondangwa a week before the strike – giving away the first principle of warfare 'surprise' – to deliver only half the tonnage on the target and run the risk of interception because they had insufficient fuel to return at low level and were forced to climb where the threat was greater.

From January 1981 until 15 June 1981 I was sent to the Senior Command and Staff Course to learn how to cross Ts and dot Is, much to my frustration while the squadron continued operations under the leadership of George Snyman. I was called away from the course on 17 March to conduct a strike with Riem Mouton as nav. We launched four Buccs for a combined strike on THTC with the Canberras. The weather was very bad on the way to the target area but, as we approached the target, the sky opened up for us and each Bucc delivered 8 x 450kgs each behind the Alpha bombs of the Canberras. Total surprise and excellent results were achieved.

24 Squadron fly low.

Fortunately I was back for our next big operation that started on 21 August when it was realised that the enemy radar activity had increased significantly over the battlefield. It was decided that the only safe way to destroy radars, and give more freedom of flight to the Mirage F-1 fighters that were used either in an attacking or top cover profile, was to use AS-30 air-to-surface missiles.

The only aircraft cleared to fire the AS-30 at that stage was the Bucc. Two missiles could be carried on the wing pylons with 4 x 450kg bombs in the bomb bay.

The AS-30 missile had an all-up weight of 520kgs with a 50kg warhead. It had a boosted burn time of twenty seconds and was manually controlled by the pilot using a joystick on the port side of the cockpit. The pilot had to steer the missile on to the target via a UHF radio link. As soon as it was launched a red flare ignited at the back giving the pilot the position of the missile, which was used as a reference point for steering.

The attack profile was to fly to a point twenty miles from the target, pitch-up to 15,000 feet AGL and attack in a shallow twenty-degree dive. The missile was launched at thirteen miles at 480 knots and then steered to hit just in front of the target.

After intense AS-30 simulator training and practice runs at Riemvasmaak weapons range in the Northern Cape that resulted in direct hits, we departed again for Grootfontein on 19 August 1981 with four aircraft.

Configured with 2 x AS-30 missiles and 4 x 450kgs in the bomb bay on my lead aircraft, with Sandy Roy as nav, and the other 3 aircraft with 8 x 450kgs, with adrenaline pumping, we took off from Grootfontein at 1007 with a temperature of thirty-two degrees for a formidable combined attack on the HQ of SWAPO (South West Africa People's Organisation) at Cahama with 1 x AS-30 and 4 x 450kgs and then on the radar installation at Chibemba (Olifant) with the same attack profile. You only get on the right side of the curve at about Tsumeb, about seventy miles away, at that temperature and load.

The safety of the rest of the aircraft was very dependent on the success of the results of the AS-30 attack. Fortunately both resulted in direct hits and the whole mission was a huge success.

The feeling that you get when that AS-30 leaves the pylon and you are in control of it is absolutely tremendous. It requires intense concentration and focus for that fifteen seconds flight time to impact. The satisfaction if it is a direct hit and the target is destroyed is quite overpowering. Knowing that you are in a ground-to-air missile environment makes the escape manoeuvre at 5g back to low level just as important. After the attack, we went round to execute a medium-toss attack on the same target with 4 x 450kgs.

During that attack I reached my 1,000 flying hours on Buccs, which was a major milestone for me.

Fact was that although the radar was destroyed on that attack, it was back on the air after about six hours with a new one and we had to mount several more attacks on the same target with AS-30s and medium toss bombing up to 28 August. Eventually the radars at that position were off the air giving us more freedom to continue with the war effort.

On some area targets we even tried combined high-level bombing flying formation on the Canberras. The lead Canberra navigator called for the release of the bombs and the aim was to saturate an area where there were known deployments of the enemy.

My last Buccaneer sortie came on 5 December 1981 on a most fitting occasion. It was during the air show for the squadron Xmas party. I was promoted out of my love affair with the Buccaneer at the end of the year when I gave the reigns over to my successor George Snyman.

My career on 24 Squadron remains the highlight of my life and the camaraderie that there was between aircrew and ground crew was exceptional. I honour those men and women that I had the privilege to work with.

My final comment: "If you haven't flown a Buccaneer you haven't flown at all."

24 Squadron air and ground crews.

CHAPTER FOURTEEN

TRAINING TALES

PHIL WILKINSON

It is 6 November 1980. As the canopy closed, snow started to fall on Honington. But as I moved out on to the runway, with 'Big Norm' Roberson in the boot, the four-ship lining up was all set to head up and away from the UK winter. We were bound for the blazing sun, burning sand, and brandy sours of Akrotiri – probably too much BS for comfort, on reflection. But there was also a real hope that Exercise Winter Watcher could put a brighter end to a year that had been marked by tragedy and the near-disappearance of the Buccaneer from service.

But back a bit. 237 OCU instructors must have had a few entertaining and probably scurrilous staff meetings in the spring of 1977, when they heard that 63 Course would include the station commander designate, and their next OC/ chief instructor – neither of whom had any previous Buccaneer experience – were both coming from ground tours via the bits and pieces of the flying refresher system. I can recall most clearly, as I look back on my introduction to the 'Banana Bomber', at the hands of those even-handed and benevolent instructors, that nobody made it easy.

But there was room for enjoyment in the general atmosphere on the ground and in the air, alongside the probing debriefs, scathing film assessments, and pithy write-ups in those Forms 5060. Cruel to be kind? Some anonymous writers with PPRuNe 'blogorrhoea' declare the OCU had built-in malevolence and unwillingness to accept occasional lapses. So many hours and so few 'mates' to the squadrons, they claim. I'll come back to that later.

Once settled in to the routine it became clear that there was very little routine about the task. Those brought up in the days before dual-control versions of front-line aircraft – Meteor, Hunter, Canberra and Lightning were all in wide squadron service for a number of years before dual-control variants came along – were prone to shaking of heads and tut-tutting when told of the challenge of Buccaneer conversion without a two-sticker. But there was a significant difference between the avuncular pat on the head and 'off you go, son', which was how the old guard sent off their young tyro, and the unsettling moment when the instructor climbs in to the back seat of the Buccaneer and has nothing to see him (and his tyro) through but faith in the Almighty, finely-modulated screaming, and –

ultimately – a black and yellow handle marked Martin Baker.

Yes, Fam 1, the potentially life-changing moment for the one in front and the one in the back. The first familiarisation ride in the aircraft, all the while looming at the end of the pre-flight training, which seemed to go on for bloody ever. This event, coming, in my own case, after seven two-hour sessions in the full-motion Buccaneer simulator and three short Hunter sorties, gave Tom Eeles a suitably invigorating start to his day in mid-December 1977. But we survived, as he had done on numerous occasions in the past, albeit, only just on one famous occasion. But for me there is one most uplifting tale of a first such 'solo'. And it is one that underlines the quality of the OCU staff, and especially the quality of those USAF and USN airmen who came to the Buccaneer fleet on exchange from their very different types of aircraft; the F-4, F-14, F-111, etc.

24 September 1979 – Fam 1 for student pilot Keith Hildred. The instructor in the back seat was USAF Capt Ken Alley, veteran of combat operations over North Vietnam in an F-111. Ken had been in the Buccaneer force for just over a year, and had progressed through all the stages of professional development, including being checked as 'competent to instruct' by one of the OCU QFIs of HQ Central Flying School. The OCU held the CFS agency for the RAF's Buccaneer fleet, thus having the uneasy 'privilege' of being the 'trappers' who could be expected to visit a squadron once every eighteen months or so, to check on operational, training, and administrative standards. Nobody expects the Spanish Inquisition, they used to say on Monty Python, and the trappers' visit was never given a whole-hearted welcome. But back to that day in September 1979.

The profile of the Fam 1 sortie was designed to demonstrate all the various elements of the aircraft's performance and behaviour. So take-off and either SID 3 or SID 5 (standard instrument departure) through the air traffic control zone set-up for Lakenheath, Mildenhall, and Honington, before a hand-off to Eastern Radar and up to Flight Level 300. High speed stuff, then a reminder of the effectiveness of those airbrakes with a max rate descent to around Flight Level 50 and then the tricky bits; flying at lower speeds, then with steadily increasing drag from undercarriage and tail and wing flaps and droop, and then with less than all those bits and pieces working.

Having got the sweat to flow by all that, it was time for a return to the radar approach path and a couple of guided attacks on the airfield with eventually an entry to the visual circuit and some self-guided darts at the ground, overshooting from some, rolling from others and eventually the full stop. But Capt Ken and young master Hildred were interrupted in all this when, half way round the finals turn with full blow on, everything dangling, and steam coming from all orifices (human and mechanical), the port engine stopped. As Bruce Chapple would have said: "It was time to rearrange the levers in a pleasing and eye-catching fashion." This was done with a very calming contribution from Ken in the back seat, well he said it was calm. Let me simply allow the words of the 'Green Endorsement' in the back pages of his flying log book tell the story:

'During the third visual circuit, at a critical stage on finals in the blown full-flap configuration, the starboard engine seized. In these circumstances only rapid and correct recovery actions can save the aircraft. Both crew members reacted to the sudden emergency with commendable speed and precision and Captain Alley calmly guided his inexperienced student through the correct recovery procedures and a safely executed single-engine landing.

'Captain Alley displayed professional skill and judgement in assisting his student to recover their aircraft safely. In recognition of his successful handling of a serious emergency he is awarded a Green Endorsement.'

Well done that man – both men. The endorsement was signed by our then AOC, AVM David Craig, later to be MRAF Lord Craig and Chief of Defence Staff at the time of Gulf War 1. He took over as AOC in July 1978. A few months earlier, on 21 April, I had completed the OCU course, and then spent some time consolidating that basic level of competence by going off to Germany and flying with XV Squadron, then – also in Germany, where they were on detachment at Schleswig – with 12 Squadron. In between I spent a lot of time in one of the OCU two-seat Hunters, being introduced to the business of instructing from the right-hand seat. The gentle tones of Bruce Chapple, from the left seat, gave me every encouragement to get it right first time.

I was to take command of the OCU on 8 June, and in my final week of irresponsibility I had a flurry of Hunter sorties, including as chauffeur to the outgoing AOC, AVM Phil Lageson. He was on a final run round all his units and needed to call in on Stornoway. I positioned the Hunter at Finningley on 1 June, taking my USAF back-seater, Captain (later Major General) Scott Bergren, with me. He and I had gone through the course as a crew, and he was similarly engaged on 'consolidation', i.e. grabbing any flying in anything going anywhere. So we had a quiet night in the Finningley mess, and I stood by to receive the AVM the following morning. The journey north was uneventful, and the broad chinagraph track gouged across an airways chart provided adequate guidance for the navigational challenge involved. Once on the ground there was much pomp and ceremony for the AVM, while I wrestled with the cartridge starter for the Hunter engine, reached via much back bending and arm manoeuvring via the lower fuselage hatch. Eventually I gave up the struggle and a hairy Hebridean shoved me out of the way to 'show me how it was done'. To my great delight he failed, too.

While the AVM finished his rounds and had a well-lubricated lobster lunch, the Stornoway metal bashers produced a piece of mild steel, tortured into a double crank shape, with which the cartridge housing could be both accessed and forced open. A great piece of inventiveness for which I was duly grateful, and carried it back to Honington, to show the engineers the model for a locally-produced tool for carriage and use any time a T7 went off on a jolly. En route, I also carried the AVM back to Finningley. He nodded off very soon after take-off and showed no signs of wishing to fiddle with throttle or stick or indeed anything. Peace and quiet reigned. Scott was waiting and we were back on the ground at Honington in time for happy hour – it was Friday and I am sure the features of those Friday evenings need no further explanation, and certainly no illustration!

So, after a long build-up, I'm in charge of the OCU, and very soon after that – in July 1978 – AVM Craig takes on his AOC 1 Group functions. Early on in his tenure, he did the right thing and offered himself for a quick acquaint course, to get to know the aircraft that his gallant chaps were rushing around in, while he sat with his staff up at Bawtry. Obviously the full training package was not necessary; in any case he could not give uninterrupted time to the process, so an abbreviated one-to-one ground-school programme was arranged, together with simulator sorties, and a couple of Hunter rides. He had been a Hunter pilot on 247 Squadron back in the mid-1950s, but acknowledged that he would welcome a reminder of its characteristics. And, in any case, the OCU Hunters, intended as lead-in and familiarisation to the Buccaneer's integrated flight instrumentation system (IFIS) display with strip air speed indicator etc, had all that lot reproduced on the left side of the instrument panel. But he had no Buccaneer background and there are bits of its cockpit design that are a little challenging.

So it was, that on the day of his intended Fam 1, with Tom Eeles in the back, that the close proximity of the standard warning panel (SWP) test switch and the engine fire extinguisher buttons, together with the application of Sod's Law, led to a discharge of engine fire extinguisher gases and fluids through the engine. The ground crew were quick to deal with it all, and a second aircraft was prepared and ready very quickly. To their amazement the AOC managed to do it again. All was eventually got right, the short sortie went to plan in the third aircraft, and the AOC was happy to step down the ladder and head for the aircrew room and a cup of coffee. I was standing outside the hangar to greet him and congratulate him on his 'acquaintance' with the Buccaneer. But wait a bit, who and what is that darting across the pan, on an intercept course looking likely to coincide with AOC's arrival at my outstretched hand of congratulation?

The engineering warrant officer on the OCU was John McBain. Mr McBain was a tower of strength, despite his short stature. He masterminded some inventive passive defence measures for the OCU, well before the start of 'hardening' at Honington, and this was but one element of his overall energy and initiative which earned him an MBE at the end of his tour. He was a driver of his men, especially the 'Flems' (flight line mechanics). They respected him, but feared some of his tongue-lashing, so much so they referred to him behind his back as the 'Lower-tollah Enema', after the then Iranian leader the Ayatollah Khomeini. Not bad for the lowest of the low. They also kept each other up to standard, instituting their own trophy, the Prick of the Week Award, given to the Flem who made the biggest blunder during his allotted time out on the line.

This POTW award consisted of a photo of the miscreant of the week, set on a plywood base inset into a standard lavatory seat. The team who were now running towards the AOC seemed to have precisely that award ready for him, and I could see my all-too brief career evaporating as they offered him their personal assessment of his skills. I managed the handshake before they got alongside, and I could then see that it was another kind of trophy. In the hour or so since his second irregular discharge, they had mounted a fire extinguisher bottle on a nicely varnished board (happily not another lavatory seat!) and I feel that his grin, and possibly his blush as he accepted it, let us – especially me – off the hook. Breathe again. Well done those Flems.

As well as these 'acquaint' courses, the OCU also had responsibility for various publicity opportunities, flying local worthies or aviation press men, usually in a Hunter. Other 'specials' occasionally cropped up: one I remember very clearly was flown with Hugh Hudson, director of 'Chariots of Fire', when he was making that classic 12 Squadron film about Exercise Open Gate, with the Vangelis soundtrack. He needed a sequence to show the back-seat operator's view of his monitor screen during a TV Martel attack on the exercise target, HMS *Kent*. The only way was to film a low-level run against the *Kent*, and he said he'd like it to be done properly, and so properly that he would be the cameraman. My log book says the sortie was on 24 July 1978, out of Wattisham. I seem to recall that Honington's runway was closed for repair at that time. What I can very clearly remember was the bulk of Hudson's camera, resting over his shoulder and alarmingly close to the ejection seat top handle. I gave a very careful brief, very careful indeed, about his need for care in that area, and that he should not try to safeguard the thing in the unlikely event of our having to eject.

Anyway, we had a plot of *Kent*'s expected track down the Channel, and got airborne at 1610 on a lovely sunny afternoon for a quick run to overhead Manston, then let down to the latest reported position. Clearly the navy were having a laugh. When we found the ship some twenty minutes later it was sixty-five miles from where it was alleged to have been. Time and fuel were running short, but we lined up and set off at 'low level' – as authorised, of course – and ran at the side of *Kent* at a representative 480 knots. I thought the final pull-up, to avoid impact, was quite late. Hugh Hudson had other ideas, and requested one last go, not the best choice of words, I thought. Anyway, the deed was done, and we landed with a tank full of fumes, back at Wattisham. The result, in the film, with Jock Frizzell's eyeballs bulging over his face mask as he looks at his Martel screen (in the simulator) shows those final seconds of the last run and proves that I should not have left the pull-up any later.

Some time after there was another encounter with Her Majesty's Royal Navy. In June 1979, three of us were heading for Greenham Common to participate in the Air Tattoo. On the way down we wired HMS *Blake*, which resulted in a formal warning. The journey back, after three days of excess, I recall was after we had called for taxi clearance and filed a flight plan as 'Tasteless Section'.

Hunters filled the ASP and the sky for a few months after that tragedy I mentioned in the opening paragraph; the loss of Ken Tait and 'Rusty' Ruston on 7 February 1980 out at Nellis, for Red Flag. With the grounding of the Buccaneer, while an assessment was made of the chances of it remaining in service, there were five squadrons and the OCU to keep alive and in some kind of flying practice. Gp Capt Ron Dick, the station commander, after discussion with 1 Group, tasked me with checking on how many more Hunters we

Phil Wilkinson in 237 OCU Hunter F6, June 1980.

could first find, and then operate. Extra two-seaters were soon being delivered, and on 28 February I flew with Paul Room, the OCU's JENGO (junior engineering officer), down to the MU at Kemble to sort out maintenance requirements for the projected batch of single seaters. In no time at all, the OCU quartet of T7A and T8B Hunters was expanded to no less than sixteen two seaters and six single seaters, and some of the 'sharper' OCU pilots went down to Brawdy for a quick F-6 simulator refresher.

The OCU ground crew now took on the task of monitoring the squadrons' techies as they tackled the business of helping operate an expanded and very busy OCU line. Eventually the squadrons took over some of these add-on aircraft, and life-long bomber squadrons like No. 12 were painting a fox head on the nose of 'their' F-6 Hunter. Pilots' currency was maintained, and navigators were re-introduced to map and stopwatch navigation. And basically all had a little fun. Especially when the annual Open Day approached in June 1980. The station commander gave his blessing to a major Hunter contribution, and the three squadrons (with 216 hanging on for grim death to their new existence) each put up a three-ship contribution to a flypast, and then the OCU's four-ship 'Green Marrows' gave their once-only show.

John Myers (later to move to the Red Arrows, and previously the Buccaneer display pilot, with Jim Crowley in the boot) led in a two-seater, with Scott Bergren adding a USAF flavour up front. On the wing was yet more USAF; Ken Alley as No.2, with Keith Hargreaves on the left as No.3. I slotted into the box as No.4, and the cavorting was disciplined but exuberant. The final pull-up led to an upward bomb burst, 2 and 3 rolling away right and left, and I going over and pulling through to join the rest downwind for a nicely spaced stream landing. Time for silly grin – job done.

And the Hunters' job was done sufficiently well for the Buccaneer fleet to come smoothly back to life when cleared to continue, albeit with reduced numbers. Back into the training cycle, and I see that I flew with young Hildred, in hiatus mode during the grounding, and sat in the back for a re-run of his Fam 1. I have only just spotted that it was on 24 September 1980 – one year to the day from his first attempt and his engine failure. Superstition has no part to play in a proper training scheme.

The business of basic conversion training was quickly re-established and once again filling 95% of the OCU working day. The tenth anniversary of the OCU's formation came up while I was still there, and the morning ops and met brief that day gave me the chance to put up a few statistics as part of the briefing. Normally, the flying-unit commanders would give a run-down on the last week's achievement against the group requirements, outline plans for the following week, etc etc. On this day, I put up a standard vufoil (for the younger readers that's a transparent plastic sheet, placed over the lamp of an overhead projector and bringing the image up on the big screen, for the recumbent aircrew in their armchairs to look and marvel at).

That vufoil had some basic simple stats, but they just tell the story of flying hours. Were those PPRuNe chaps right? Lots of hours, not enough products to the front line? I think not. Those first ten years of OCU operation had concentrated on full conversion training, and during the period 168 RAF pilots had arrived on course and 176 navigators. Seven USAF and four USN pilots, and seven USAF with six USN navigators came through as well. (Very soon after that tenth anniversary, we received the first of the Australian exchange aircrew, in return for which people like Dave Cleland-Smith and Tim Aaron had the chance to operate RAAF F-111s. The aircraft that the RAF was to get instead of TSR2, but which eventually gave way to the Buccaneer. What goes around.....!)

FLYING ✕ ACHIEVEMENT 237 OCU		
10 YEARS COMMENCING 1 APRIL 1971		
	SORTIES	HOURS
Buccaneer	26509	32465:10
Hunter	11534	9971:20
DCO: YES !		

237 OCU flying hours.

But those long courses, with absolute concentration on the main lines of professional development of trainee aircrew, were always sharing instructor and ground engineering time in support of the specialist and post-graduate training tasks: weapon instructor and instrument rating examiner courses; more of those senior 'wheels' acquaint courses; and so on. Adding all that lot up, 612 aircrew came through for basic conversion, refresher or specialist flying courses: 332 pilots and 280 navigators. Twenty pilots and twenty navigators failed to reach the required standard: failure rates of 6% and 7.1% respectively. I suggest that a success rate of nearly 95% is a suitable tribute to the work, over those ten years, of some 100 staff aircrew and the more than 1,000 ground crew involved.

'Panache et Precision' indeed.

Finally, a great tour in command came to an end on 5 June 1981 and after landing from my final sortie I was offered a glass of champagne. Although I had flown with Ron Pegrum, Jock Frizzell could smell the champagne from 100 yards away and was in there for a

Jock Frizzell is the first to share a glass of champagne to mark Phil Wilkinson's final flight as OC 237 OCU.

glass sharpish (still sporting the after effects of a 'perm' he'd had for a fancy dress party a few weeks before). Dave Mulinder took the reins that evening, a Friday. And so it was, that on the Monday morning following, Dave's first day, I was in the station commander's office for a farewell chat, when there was an ejection as a Buccaneer left the runway. Thus I had got through three full years without an accident or even a serious incident. *Allah akbar!*

CHAPTER FIFTEEN

THE BUCCANEER IN ITS ELEMENT

ROB WRIGHT

It is 1979 and I am serving with the US Navy as an exchange pilot on the Phantom F-4J. I note the entry in my log book for 4 April is for a four-versus-four air-to-air combat sortie against VF-43 'Aggressor Squadron' operating Skyhawks in the Naval Air Station Oceana Air Combat Manoeuvring Range in Virginia, USA. I turn over the page to 8 June and, only two months later, I step into another brave new world – I am flying Buccaneer S.2 XT 283 out of Honington on my first familiarisation sortie with a USAF pilot, Ken Alley, in the back seat. I am his first student, and I suspect he is more nervous than I am, but at least I can speak his language.

As an ex-Hunter and Phantom pilot I had viewed my unexpected posting to the Buccaneer force with mixed feelings. Whilst serving on 17(F) Squadron at Brüggen in 1972 we had a very good social link to the Buccaneer Boys at Laarbruch, and in 1977, during the Queen's Jubilee Year I had helped host the *Ark Royal* Air Wing, along with a RN Buccaneer observer, Brian Jackson-Dooley, who was also on exchange at Oceana flying the A-6 Intruder. 892 and 809 Squadrons were forced to deploy ashore for a week's training whilst the *Ark*, on her last commission, and having carried out intensive training in Jacksonville, unexpectedly sailed into Norfolk, Virginia for its boilers to be repaired (again). All to enable the ship to stagger to Gibraltar before returning home, but nonetheless the fine reputation of the Buccaneers (and indeed the whole of *Ark's* Air Wing and its crews) certainly preceded them wherever they went.

Little did I realise that I was about to join this band of brothers. I had been expecting a posting to Jaguars but the hints had not materialised; ex-Buccaneer pilot Graham Smart, my Washington wing commander (now there is a man who knows how to party), had just visited during this memorable Royal Navy deployment and perhaps he got involved but

Flight line at CFB Cold Lake for Maple Flag 1980.

after three years with the US Navy, I was unexpectedly informed of the plan to make me the deputy squadron commander of 208 Squadron, which had the first fast-jet navigator boss; I do not think this had been spotted in the Air Secretary's crystal ball, but on second thoughts, perhaps it had.

During my two years on 208 I grew to love the Buccaneer. In that time there were deployments to Nellis AFB, Cold Lake in Alberta, northern Norway, Germany, Decimomannu and to Cyprus. This aeroplane surpassed all that I had ever encountered particularly when travelling away from base. It had exceptional range, even greater with overload fuel tanks and air-to-air refuelling, outstanding load-carrying capacity, cockpit comfort, excellent serviceability. And it was very much at home in all environments, whether on long-range missions into Northern Norway, landing on packed snow at Bodø or dropping bombs at Capa Frasca where its stability as a weapons platform was exceptional.

Whilst the nav kit was a little vintage, it seemed to serve us well and the boys in the back seat performed wonders in the black art of using the GPIC and some geriatric nav gear. I remember vividly calling up Laarbruch ATC tower prior to a pre-planned exercise airfield attack to be told there was no flying as the airfield weather state was amber. As my formation was only one minute out at 250 feet I had no option but to force their hand and we carried out a successful attack whilst the base was on radar recoveries only. What better example of the skill of the GIB?

There is no doubt this was the best aircraft I had ever flown at low level and at high speed; it was an aircraft that could sustain high speeds for as long as you had the energy to fly it: 480 knots cruise, 540 knots dash and egress at 580 knots. It could go faster as most Buccaneer aircrew will know.

Reflecting on the two-year period since leaving Oceana, and leafing my way through my log book to May 1981, my last year with the Buccaneer, I find myself positioned at the front of an eighty-aircraft mission launching out of Canadian Forces Base (CFB), Cold Lake, Alberta in Northern Canada on the final strike of Exercise Maple Flag 81. Prior to this demanding exercise, the squadron had completed two weeks of ultra-low-level (ULL) training from Lossiemouth and all the crews had been cleared to operate at 100 feet overland. This was followed by a week's acclimatisation at Cold Lake. We were all very comfortable operating at ULL and felt able to compete with any threat that was put up against us; a very capable aircraft, a huge amount of tactical 'nous' and experience on the squadron and everyone, aircrew and ground crew, felt on top of the job. It was a great feeling.

The Cold Lake Air Weapons Range was about 100 miles long by forty miles (eleven minutes by four) but a vast area of uninhabited land where ULL was fair game surrounded it. The whole area was covered by stunted silver birch and dotted with countless lakes, a less glamorous venue than the Red Flag exercises in the Nevada desert but, nonetheless, a realistic opportunity to fly over terrain and targets more akin to those over Northern Europe, the squadron's assigned area of operations.

The range was covered by electronic emitters and anti-aircraft sites (to be avoided) and dummy tanks and airfields (to be attacked) and, whilst the targets lacked the elaborate scoring facilities of its Red Flag cousin further south, the free flying environment was excellent value.

I remember that trip on 14 May in XX 901 quite clearly. It had been a good two weeks so far, now culminating in this last final mass launch, of which I had the honour to lead, and by which time tactics and ideas had developed to a fine pitch.

Airborne with Roger Stone in the back, and seven Buccaneers behind us, we took off earlier than the main package, turned north and headed for a start point some 300 miles north of the range, much further than on previous missions, flying in wide battle formation at 100 feet. Accompanying us were the A-7Ds of the US Air National Guard who were flying much higher to act as bait and draw Red Air out towards the edge of the range while we dashed in from a different direction with the rest of the attack package joining on behind to concentrate, in time, the whole attack.

The A-7Ds too had a Spey engine and the range to outrun the fighters (F-16s) with the intention of running them short of fuel. As they were intercepted, the A-7s turned hard and dropped to low level to draw the F-16s away before turning about to hit their assigned target time. The plan worked; we had sneaked in successfully.

Ingression now and the pace picks up, accelerating to 540 knots, trees and lakes a blur at 100 feet and one mile every seven seconds. Avoid overflying the lakes (aircraft being easy to spot from above) approaching the target, an airfield complex, jinking to avoid being locked up, airfield in the sights, open the bomb door, each of eight Buccaneer crews heading for their own pre-selected aiming point, very aware of the cross overs as we all hit the airfield all looking for deconfliction, all looking across the flat terrain to the horizon where we could see the other groups of the attack package, F-111s, F-4s, CF-104s and our friends the A-7Ds hitting their associated targets, SAMs, convoys, ammunition dumps, all of the package co-ordinated across the target area within a few minutes. Adrenaline

Fantastic! Buccaneers take the honours

TAXYING out for action ... 208 Squadron's Buccaneers

THE NOSE of a Buccaneer and an F4 Phantom in front of a line-up of F16s and A7 Corsairs.

ARRESTING moment for 208 Squadron commander Graham Pitchfork during a visit by members of the Royal Canadian Mounted Police

NORMALLY an operational pilot would not expect to discuss tactics with the enemy — still less in a friendly, relaxed atmosphere over a pint in the bar.

But the apres-battle discussion between friend and foe is a very important part of the 'war' fought in Canada during May. In reality, of course, it was an exercise, named Maple Flag, planned to produce conditions as close as possible to actual combat.

More than 100 aircraft from Canada, America and Britain were taking part in the seventh Maple Flag over the Primrose Lake Air Weapons Range, which spans 100 miles by 40 miles of wild forests and lakes of northern Alberta and Saskatchewan. The Canadian Armed Forces base at Cold Lake, Alberta, hosted the aircraft and 800 personnel.

Buccaneers of 208 Squadron, Honington, were taking part together with United States Air Force F4s, F15s, F16s and A7s and Canadian Armed Forces F101s, F104s and F5s, in various combinations as friends and foes. Providing full-time opposition

fighters simulating Russian weapons and using Russian tactics the freedom to operate down to 250 feet over an area four times as large as the British Isles.

In all, 1039 sorties were flown by Maple Flag aircraft during the first two weeks (the first time that the 1,000 sortie in two weeks had been passed). A planned 2,080 sorties were planned for the whole month. The Buccaneers, which took part in only the first two weeks of flying completed 115 of their 118 assigned sorties.

Some units, squadrons and individual aircraft, like the Buccaneers, we rotated during the exercise. At any one time

Report in the RAF News *(Editor RAF News).*

rushing, hit the target, roll the bomb door shut, accelerate to 580 knots for egress, weave, jink, threat locks up, jink harder, break lock, watch for the lone pine tree that sticks out at thirty feet above the tree tops in this otherwise featureless terrain, hit the edge of the range area, see the team appearing from either side as we join the infamous Buccaneer timeline; no R/T required here, just confidence in your colleagues, in the knowledge that they would appear on time, at the right place, in wide battle formation for cross cover. Throttling back as we hit the edge of the area, 420 knots, climbing to 500 feet, feels like 10,000 and as if I could step outside and walk back, the pace has slowed so much.

Back at Cold Lake, mass de-brief, videos, good plan and effective co-ordination, extremely good low flying and tactics, effective jinking, some kills, but none against the Buccs, targets hit, excellent results, congratulations from the USAF commander of Tactical Air Command, and all in front of our own visiting Chief of the Air Staff. The Brits are seen as being very professional and leading the way. The old Banana jet had served us well.

Two days later and the squadron is en route to Goose Bay staging through CFB Trenton carrying out aircrew turn-rounds (which seems almost unbelievable to me now) but the whole squadron cycled through successfully in a daisy chain over ninety minutes before carrying on to Goose Bay whilst the rear party swept up behind us in a Hercules. Thanks to superb and enthusiastic support from our Canadian colleagues at Trenton we had no need to call on the engineering support from our own team. Landing at Goose that night, we had a twenty-four-hour rest up and then tanked back to UK with our ever reliable and efficient Victor tanker colleagues to land back at Honington five hours later. You have to have a bit of luck some of the time but it must have looked impressive back at 1 Group Headquarters to see such an apparently effortless withdrawal from Cold Lake. In my more recent times on Tornado, I don't think we ever saw quite that success in recovering home from a major exercise. Absolutely knackered yes, but very satisfied with a job well done, and we all felt at the peak of our professional capability, thanks to the benefits of our work-up in Scotland, thanks to the Red Flag experience and this Maple Flag, thanks to determination, a good aircraft and great organisation.

We needed all of that because, as we landed, we were welcomed back by a signal from AOC 1 Group, AVM Mike Knight, to say that we were to take part in the Tactical Bombing Competition (TBC) at Lossiemouth. This was not a problem to us until we were told that it was a last-minute decision and that this important and prestigious event was taking place in two weeks' time. Well, what do we do, plan the usual work-up? No! The squadron motto is 'Vigilant' and we had just had the best work-up possible, so we relaxed, focused on getting ourselves back into the UK weather patterns, and we dropped a few bombs to just fine-tune those particular skills.

Unfortunately, I overdid the training by inadvertently rolling the bomb door as I ran up to the target at Cowden Range en route to Lossiemouth to take part in TBC. This is standard operating procedure on a weapon's detail in the Buccaneer – although not when carrying the baggage for the eight deploying aircrew in the bomb-bay pannier. On this occasion the bombs were on the wing station. However, some good comes out of everything. Only two suitcases fell out over the sea (albeit, they belonged to the boss and my navigator). After submitting their respective claims, and some unusual queries from their insurance companies, they were both feted for their sartorial elegance – not something normally associated with Buccaneer navigators!

And so we took our Maple Flag training with us to Scotland to enter into the fray against the newest kids on the block, flying shiny F-16s (whose specially selected crews had been working up for three months for their debut [sales?] mission in Europe), and against RAFG Jaguars and USAFE F-111s on this very intensive and high profile competition. This was an exceptionally stimulating and realistic exercise, focused on tactical targets at the Spadeadam and Otterburn ranges with Lightning and Phantom fighter caps covering several mandatory entry gates. There was a points scoring system for kills against and kills for, and points, of course, for the successful bombing on Otterburn range. The tactical targets consisted of an airfield and various convoys, all protected – over protected in truth – by radars, ground observers and several Rapier units.

Most of the early sorties for all participants involved standard coordinated attacks approaching from each end of the target complex by flying down valleys, but the RAF Regiment Rapier Squadron had set themselves up extremely well to cover this tactic. I led this series of missions with Roger Stone along with Eddie Wyer, who had the boss, Graham Pitchfork, in the back, Geoff Frankcom had Charlie Wrighton and Terry Heyes had John Plumb operating the kit in the back of his Buccaneer.

By the time we launched for the final mission, the team decided to do something different and put the Rapier units in their place so we elected to carry out an unconventional attack from the south, over a ridge and across the main valley at 500 knots in 'wadi' formation (from my Middle East Hunter days, twenty-five metres apart in finger formation although I am told by those at the back that it was a hell of a lot closer than that) on a cluster-bomb attack and for us to drop simultaneously on the convoy that was ranged on the south-facing slopes on the northern side of the range.

Inbound to the target we tracked the edge of a distinctive forest, skimmed over the ridge as one unit, dropped down rapidly to bombing height, spotted the target, and then all bombed on my call; immediately off target, we each selected a 'furrow' that we flew down to escape. It was the most amazing ten minutes I think I ever had in an aircraft, the team hanging on, all bombing the target effectively (the adjudicators deemed it to be completely destroyed) and then egressing, weaving, jinking, hiding, each to his own furrow before forming up on the timeline and heading home.

Hardly a word had been spoken, all our tactics against the fighters revolved around an innate knowledge of the opposition's own strategies and capabilities, and of what each member of our team would do, dropping a wing to indicate a move, staying low, covering each other, widening when needed and, if necessary, taking separate valleys and re-joining on the timeline. Again there was a huge feeling of satisfaction as we headed back to Lossiemouth on a job well done; there is not a single person in that formation who will ever forget that sortie.

In the de-brief, the comment on the Rapier video had been, "I can hear them, but I can't…see them…", followed by an expletive and a single ear-splitting noise…and then silence. And that was it. Not a single hit on the team, either air-to-air or ground-to-air, and four direct hits on the convoy. It was the same feeling of satisfaction and professionalism that we had experienced at the end of Maple Flag.

What a month, what flying, what a team of aircrew, engineers and support staff, and what an aircraft. Five months later and I bade farewell to Graham Pitchfork, after a memorable final sortie mounted from Lossiemouth, and saw in Ben Laite as the new boss, another navigator, so clearly the formula worked. Ben's inauguration was an unforgettable one based around a full-blown Taceval – culminating with the award of the highest ratings – and then I too departed the team and headed for Staff College.

CHAPTER SIXTEEN

FROM THE F-111 TO THE BUCCANEER – THAT'S PROGRESS!

GARY GOEBEL AND KEN ALLEY

Both the Fleet Air Arm and the RAF enjoyed the company of some outstanding characters on exchange programmes from their parent service. In this chapter, two USAF pilots outline their memories of exchange tours with the RAF.

GARY GOEBEL

I am an Anglophile, have been since the early 1950s. My old man was a World War 2 Mustang 'ace' and later served with the USAF in Oxfordshire when I was a small kid. While living at Witney, the Coronation occurred, and I was impressed with the nationwide celebration, the hot-crossed buns and the commemorative mugs handed out. A truly grand time, and when I finally left England on the SS *United States*, I did so with fond memories and a strange accent. So, I suppose I was destined to return one day.

In 1975 I was stationed at Nellis AFB flying F-111s, and the next posting offered to me was an exchange tour to the RAF on Buccaneers. I had to go to Jane's *All the World's Aircraft* to see what it looked like; a strange, fat aircraft with a bumblebee's stinger at the back. Given the previous youthful experience, there was never any doubt; off to the United Kingdom I went, first to RAF Brawdy for Hawker Hunter lead-in training and an aviation culture shock. The other students on the course were primarily squadron leaders re-qualifying in the Hunter, and they breezed through the course.

For me and a fellow exchange pilot it was all new: "What the hell is Avpin?" Taxiing out for take-off, the wind moved the rudder, and the pedals moved, no hydraulics involved at all. No nose-wheel steering, but differential brakes relative to the rudder position, applied by squeezing a paddle on the stick. My father had used the same brake system in the Spitfire for heavens sake! I had flown tape instruments for 2,000 hours in the F-105 and the F-111, now it was back to round dials. Limited panel instrument approaches were now to be needle and ball instead of a backup attitude indicator. Not this boy; I'd probably be over the side first. When I fired the 30mm cannon, I could see the bullets coming out the front and dropping rapidly. Yet for all that, the airplane was great, considering its age, very fast down low, and really a good-looking ride. The Hunter shags were a good bunch and at the end I was sorry to leave.

On to Honington and the Buccaneer OCU. The simulator introduced me to the aircraft cockpit, and the rather neat visuals provided by a model village with a camera poised above it. I had never before seen anything like either. The cockpit description as 'an ergonomic slum' was a little harsh in my view, but many of the indicators and switches were scattered apparently randomly. 'Outside in' or 'inside out' are human factor terms used for attitude indicator presentations and I can't remember which was used by the Buccaneer, but it was the reverse of what I was accustomed to. At least there was a standby instrument, no more needle and ball. It was strange, but the flying tactics, instrument presentation and terminology seemed to me to be easier to adapt to.

Some of the kit was outstanding, the exposure suits for instance, even though the roll-up part was too short, but I hated those damn entangling chains on the flight mask till the day I departed. With reference to the roll-up portion of the exposure suits, I guess it was designed on the basis it should fit 96% of your targeted users. When I was on the Hunter course, a student group captain told the rest of us that after he had completed test pilot school, he was detailed to Farnborough. Entering the pilot lounge of that famous place, he expected to hear esoteric discussion of aerodynamics, aircraft design, etc. Instead, they were gathered around a table with rulers measuring their private property. I can only assume they were doing a human factors design for the exposure suits, resulting in the rather short roll-up.

Airborne in the Buccaneer on the first flight with an incredibly brave instructor in the back seat without flight controls. In spite of the instrumentation the aircraft was a sweetheart, quite honest and performing to the limits of its speed envelope seemingly without effort. The speed brake was extremely effective, and the rotating bomb bay was a slick innovation. Later on when I carried 1,000lb weapons internally, there seemed to be very little decrease in performance. Try carrying four 1,000lb bombs externally on an F-4 and see how much range you end up with! I really believe an internal weapons bay is the best option for a fighter, and it is fortunate that stealth considerations have forced modern aircraft designers into including them. I wish they were as smart with forward-firing ordnance. It doesn't have to be a gun, it just has to be always there, un-jammable, point and shoot, and usable air-to-air and air-to-ground.

My GIB (guy in the back) on the OCU was a large amiable Irishman, Mike Cunningham. We got along famously, in spite of our 'Jalapeno incident'. He had joined me for lunch at my place in base housing on the square, the wives were off somewhere, probably shopping, so I made up sandwiches, and got out a jar of south-western US Jalapenos. I warned him they were hot, but he had to try one. The sweat broke out on his forehead, and his eyes began to tear up. He wiped them with his hand, but of course the Jalapeno juice was still there on his fingers and began to sting his eye. Dashing to the sink and throwing water into his face, he received no help from me at all, beast that I was, busy rolling on the floor with laughter. I did hand him a towel eventually...

I went to 12 Squadron, which was an overwater ship-attack squadron. I was crewed with Alan Dyer-Perry (DP) for the duration of my tour. I was somewhat familiar with the overwater aspect, flying F-105s out of Kadena AB, Okinawa (coincidently with 12 Squadron USAF), but except for shooting up a couple of fishing boats off the coast of Vietnam, ship attack was all new, particularly the night flying aspect of it. Whoever thought of tossing Lepus flares and rocketing a splash target at night ought to be lynched.

I discovered some language differences: A/B to the Buccaneer force was airbrake; to the USAF it means afterburner. 'A/B Now' in an international formation would have been very interesting! Other terms, such as 'downwind, roller' were self explanatory and easily understood. Words that look the same were more of a problem, but have subtly different meanings. To an American, a gentleman is someone who holds doors open, and helps little old ladies cross the street. To a Brit, a gentleman is someone who talks with an Etonian accent, and cheats his tailor. Doc Read, rest his soul, was deploying to Nevada and asked me how to meet American girls. Doctor in the UK means a sawbones working for the National Health, but for Americans who worship the body, any doctor is a High Priest. I told him to introduce himself by saying in his finest accent: "I am an English doctor!" On his return he sought me out and said that it had really worked!

I had done a large number of air-to-air refuelling sorties prior to arriving in the UK. For a variety of reasons, some of them good, the USAF standard is the boom and receptacle and, flying the F-111 in SE Asia, I used it on almost every flight. The design of the F-105 was more versatile, and we could use the probe-and-drogue method. I found that an absolute requirement was to first and foremost fly formation on the tanker, never look directly at the drogue but observe it in my peripheral vision. Looking directly at it always resulted in a pilot-induced oscillation chase that did not result in a hook-up.

On one occasion I was leading a group of newbies on an air-refuelling mission in the Buccaneer, and was determined to get this point across. I set up a representation of a tanker on the wall, hung a proportionally-sized circle from the ceiling to represent the drogue, and had the potential receiver hold up a pencil, then walk forward. While he focused on the tanker, the pencil was to go in the basket, which was never to be looked at directly. I positioned myself to the front where I could watch the receiver's eyes and could immediately correct him if he looked at the drogue representation. Sure enough, even after stressing the point in the briefing, every pilot in the flight at some stage looked at the circle and was suitably chastised. As I recall, the mission went well and everyone got hooked up, and I know the pencil simulation was effective, but the sense of the ridiculous was so strong during the use of this fabulous air-refuelling simulator that I never tried it again.

One of the most enjoyable aspects of my entire exchange tour was the many detachments

12 Squadron Buccaneer at Gibraltar.

to locations in Europe. Gibraltar (Gib) was a unique place with the road to Spain closed. In spite of that, the touristy things to do were interesting: walking the honeycombed Rock tunnels; climbing to the top with the spectacular views; watching the Barbary apes; and visiting the cemeteries with many of the fallen from the Battle of Trafalgar buried there. The flying was also special, trying to penetrate the Hunter detachment CAP while inbound from the Med to Gib, or attacking the *Kennedy* or the *Enterprise* on the Atlantic side. I recall one low-level attack when we were inbound to the carrier target and went right through the dive-bombing pattern of a group of A-7s, then on exit seeing the belly of an F-14 dropping into gun attack range on my wingman out of a 500 foot overcast. I'm not a USN fan, but that was impressive. Recovery at Gib was also interesting, with Spanish airspace limiting approaches from the west to VFR patterns only, water on both ends and sides of the runway, and a road across the middle.

The detachment to Nancy in France was of some historic importance to 12 Squadron, with the squadron silver supposedly buried somewhere about, just prior to Dunkirk, where it still remains. The hosting squadron was equipped with Jaguars. An individual host assigned to us gave the local area brief and was available during the daytime, but seemed to disappear at night. After a few discreet inquiries, it turned out that our host was on work release in the daytime, but at night had to return to confinement. Apparently, he had been taxiing out as No.2 in a flight with his squadron commander leading, and dropped his checklist to the cockpit floor. He bent over to pick it up, just as his squadron commander stopped, and the pointy end of the No.2 Jaguar went right up the blunt end of the No.1 Jaguar.

The flight evaluation board met and sentenced our host to confinement for something like six months. That seemed to me to be a uniquely French solution to an incident and I subsequently considered how the USAF and the RAF would resolve something similar. The USAF is famous for its checklists and procedures, and would probably rearrange or create a new checklist to include an 'avoid taxiing into other aircraft or vehicles' step. We also are great believers in technological solutions; so all Jaguar aircraft would be fitted with stoplights on the tail, wired through the brake pedals. The RAF would not have penalised the pilot, but would have blamed the officer at MOD for placing him in a posting beyond his capabilities. He might get further training, or be assigned to Victor tankers, but that would be the end of it. Ever after however, he would be known throughout the RAF as 'Charlie up the Chuff', or 'Backend Bob'.

On a deployment to Kiel, visiting the German naval air arm the flying was great. There was the inevitable simulated attack on the Möhne Dam, and low-level flights over the North German plains below a solid overcast, bouncing any number of Belgiques, Germans and even other Brits. In fact the only air force missing seemed to be the USAF; the F-15s apparently had higher headquarters' restrictions against low flying and refused to play (shame). Off duty my squadron mates taught me the words to 'For tonight we march against England' and in the Kriegsmarine Officer's Club (now Bundesmarine as I was gently informed by our hosts), I discovered that a Honkatorium was a porcelain fixture resembling a urinal positioned for a nine-foot giant in which to puke a beer overload so he can continue drinking.

Decimomannu (Deci) on Sardinia was the destination for wintertime weaponry; the sunshine and good flying weather was always a welcome respite. The resorts on the island were a great place to relax off duty, although Buccaneer crews were not allowed in at least one of them following an earlier incident involving a golf cart and a swimming pool.

Among the weapon attacks we would perform VFR laydown, high-drag deliveries with practice bombs. I had been weapons officer in F-111s, and knew that the key release parameter with high drags was range to the target. High drags do not go very far; think of a badminton shuttlecock thrown forward. My normal technique was to figure the release altitude and the associated bomb range, measure off that distance on a map or photo to obtain a reference point, track the pipper toward the target, and release when the reference point came up off the wingtip. At Deci I didn't bother with measuring, on the practice runs I would call out "ready, ready", and "release" as I hit the pickle button, and DP in the back would line up a prominent feature with the release call for the good scores. When it came to competition, DP would call out "ready, ready, release" relative to his reference point, and I would average out his calls with my forward sight picture. It resulted in some very good scores, and I didn't consider it cheating since I could use the same technique in combat.

For me the Buccaneer was great, and I cannot recall one major aircraft-related incident that occurred to me that could be made into a tall tale. I had good luck and great maintenance troops. After three very short years, the Goebel family bid the UK a fond *adieu*, and headed back to the States, a posting to A-10s at Tucson. For a short time after our return, everything seemed very provincial to me. No European news in the local paper, really no world news at all. After a few months back everything seemed normal again, and the kids had mostly lost their accent.

I did manage to get back to the UK in 1996 to visit my son who was working in Southampton. We went up to Bury St Edmunds visiting the familiar sights and on to RAF Honington to look the old place over, and there next to the gate was a Buccaneer looking rather tired and lonely. I used to tease my father when all his aircraft went up on posts, now mine are all there. Uncertain of the alert status I went up to the guard at the gate to ask him if it was permissible to take a picture of the Buccaneer. He told me "for 50p you can have it". Thus passes Glory!

_____

Following Gary to RAF Honington was KEN ALLEY

I was flying the F-111E at Upper Heyford when I volunteered for an Allied or inter-service exchange assignment as an exit strategy from the F-111 (after 1,500 hours in the Aardvark). Then a bolt of lightning must have hit the personnel office in Texas as suddenly I had an exchange assignment to the Royal Air Force flying the Buccaneer. I rushed out to buy a book on RAF aircraft to see what the Buccaneer aircraft looked like.

I arrived at Honington in December 1977 and stored my goods at the current exchange pilot's quarters (Gary Goebel). Then off to the colonies for Christmas before the foreign pilot's course at RAF Brawdy in early January 1978. I had a lovely time at Brawdy on the course but suddenly it was announced that I would have to go to RAF Valley for the normal Hunter weapons/fam course. (This was because the courses at Brawdy were full and I had flying experience in the UK flying system already.)

The Hunter check out was wonderful (what weapons!) but I was back in the basic flying training world, which could not tell the difference between an experienced pilot and a student. In other words they treat you like crap much like the USAF pilot training world. I still wonder why you take a full instrument check on needle, ball and airspeed (must be in case the WWII aircraft ever came back into service). I survived to enter the 237 OCU Buccaneer course in March (after I almost drowned in the Irish Sea at Valley Sea Survival School, but that is another story).

The Buccaneer conversion course was a much more hospitable occasion than the Valley course and the family moved on to the main married patch at Honington. I occupied one of the exchange officer's houses that had a transformer to convert some of the outlets from the UK standard voltage to 120 volts. The front door of this house was the closest to the back gate from the officers' mess (funny thing). My dear wife Liz still says that I planned it that way as I always had chaps stopping by for a Budweiser. The course progressed successfully and then came my last ride as a student.

This was a two-ship, strike-progression sortie to land at Leuchars in Scotland on a Friday afternoon. Since the statute of limitations has long expired (I hope), I shall divulge the characters involved. Mike Heath was in my back seat and the No.2 was John Myers and Jim Crowley. John and Jim were scheduled to put on the Buccaneer aerial display the next day for the Leuchars Open Day. We showed up at the mess and commenced to consume a large quantity of beer. There were numerous crews in attendance to represent all the types of aircraft for the next day. Not surprisingly we forgot to eat until we found out that the kitchen was closed. That did not stop some of the other aircrew from contriving a way to enter the kitchen and cook their own food. As would be expected, we four fell in line and took the food back to our rooms for consumption. Someone came up with the bright idea to throw the plates out of the window so as not to have them discovered in our rooms (although this did not work). The next day went off as planned and we departed. I was in my quarters on Monday when the other three criminals stopped by to tell me that they had been summoned to the squadron commander's office, but for some reason, I was granted diplomatic immunity from the expected bollocking for the time being. When the three returned (minus some fabric from the rear of their flight suits), I was informed that we were being charged with paying for the meals and associated dinnerware, as well as a fine for the station commander's fund. Apparently we ate the food that was to be provided for the AOC's formal dinner on the Saturday night. I don't think we would have escaped that easy in the USAF!

After paying my penance for the guilty crime, I escaped to 12 Squadron where I had expected to spend the remainder of my time as an exchange pilot. Peter Harding ran an outstanding outfit and I thoroughly enjoyed my check out on the maritime attack squadron. One notable incident occurred on a four-ship flight to the Victor tanker. As we were starting to taxi out, someone in the flight radioed lead (not to mention names but he is Scottish, a retired group captain and an erstwhile air attaché to Poland) and politely inquired how lead was going to air refuel without a refuelling probe. Seems the aircraft had been on a ranger and the probe was removed due to the barrier configuration at the NATO base.

I was returning from a detachment to Gibraltar flying with the late Tony White (a wonderful chap and a dear friend). As we taxied into the pan at Honington, I saw Sqn Ldr Tom Eeles coming across the flight line. When I exited the aircraft, Tom informed me that I was really supposed to be assigned to 237 OCU, so I had better pack up my 12 Squadron gear and report for the start of my QFI check out. As he dragged me back to the OCU (with heel marks on the tarmac), I knew it would be enjoyable to check out in the Hunter again. I really enjoyed flying the maritime mission, but I was about to embark on the best twenty-one months of flying, fun and camaraderie I experienced in my air force career (except for my squadron commander days). Apparently I had been forgiven for my transgressions of eating the AOC's food as the boss, Wg Cdr Phil Wilkinson, welcomed me into the OCU family. With the likes of Wilkinson, Myers, Crowley, Waddington, Eeles, Heath, Dave C-S, Coop and Moore (to only name a few), there was bound to be constant comedy, and there was.

The fun started when I was unlucky enough to be in the back seat of the Buccaneer on a Fam 1 when we lost an engine on the final turn with full droop and blow. We did make a recovery without ejecting, which as I understand was not the common outcome in such a situation. Tom Eeles had been gone for the day and had missed the whole event. However, I was in the mess bar (not normally) when Tom appeared. I approached him in a somewhat subdued manner and informed him that we lost an engine on Fam 1 during the final turn. His face turned ashen grey as he searched for words but recovered quickly when I informed him that we landed successfully. Finally got one back on him for dragging me away from 12 Squadron.

John Myers and Jim Crowley were doing the air show demonstration circuit in the Buccaneer and I was lucky enough to fly the spare aircraft to almost all of the shows. Too many wonderful memories to recall here but one event does need mentioning. My fellow American, Scott Bergren, was my navigator on the trip to Glasgow, Scotland. After a quiet night on Friday (not) Bergie and I assumed our post at the spare aircraft for the static display. We both had a small American patch on our flight suits. The weird looks and questions that came our way were very comical. Such as, "So this is an American Buccaneer", "Did you bloody Yanks steal this aircraft", "What the ---- are you two doing with a British aircraft."

On another occasion, Wg Cdr Wilkinson asked me if I would mind taking a Hunter to Cottesmore and fly the AOC (Sir Mike Knight) to Lossiemouth. Of course I said yes. As the day approached, he told me not to let the AOC fly in the left seat, as he would have been drinking champagne at the ribbon-cutting ceremony for the Tornado OCU. As I started up the left ladder at Cottesmore, a loud voice roared "Captain, whose air force do you think this is?" In other words, get in the right seat. We proceeded to Lossiemouth and Sir Mike decided to land the aircraft. On the approach the crosswinds were fairly severe and a gust before touch down forced us to go around. The AOC, disturbed that he had to abort the landing, said, "Here you land the damn thing". The wind gods had taken mercy on me during the next approach and the landing was a grease-on. I dropped the AOC off and returned to Honington. The next morning, Phil Wilkinson (with a sheepish grin) asked me if Mike Knight flew in the right seat. At this point, I realised I had probably been set up and it was a given that the AOC would fly in the left one.

Sadly, a Buccaneer was lost in 1980 at a Red Flag exercise with both crew killed when a wing pin failed. The Buccaneer was grounded for a considerable time and we received several more Hunters to keep some resemblance of a flying organisation. Since Honington was having an Open Day that summer, we were given permission to form a Hunter four-ship for a fly by for the event. Lead was a two-seater with John Myers and Scott Bergren,

The Green Marrows. L-R: John Myers, Ken Alley, Scott Bergren,
Phil Wilkinson, Keith Hargreaves.

rounded out with Keith Hargreaves on right wing, myself on left wing and the boss in the No.4 slot. The Green Marrows (as we were named) performed on the given occasion without incident or numerous laughing remarks about our formation.

My tour remarks would not be complete without mentioning the American Christmas function at the mess with the ladies, the summer balls and the Queen's visit. I am sure many of the wives are still wondering how they consumed so much champagne in such a short time. Of course there is the famous, 'carry me out on a stretcher' event. I did not know I could party all night at the summer ball and then play tennis at sunrise. I also learned not to attend a pre-party party at Dave Herriot's house, which shortened one summer ball for Mrs Bergren. Of course the Queen's visit was an extraordinary event to remember, including our practice dinners prior to the real event.

In summary, it would have been impossible to have any more wonderful flying, fun and camaraderie and still have been legal.

CHAPTER SEVENTEEN
AT LONG RANGE

Mike Rudd (right) meets
CAS, MRAF Sir Keith Williamson.

MIKE RUDD

Dawn, 14 January 1983. Height of the Cold War. Six Buccaneers of 12 Squadron on the dispersal at their main operating base at RAF Lossiemouth. I was Vixen leader and, like the others, I had started my Spey engines and completed after start checks.

"Vixen check-in"
"Vixen 2"
"3"
"4"
"5"
"6"
"Lossiemouth Tower Vixen, six Buccaneers taxi"
"Vixen, good morning, Lossiemouth tower. Taxi Runway 05, QFE 1009"
"Vixen, Roger."

We took off and the mission was completed as planned. Vixen formation executed a copybook Martel and toss bombing attack on the simulated enemy, the strike carrier USS *America* and her escorts over 500 miles into the stormy North Atlantic Ocean. As so often a Russian navy warship, in this case a Kashin class destroyer, observed proceedings closely. We in turn recorded the Soviet radar data and took pictures for the intelligence folks back home.

Later in the officers' mess bar at happy hour the ATC tower controller from our early morning launch said, "You 12 Squadron guys are so arrogant you even taxi arrogantly". "Good!" I replied.

Our job was to attack and destroy major Soviet warships anywhere from the North Cape of Norway through the Iceland-Faeroes Gap and the Atlantic Ocean and as far south as the Mediterranean Sea. The challenge was formidable but we believed we were up to it.

We had the weapons, the training and tactics but above all we had the mighty Buccaneer. We also needed chutzpah and we were pleased to be perceived as arrogant because it reinforced our self-belief. We were right at the sharp end of the Cold War mind game called deterrence.

I can identify the start of my personal journey, which took me to this point in the Cold War. Nine years earlier I was a twenty-four-year-old flying officer QFI on the venerable Jet Provost at the Royal Air Force College, Cranwell. Approaching the end of my three-year 'creamie' (1st tour instructor) tour the boss, Sqn Ldr Colin Richardson, told me that my posting instruction had arrived: Buccaneers.

At last I was on my way to my version of nirvana ('release from a state of suffering after an often lengthy period of committed spiritual practice') – operational fast jets. I was elated but uncertain of any real facts. My QFI colleagues were predominantly from the heavier, multi-engine brigade. They were a great bunch and delivered excellent skills to the hordes of student pilots that the numerous BFTS (basic flying training schools) trained in those days for the very substantial front line of the RAF. And there were many amusing and fascinating 'war stories' in the crew room of V-Force co-pilots dressed like astronauts refuelling Blue Steel missiles with the lethal rocket fuel hydrogen peroxide. Others spent weeks 'down the route' in Masirah, Gan, Nairobi and many other exotic places. But I had not met one person who had personal knowledge of the Buccaneer or its roles. But it sounded great to me – just the job. My optimism, whilst naïve, proved to be well placed.

The route from Jet Provost QFI to squadron Buccaneer pilot was demanding and it contained several distinct but well trodden steps. After a Hunter conversion at RAF Valley and Tactical Weapons training at Brawdy, also on the Hunter, I was deemed ready to take on the Buccaneer.

No. 49 Long Buccaneer Course started with three pilots and three navigators. But, for one reason or another, only myself and two of the navigators, Mike Kennedy, first tourist and Al Laidler, Vulcan ace nav radar, were there at the end. Others in this volume will explain the conversion training delivered by 237 OCU. Suffice to say it was excellent and tough, as it needed to be. The aircraft itself was quite something. It was a man-sized jet but the two Spey engines and the unusual airframe design combined to produce a powerful, fast load carrier with very long legs and surprisingly nimble handling. It was a bomber built to a fighter specification. With no dual-control trainer version the first sortie for a pilot was also his first solo. My intrepid instructor, for what I assume was a more anxious experience for him than it was for me, was the CFI, Peter Norriss. Peter had preceded me at Cranwell as a QFI and we saw a lot of each other in later years during our time on the Buccaneer. First impressions flying the Bucc were on the whole very positive. The aircraft handled beautifully above 360 knots but as speed reduced towards landing (around 135 knots) the Bucc became twitchier particularly in pitch, yaw and speed stability. It was in the approach configuration and around the radar and visual circuits that the aircraft took a bit of mastering. But the Bucc at low level doing anything from 400 to 580 knots was an absolute joy. The high-wing loading and the area-ruled fuselage both contributed to the smooth, leggy and easily-controlled flight of this wonderful aircraft doing what it was designed to do.

The other 'new' experience for many of us was the extra dimension of flying with a navigator. From the start, I was very comfortable with this. In the days before we had any form of reliable navigation kit, especially in our low-level, over-sea domain, it was vital that someone worked out where the hell we were. This was even more important in the low-level, all-weather, day/night-attack role when the workload, even with the more modern kit, was too high for one person.

I was very lucky throughout my time as a Bucc Boy to fly with great navigators. On the OCU Mike Kennedy belied his lack of experience and we worked hard together as a student crew to succeed and enjoy the challenging OCU course. On 809 NAS, aboard *Ark Royal*, Lt Arthur Davies was a great operator but was also terrific fun to be with. Leading the late-night, on-board marching band to the tunes played through a nose-aspirated recorder was one of his many talents. Then Roger Carr, like me one of the RAF 'crabs' serving with the Fleet Air Arm, joined the squadron and we were crewed up. Thus started a lifelong friendship.

Roger was a real expert in the cockpit and appeared to me to be completely without fear for his personal safety. With both of us complete novices to carrier night ops, at the end of a 'duskers' (day into night) sortie in mid-North Atlantic, I managed to misunderstand an instruction from Flyco and put the arrestor hook down during what everyone else in the world, including Roger in the back, thought was an approach to the deck for a touch and go. As we appeared over the round down the arrestor gear operator who had two buttons – one for lifting the wires on bow springs and one for resetting the cables after it was pulled out on landing – saw the hook down and quickly hit what he thought was the bow spring button to enable us to engage a wire. Less than a second later, having successfully 'trapped', we found ourselves being propelled backwards towards the stern of the ship at an alarming rate of knots. My recall of the drill for this occurrence (known as 'caught in a resetting cable') was reinforced by Flyco shouting: "POWER!" on the radio. I calmly (relatively) applied the throttles and we stopped in time to avoid a wet finish. My entire fault but Roger as ever was reassuring and uncritical.

809 Squadron and the Fleet Air Arm in general were a real can-do, skilful and dedicated bunch of operators who got the job done often in very tricky circumstances. They also proudly possessed a sense of fun, which they believed with some justification that their younger, sister service in light blue lacked somewhat. It is this very intimate, slightly competitive relationship between the dark and light blue Bucc Boys that I believe is the special bond responsible for the unique, lasting brotherhood demonstrated each December at the exceptionally well-supported Bucc Blitz.

Rising up in the world in terms of experience I was fortunate to fly on 12 Squadron with my flight commander, Barry Dove, another diamond man in the air and on the ground who had also been through the aircraft carrier experience. 12 Squadron flew much the same role as 809 but from land bases and under the command of 1 (Bomber) Group, whose main task was overseeing the RAF's nuclear deterrent of the V-Force. Life compared with that on 809 was like chalk and cheese!

But 12 Squadron had evolved an impressive approach to maritime attack involving a standard-load six-ship, which required precision and discipline. It was hugely satisfying to be a part of this superb outfit and, as a third tourist and the flight commander's nose gunner to boot, I soon qualified to lead six ships. After a short tour on XV Squadron at Laarbruch flying in the overland role with the guidance, support and comradeship of some great, fellow Bucc Boys – Crispin Edmunds, John Cosgrove, Trevor Nattrass, Steve Fisher and Steve Parkinson just to name a few – came a return to 12 Squadron which by then was based at the wonderful RAF Lossiemouth on the Moray coast in north-east Scotland. It was also a reunification with one of my best mates, Brian Mahaffey, ex 809 partner-in-crime and now fellow pilot flight commander. 'Shiny 12' was always blessed with charismatic and lively bosses; Graham Smart and Peter Harding at Honington on my first tour and Jerry Yates followed by Martin Engwell at Lossiemouth. All were real role models in their own ways.

That brings me back to how I came to be hearing that comment about 12 Squadron's arrogance in the officers' mess. Now as OC 'A' Flight, and extremely proud, I was for the first time in a position to choose my back seater. Pete 'Bins' Binham had always been an impressive, young operator in the Buccaneer; largely through his knack of finding the target ship far more often than anyone else. Using a combination of excellent radar skills, detective work, assembling the many scraps of information available and a healthy dose of his intuition we worked well as a crew. I recall a ground-training day during which all aircrew were required to deliver aircraft systems lectures to the others and Pete was briefing on the flying-control system. He put up his first vufoil showing the overview of the system and said "the flying control system includes the pilot who is part of the set of mechanical components needed to link the navigator's brain to the aircraft". I reckon that Bins' view was that the only thing required to make the Bucc a single-seater was a better autopilot. With Pete's departure for better things, Andy Hext and I formed a constituted crew. After a few months together, things warmed up considerably for us both.

It was February 1983, a few months after the end of the Falklands War when 12 Squadron was tasked to prepare two Buccaneers plus a spare to deploy to RAF Stanley and return. There would be only one stop each way, at Ascension Island. The objective was to prove and demonstrate the feasibility of reinforcing the relatively light forces already in place in the South Atlantic. It was the clear but unstated intention that, as well as proving the deployment for UK purposes, a message would be sent that the British armed forces could very quickly add serious offensive capability. As the senior flight commander I was selected and Andy and I found ourselves lifting off from Lossiemouth on 3 March 1983 to rendezvous over Cornwall with the Victor tankers. In the other two Buccs were Cas Capewell flying with Nigel Yeldham and Dave Lord with Martin Taylor. Tony Burtenshaw and Dick Aitken were on their way as a spare crew in the Hercules with the ground crew. The planning for the very long deployment had raised some novel concerns. For example, average engine oil, hydraulics and oxygen consumptions indicated that the planned ten-hour flight could give us some problems. In the end we reasoned that it was better to find out during the first leg, which was stacked with friendly diversion options thus reducing the risk on the second, Ascension-Falklands leg, which was for the most part non-diversion flying.

Buccaneer detachment at Stanley, Falkland Islands.

The first seven hours or so of the flight to Ascension consisted of flying formation and air-to-air refuelling from the Victors. There was a fair bit of weather and turbulent cloud en route so much of the formation flying needed to be close (a few feet) rather than relaxed (100 yards plus). The refuelling workload was at the top end of degree of difficulty with the Victors' wings, hoses and baskets bouncing around merrily during the three refuelling brackets while we manually manoeuvred thirty tons of Bucc in thick cloud to get the fixed AAR probe engaged.

Eventually, off the coast of Senegal, the last Victor turned away towards Dakar and wished us well with the remainder of the flight, a mere 1,200 miles of ocean to cross with no land or navigation aids until the completely isolated volcanic pin-prick of Ascension Island. Easy! Well it would have been if we had any nav kit on the Bucc that could reliably let us know which hemisphere we inhabited. So Andy and the other navs proceeded with their best nav school air-plot working on met winds and we hoped for the best. We needed to be within 200 miles of track to find Ascension by TACAN, Blue Parrot mapping radar or UDF.

The weather as we approached the equator was CAVOK and very smooth flying conditions. The peace was broken suddenly, and unexpectedly, by a radio call to us from an RAF Nimrod. We had been told Nimrod SAR cover was not available for the deployment but here it was. The Nimrod gave us an extremely valuable navigation update with the information that we were thirty miles off track. Thanking them for their assistance, we reset course and after another 400 miles achieved a solid TACAN lock at 200 miles and we were home and dry. On the dot of ten hours flight time the three Buccs touched down safely in the late afternoon at Wideawake airfield. I hesitate to claim a record but I have not heard of a longer Buccaneer flight.

Aircrew just landed at Lossiemouth after the direct flight from the Ascension Islands.
L-R: Nigel Yeldham, Tony Burtenshaw, Mike Rudd, Andy Hext.

A few beers in the evening at the American facility on Ascension and a good night's sleep in Concertina City left the crews ready for one day of rest and planning. This included a single hole of golf played on officially the worst golf course in the world (all volcanic rock) and a mercifully short sightseeing trip of the equatorial, volcanic island. Having been briefed by what seemed like the entire Victor force headed by Wg Cdr Andy Vallance we launched from Wideawake in a large formation of Victors and our Buccaneers on the second and final leg to Stanley airfield. The spare Buccaneer accompanied us until the first refuelling bracket before turning back reluctantly to land at Ascension. Meanwhile the main formation continued and rather like the famous Vulcan Black Buck mission, the Victors gradually thinned out until there was one full of fuel that led us as far south as possible into the wide wastes of the South Atlantic.

However, some time before we parted company intentionally we had a rather worrying episode. Flying through the heavy thunderstorms of the Inter Tropical Convergence Zone, our lead Victor told us, "climbing out of the weather". The cloud was exceptionally thick and since we were heavy and flying low on our drag curve we immediately started to slip backwards. I asked the Victor to 'toboggan', which meant to increase speed by lowering the nose. This ploy failed and we lost visual contact completely with our tanker. We eventually burst from the cloud into blue sky and...no tanker!

It took about twenty, very long, minutes of radio discussion and anxious visual searching to regain contact. It was a most uncomfortable feeling. Having finally topped up we then flew another two hours or so before a planned rendezvous with a Hercules tanker operating out of Stanley, a further top up and an arrested landing onto the excellent runway matting of RAF Stanley's 6,000 foot runway.

After ten days of outstanding flying and exercising with the Royal Navy units, Phantoms, Harriers, Hercules and other units of the standing garrison forces we returned to Lossiemouth using the same route. By now we had improved our long-range transit techniques and confidence so the rendezvous in mid-South Atlantic with Andy Vallance and his airborne gas station was made very smoothly. We eventually touched down at Lossiemouth feeling a great sense of satisfaction and admiration of our trusty Bucc steeds as well as for the RAF teamwork that had completed a tricky and somewhat risky operation faultlessly; a total journey of over 16,000 miles without a problem and the first fast jets to fly the return journey from UK to the Falkland Islands.

A few months later the Lossiemouth Buccaneer Wing was called upon again to deliver capability far from British shores. In Beirut a multi-national force (MNF) was attempting valiantly to stabilise a complex and dangerous situation. The British Army unit from the Queen's Dragoon Guards had requested air support on hand to assist should their precarious position deteriorate at short notice. The tasking arrived for six Buccaneers from 12 and 208 Squadrons to deploy immediately and provide on-call support. Wg Cdr Ben Laite was the detachment commander and I was selected to lead the flying operations. After twenty-four hours of preparation we took off on 9 September 1983 with operational loads from Lossie and headed for RAF Akrotiri on the Mediterranean island of Cyprus. Five-and-a-half hours and a couple of top-ups from a Victor tanker later we landed as planned and after refuelling assumed immediate combat readiness.

The next morning I received operational and intelligence briefings from the air commander, Air Cdre Ray Offord, at the headquarters in nearby Episkopi. At the same time the crews were studying detailed imagery and threat information at Akrotiri. The job was a challenging one. The eighty British soldiers were based in a single, multi-storey building in the Beirut city outskirts. Artillery units operated by various opposing factions were active in the vicinity from urban locations. The decision was made that we should launch the following day in pairs for an armed show of strength mission over Beirut, which was intended to deter any attack on our troops. A route through the rooftops of the city at ultra-low level was chosen to make the most visible and audible demonstration of intent. Defences expected were Russian-made AAA including ZSU23-4 and the latest SA-8 missile system. There was, to say the least, an atmosphere of tense excitement as we prepared for the sortie.

Dick Aitken was my nav for the mission and, after a radio-silent launch for security reasons, we transited through the formidable naval elements of the MNF. It was not a straightforward process as no formal procedures had been established. Coasting in near Beirut airport we descended while fire-control radars lit up the RWR and we roared through the rooftops at 540 knots. Following our street-by-street route and navigating visually we emerged unscathed exiting to the north of the city over the harbour. Flying past the awesome bulk of the battleship USS *New Jersey* we returned to Akrotiri. Back home BBC News showed us flying through the city with the sound and sight of nonstop AAA activity firing. The mission was a success.

With additional time for planning and assessment of the threats deployed we were able

◎ NEWS

INSIDE
★ "Star Wars" feature — P10/11
★ The Sea Searchers — P12/13
★ Horse of the Year Show — special offer — P17

No. 582   SEPTEMBER 24-OCTOBER 7, 1983   FORTNIGHTLY 12p

Lossiemouth Buccaneers in show of air support for British troops

The Buccaneers over Beirut as seen by viewers of ITN

RAF OVER BEIRUT

Report in the RAF News *of the Beirut 'flypast'* (Editor RAF News).

to develop more appropriate, medium-level deliveries of our precision bombs to overcome the difficult acquisition at very low level of urban targets. Norman Browne, the Pavespike king, played a big part in this tactical thinking. Who knows whether or not our warning flight had the desired effect but I do know that our soldiers remained free of serious attack. Later, I flew into Beirut by RAF Chinook for a few hours to walk the ground and discuss operational issues with the ground commanders. The detachment refined its tactics, procedures and weapon deliveries and remained on operational alert for several months into the winter of 1983. The mighty Buccaneer and its proud operators demonstrated, not for the first or for the last time, their firepower, adaptability and long reach.

The Buccaneer was designed for a very specific role against major Soviet navy units. But the sheer size and unusual, transonic airframe design of the aircraft gave it range and payload characteristics totally unmatched by other RN or RAF tactical aircraft. It was routine for Buccaneer squadrons to deploy over very long distances to destinations in the Mediterranean, Asia, Canada, the USA and the entire European continent. The aircraft in its ferry configuration as we flew with to the South Atlantic could fly over 2,500 miles unrefuelled.

Our Buccaneer, which all we Buccaneer Boys are so fiercely proud to have flown, was peerless in the business of projecting serious tactical airpower on a global scale. Among the many special attributes of the Buccaneer, its ability to deploy long range was key.

CHAPTER EIGHTEEN
JOINING THE BIG BOYS

JERRY WITTS

As a young Air Training Corps cadet in the 1960s, I was taken to an air display at RNAS Yeovilton and can vividly remember spectacular flypasts by Scimitars and Sea Vixens, but the aircraft that really caught my interest that day was the relatively new Buccaneer. I had already made up my mind that I wanted to be a military pilot and thought that this was definitely the jet for me. As soon as I was old enough, I wrote to the Royal Navy and enquired about joining the Fleet Air Arm as a fast jet pilot. They were very polite but regretted to inform me that they would be giving up their fixed-wing carriers and that, unless I was interested in helicopters, I would probably have better luck applying to the RAF. I took their advice, persuaded the RAF to take me on and, in early 1972, graduated as a pilot, although not at that stage a sufficiently confident enough one to cope with fast jet advanced training.

In due course, after multi-engine advanced training, I found myself in Cyprus as a co-pilot on 35 Squadron flying the Vulcan B2, a wonderful aeroplane but not quite a fast jet. However, one beautiful Cyprus day in May 1974, I managed to blag a ride in a Lightning T5 with Wg Cdr Martin Bee, the CO of 56 Squadron, the resident Akrotiri air defence team. He let me fly most of the sortie, which rapidly rekindled my ambition to somehow become a fast jet pilot, although there was no obvious pathway to achieving this at the time. Anyway, it seems that I wasn't too bad a Vulcan pilot because in 1975 at the age of twenty-five, I found myself posted to 44 Squadron at RAF Waddington as a Vulcan captain. They weren't taking too many chances though: my co-pilot was an ex-Canberra pilot, who was older than me and my navigator plotter was the squadron commander. He certainly looked after me and, after a couple of years, the RAF started to wonder whether it would be able to retrain some of the V-Force aircrew eventually to join the Tornado force that was ultimately due to replace it. Somehow I found myself in the role of guinea pig with a posting to the Buccaneer, contingent upon successfully completing a foreshortened fast jet advance training course on the Hunter at Valley followed by the usual Tactical Weapons Course again on the Hunter at Lossiemouth.

I was exceptionally fortunate in the instructors allocated to me along the way; at Valley, Al Beaton took on the challenge followed by Graham Bowerman at Lossie. Both were experienced Buccaneer pilots and could not have been more supportive and encouraging in gradually altering my thinking from a necessarily procedural and staid V-Force perspective to that of a 'disciplined rip-shit' as I have heard it described. It was all huge fun.

I did, however, make one major, albeit unwitting tactical error. Probably because, with my posting already known, I was pretty relaxed about the outcome of such non-Buccaneer training as air-to-air gunnery, I seemed perversely to be pretty good at it and actually won the Aden Cannon trophy for my course. (Dennis Caldwell, who was the station commander at the time and whom I led on the winning sortie, still maintains that I stole his scores, but don't believe him!) This success prompted my flight commander to enquire whether I would consider changing my destination to air defence Phantom F-4s and swap my Buccaneer slot with another student. "Not on your life" would be the politest version of my actual response.

Anyway, in April 1979, I duly pitched up at 237 OCU at Honington to start 69 Buccaneer Conversion Course. Here, I was crewed up for the course with a very experienced navigator, Norman Roberson, who was undertaking refresher training, but not until I had used up a few of my pilot instructor Norman Crow's heartbeats on my Fam1 Buccaneer flight, when the intercom failed. I loved the aircraft, but there was a lot to learn, including the mysteries of the various Buccaneer weapon delivery profiles. Eventually, I was signed off by the chief instructor, Phil Wilkinson, and posted to 16 Squadron at Laarbruch in Germany with Dave Cousins as the boss.

It was a great outfit, and continued to be so after Peter Norriss took over command from 'DC' in 1980. Warm and friendly and, excepting myself, pretty good professionally by any standards. I couldn't believe my luck, especially when I discovered that I was about to be promoted to squadron leader, albeit without portfolio for a time while I learned the operational ropes. All in all it was the perfect environment in which to continue the transition from necessarily prescriptive and pre-planned V-Force operations to think-on-your-feet tactical mud-moving, especially when leading a formation and not just worrying about a single aeroplane. The only disadvantages that I could see were three less blokes on the crew to buy rounds in the bar and slightly less space for luggage in the bomb bay.

Ironically, having just come from the V-Force, the first priority was to get operational in the strike role so that I could do my share of QRA. Except on exercise, we didn't do QRA in the V-Force, so this was all new as well. Not that it wasn't taken seriously, but a twenty-four-hour shift now and then was quite a relaxing change from roaring around Germany at 250 feet and 450 knots on a daily basis. In between the routine of the daily QRA weapons checks and the occasional practice scramble, there was plenty of time to catch up on paperwork or just watch television; Deutsch 3 could be particularly entertaining after about 2300 hours – at least, that's what I've been told!

For most of this period, I was crewed with 'John Boy' Sheen, a great navigator, a demon at playing Risk in QRA and an all-round super bloke. Sadly, he was killed several years

Two 16 Squadron aircraft airborne at Nellis AFB.

later in a Tornado GR1 training accident but an abiding memory of John Boy was of him occupying a rear seat on the last leg of a transatlantic deployment to Red Flag that took a nine-ship of Buccaneers, led by Peter Norriss on a beautifully-clear Sunday afternoon, at low level from Bergstrom AFB, Texas to Nellis AFB, Nevada via the Grand Canyon. It was my turn to take a ride in the Hercules for this leg but as the nine-ship roared in diamond formation along the canyon and 1,500 feet above its lip, John's pilot could see in his rear view mirror that he had removed his helmet and oxygen mask and replaced them with a Stetson! What a character, now very sadly missed.

The temporary Buccaneer grounding in 1980 slowed things down for a bit, but there were many highlights such as taking the first Buccaneers to participate in the NATO Tactical Leadership Programme (TLP) at Jever in August 1981. John Boy and I got a bit carried away on one of the TLP trips: we were getting fed up with being claimed by German Hawk missile batteries after we had loosed off the single shot of self-protection chaff that we were able to carry in the Bucc's airbrakes. Someone had suggested that we tape another bundle into the rotating bomb bay. Well, on the next sortie it worked a treat, but there was a snag, in fact, it was a big one. A few seconds after the chaff drop, every warning light in the aircraft came on so we quickly put the aircraft onto the ground and into the arrestor gear at RAF Gütersloh. I swear that even after I had shut down and disconnected the battery it was still ticking. Of course, what a more sensible and knowledgeable Buccaneer operator would have known was that the upper surface of the bomb bay was covered in electrical busbars and connectors which our tinfoil chaff bundle had promptly shorted out. Whoops!

Shortly afterwards the Royal Netherlands Air Force TLP support helicopter arrived to ferry us back to Jever. At my request, he very kindly agreed to go via Laarbruch, where I quickly changed in to my best uniform and presented myself at the station commander's office to tell him what I had done. Graham Smart was incredibly decent about it and told me to get back to TLP. It did cost me a lot of beer though, not least for the ground crew who spent days clearing up the mess we had made of the aircraft.

Happily, TLP was followed by a Red Flag in October that year during which Dave Herriot, who was the boss's nav, was often seen displaying a t-shirt emblazoned with a logo: 'Buccaneer, Fly by Wire!' Whenever asked why, he would say, "Flying with the boss! He's always asking 'why are we doing this? Why are we doing that?'" Needless to say he only showed it when the boss wasn't looking and I know that the two of them had an excellent relationship both in the air and on the ground, so I am sure that he was only joking!

Later, in December, I was sent back out to Nellis AFB with Geoff Thompson (a former Nimrod navigator captain) on a mission to repatriate a Buccaneer that had been left behind after Red Flag having had a problem with its wing-fold system. The aircraft was cleared for transit in level flight only not exceeding 1g, so who better to ferry it back across the Atlantic to RAF St Athan than a couple of ex four-jet captains. After an air test at Nellis to make sure the wings stayed on, we duly set off via Offutt AFB, Nebraska, CFB Goose Bay, Labrador, and Keflavik AFB in Iceland, arriving four days later at St Athan, where the aircraft was due to be scrapped. Geoff had learned that the *Ark Royal* was being torn apart up at Cairnryan, near Stranraer so on the last leg we felt obliged to drop down to low level to pay due respect, albeit not exceeding 1g of course.

Peter Norriss managed to persuade the powers that be in 1982 that he should form a five-ship formation team for a Laarbruch Families Day. Christened the Black Saints (derived from the squadron's logo 'The Saint' based on its founding at St Omer in 1915, and our day-to-day call sign 'Black'), and led by the boss, we put together a routine which included an opposition singleton flown by Ron Trinder and Ray Horwood. With Colin Buxton in the boot, I had the easy job flying as No.2. This all went down very well and we performed at several other venues thereafter.

Like most strike/attack squadrons, we visited Decimomannu in Sardinia on a regular basis for armament practice camps and from there the lucky ones might get a weekend ranger flight to one of our Mediterranean bases whilst the rest of the boys practised their golf at Is Molas, cruised the Via Roma and kept the Pig and Tapeworm Bar in the officer's block in business. I think it was Peter Norriss who rather foolishly left me in charge while he went off one weekend to Cyprus whereupon the boys thought it would be a jolly jape to see how many of them could fit inside the RAF Mini set aside for the boss's use on official business. Predictably, this didn't do it a lot of good but with some help from the ground crew, I think we got away with it and returned it looking more or less like a Mini on Monday morning.

Another exciting development was the introduction of a Pavespike laser designation capability largely overseen by Nick Berryman and Norman Browne. This seemed to be a great excuse for them to roar around 2 ATAF working, in particular, with the Brüggen

The Black Saints, March 1982.

Jaguar Force. A few others, including me, got a go now and then, which paid off big time years later during the 1991 Gulf War when Buccaneers arrived in Bahrain to designate for the Tornado GR1 detachments, such as mine, that were engaged in Operation Granby. Having one or two people around, who had done at least some of it before, and who knew the Bucc team, undoubtedly made the difficult job of introducing a new capability on the operational hoof slightly easier. The results we achieved speak for themselves and show the value of being part of a close-knit community who knew each other's capabilities.

In May 1983, there was a joint XV/16 Squadron deployment to Maple Flag at CFB Cold Lake in Canada led again by Peter Norriss. The team arrived back from their work up at Lossie on 29 April and were due to fly to Edmonton two days later for seven days acclimatisation. However, 38 Group had messed up the airlift plan and no VC10s were available for over a week. The boss dug his heels in firmly and gave RAFG an ultimatum saying that "OK! If we don't get airlift and time to acclimatise we're not going to Maple Flag". After a few days of debate over the weekend RAFG capitulated and twenty-six Bucc aircrew eventually left 16 Squadron by MT coach at about 0630 on 2 May with the plan to fly by civilian airlines to Edmonton via Düsseldorf, Heathrow and Toronto with no overnight stopovers in between.

We had been informed that the three legs would be in Club Class and, on arrival at Düsseldorf, we were soon checked into our Lufthansa Club Class seats and settled back to enjoy a few G&Ts on the short morning flight to Heathrow. Davie Paton, one of the 16 Squadron navigators and a Scotsman, had chosen to travel in full Highland dress. However, much to his chagrin and the delight of his watching peers, he was very quickly ushered out of the Düsseldorf security line by a very large *Brunhilda* who escorted him into a female security check area and gave him 'the full works'.

Club Class all the way to Edmonton seemed too good to be true, and so it proved. On arrival at Heathrow, we soon discovered that the transatlantic leg would see us occupying seats at the very back of the British Airways Jumbo. With the prospect of having to pay for drinks for eight hours across the Atlantic in 'Cattle' Class (this was 1983 in the days when alcohol was not free on board), the team very quickly established themselves in the Duty Free Lounge at Terminal 3 to await our call forward to board Flight BA001 to Toronto.

As the Boeing 747 lifted clear of Heathrow's runway and climbed in a north-easterly direction for Toronto, the cabin service manager announced to the 200 plus passengers: "Ladies and Gentlemen, Welcome aboard Flight BA001 for Toronto. We have travelling with us today members of the British Airways Canada Club and because of their esteemed presence, all drinks on board this flight will be courtesy of British Airways." I don't think he realised that he had a bunch of Buccaneer Boys who were well practised at enjoying any free hospitality. Some seven hours later, and whilst still about 500 miles from Toronto, he was once again forced to use the PA system to let us know that: "Ladies & Gentlemen, I'm afraid to inform you that we have run out of alcohol but we still have some bottles of Tia Maria left, so if anybody would like..." He didn't manage to complete his announcement before twenty-six hands at the back of the aircraft hit their call buttons. After a short stop in Toronto, the team were once again airborne in Air Canada's Connoisseur Class to Edmonton but now tired and emotional after a strenuous day in the air were relieved when the purser on that flight used the PA system to let the passengers know that he was closing the bar because some passengers were becoming a little rowdy. What? It wasn't long before most of the team were sound asleep.

Towards the end of the Buccaneer's time in Germany, whilst partaking of a few beers at happy hour one Friday evening, Dave Herriot and I were approached by the station commander, Graham Smart, who was keen to know what 16 Squadron planned to do as a farewell tribute to the Buccaneer's service in RAFG. Caught on the hop, we responded to his challenge to come up with something 'big' by insisting that we would work on it, if he agreed to meet us in the bar in seven days time to hear our proposal. There was some talk of him buying the beers, but we both knew that that was one demand too far! So, as it happened, Dave and I were programmed for QRA the following week and resolved then and there to make best use of the twenty-four- hour duty by coming up with a 'Cunning Plan'.

The Buccaneer has, for a two-seat fast jet, got very long range. At low level cruising speeds it burned about 100lbs of fuel per minute but with judicious handling of the throttles, and the selection of appropriate cruising altitudes, this could be reduced by 33% at high level. Dave arrived in QRA with all the necessary equipment that a professional navigator needs to complete what was an audacious plan. En route documents that covered every continent, a copy of the planning document (the equivalent of the aircrew's bible), statistical meteorological tables, en route high-level navigation charts and all the usual planning detritus that clutters the average navigator's bag. Within about three hours, we managed to plan, work out and convince ourselves that it was possible to fly a Buccaneer around the world without the use of air-to-air fuelling.

16 Squadron aircrew at Laarbruch, early 1983 (CO Wg Cdr Eddie Cox).

The greatest area of difficulty was getting across the Pacific but with the skilful use of 'island hopping' and the occasional partial back-track it was possible to get to Hickam AFB, Hawaii without too much trouble. One possibly difficult stop-over on the plan from Auckland to Hickam was the US Army's airfield, Bucholz, on Kwajalein in the Marshall Islands; a strip of only 6,000 feet but with an arrestor system, which we knew we could handle having visited Gibraltar on many an occasion – and Bucholz wasn't wet at both ends. The real problem was the last leg across the Pacific. The Buccaneer with full internal fuel plus underwing tanks, bomb-door tank and bomb-bay tank will hold 23,000lbs of gas. The leg from Hickam to McClellan AFB, near San Francisco, was 2,300 miles long. With greater fuel consumption in the climb and less in the descent it was pretty obvious that the leg would be a tight one and could be a show-stopper. However, the statistical met winds were favourable and we calculated happily that as long as we made an early decision to divert to San Francisco International, which was en route, the plan was viable. I left Dave to undertake the minute detail of the plan over the next twenty-four hours and to prepare our case for presentation to the station commander in the bar, which by necessity, would have to be a quick and dirty affair as 'briefings' were not the prime purpose of a happy hour.

True to his word, Graham Smart challenged us with the words "This better be good". It took us no more than five minutes to let him into our plan to take two Buccaneers plus support equipment in a VC10 for thirty days across the globe, via Sardinia, Cyprus, Egypt, Bahrain, Bombay, Sri Lanka, Darwin, Sydney, Auckland, Bucholz and Hawaii to California, from where it would be easy to fly across Canada then on to Keflavik, Lossiemouth and back to Laarbruch. We won! He was overwhelmed and fully supportive, even to the point of agreeing that he would fly with Dave, whilst I would fly with the navigator of my choice. Now, the problem was to convince the powers that be at RAFG that the plan was robust and achievable. Sadly, they agreed that both these facts were so but their negative response was related to the fact that to 'fly the globe' with an aircraft that was about to be taken out of service and replaced by an aircraft, the Tornado GR1, that could not make the same trip would not send a particularly positive message. So, we had utilised our time in QRA well but it was, sadly, all for nought. However, it was an interesting planning exercise and highlights graphically the capabilities of the mighty Buccaneer, not least its long-range reach, something it demonstrated when it deployed to the Falkland Islands in 1983.

In mid-1983, as the Buccaneer was being withdrawn from RAFG in preparation for the long-awaited arrival of the Tornado GR1 at Laarbruch, the rump of our sister XV Squadron was amalgamated with 16 Squadron and OC XV, Eddie Cox, took over as leader with me as his deputy. We even managed to reform the Black Saints briefly as a four-ship with me leading. Sadly, the fun had to stop eventually, and in early 1984, we started the handover to the new 16 Squadron Tornado team. What a privilege it had all been. Nearly five years on a front-line RAF Germany squadron flying nearly 700 hours on the aircraft of my boyhood dreams, as well as 300 hours on the trusty squadron Hunters, alongside as fine a bunch of operators as one could ever wish for.

Anyway, it was off to HQ Strike Command at High Wycombe for me as Tornado 1 working for another Buccaneer mate, the inimitable David Wilby. And thus to the Bucc Blitz, but that's another story.

CHAPTER NINETEEN

FINAL YEARS AT SEA

David Thompson on Ark Royal.

DAVID THOMPSON

I re-joined 809 Naval Air Squadron as the senior observer in August 1977. Interestingly my first pilot, with whom I had flown for a year embarked with 800 Squadron in *Eagle,* was Frank Cox who joined as the senior pilot at the same time. This set in motion a series of 'lasts' that concluded with the squadron's final disembarkation directly to RAF St Athan on 27 November 1978 and its disbandment some two weeks later.

These events were a far cry from the situation that existed in the mid-1960s when my long association with the Buccaneer began. The year I flew with Frank on 800 Squadron off *Eagle* coincided with the continuing build-up of Buccaneer squadrons, conversion to the Mark 2 and with four carriers still in commission. Furthermore, there were plans for a new fixed-wing carrier (CVA01) and an upgraded Buccaneer Mark 2 Star, which aimed at combining the excellent airframe qualities of the Mark 2 with an upgraded nav/attack and weapons system. However, that moment signalled the high water mark of naval Buccaneer development as the 1967 Defence Review announced the planned withdrawal of British military forces from 'East of Suez'. As a result, the programmes for a replacement aircraft carrier and its upgraded Air Group were cancelled.

During the next twelve years or so I had been appointed to 809 Squadron four times operating from *Hermes* (once) and *Ark Royal* (three times). I only mention these statistics as they permitted me to live through the inexorable drawdown in the fixed-wing carrier programme. What was pertinent, however, was that although the 'writing was on the wall' and the end was in sight, there was no change of attitude either amongst the aircrew or the ground crew. Spirits remained high; we had a great aircraft, a challenging mission and a testing flying environment. It was business as usual for everyone.

The draw down of the carrier force impacted 809 Squadron almost immediately. Having got back from a six-month deployment in 1966/67 covering the withdrawal from Aden, we had returned to Lossiemouth for a rapid turn round before redeploying. However, following a minor fire whilst alongside completing her refit, the decision was taken to scrap *Victorious*. As a result, 801 Squadron, which was about to deploy was redeployed to *Hermes* leaving 809 Squadron without a carrier.

However, nothing ventured nothing gained, it was decided that the squadron would create a five-aircraft aerobatics team and share a spot with a similar number of Sea Vixens at the 1968 Farnborough Air Show and the Yeovilton Air Day. Now, however much one can extol the qualities of the Buccaneer, formation aerobatics would probably not be at the top of the list. However, Dave Eagles, our superb senior pilot, put together a challenging routine including barrel rolls, wing overs, clean and dirty passes and the 'twinkle roll' amongst a variety of other manoeuvres and the display completed with a very low, very fast and very noisy series of low passes! Pete Sturt, Paddy Meiklejohn, Robin Cox and Dave Beddoe made up the team led by Dave with Igy Milne flying the airborne spare aircraft. Tony 'Biggles' Richardson acted as our ground manager and flew the seventh aircraft. I had flown with Biggles during the previous six-month deployment and I have to admit that we went through every emergency in the book that did not require an ejection. The boss, Arthur White, Pete Mathews, Peter King, Twiggy Cunningham, Ian 'Nick' Nicholls and Andy Evans 'volunteered' to fly in the back seats. I flew with Robin Cox in the box position.

Actually, the work-up of the display went pretty well with only a couple of iffy moments. The first was when we first tried the twinkle role. Initially, aircraft were to twinkle simultaneously. However, at the first attempt we discovered that not only did the aircraft lose some 200 feet in height but it shifted sideways some 500 feet. This resulted in aircraft being canopy-to-canopy half way through the roll. So, it was back to the drawing board. The other 'moment' was when Igy, flying in the No.3 position, slipped back and touched our wing half way through a barrel roll. RAF Chivenor, over whose airfield we were practising at the time, was thus treated to a 'bomb burst' of Buccaneers from a number of unusual attitudes. Still, no real harm done and the actual Farnborough display days and Yeovilton Air Day seemed to go pretty well. I have expanded on this period as it proved once again the spirit, adaptability and flexibility of being part of the Buccaneer world. One day preparing for re-deployment, the next working up an air display routine.

One footnote to add was that Biggles had been tasked to obtain some squadron transport for our couple of weeks at Yeovilton. With limited funds he produced a 1950s Austin Westminster ambulance, which when decorated with a couple of fried chickens (Phoenixes) and the squadron motto, it looked just the job. So, first outing, all aboard after an excellent evening, Biggles started up, put the ambulance in gear and tried to accelerate away. Unfortunately, the ambulance stayed put. Lots of cries of "try another gear", "try reverse" and "we're not paying for this bunch of crap". Little did Biggles know that Evans and Beddoe had discovered that there was a set of hydraulic ramps which could be lowered thus raising the wheels some six inches off the ground to allow the ambulance to be used as a temporary operating theatre. It brought a whole new meaning to the phrase 'spinning your wheels'.

Phoenix 5 and the Westminster ambulance (CO Lt Cdr Arthur White).

Somewhat belatedly, the authorities finally recognised that lookers had a fairly large part to play in operating the Buccaneer weapons system. This resulted in two of us (the other was New Zealander, Noel Rawbone) joining two pilots on the Air Warfare Instructors Course. Robin Cox and a Vixen pilot made up the foursome. After three months of fairly boring but necessary ground school at HMS Excellent, we were rewarded with four months of Hunter flying with 764 Squadron at Lossiemouth. Mike Layard (future Second Sea Lord) was the boss and Dick Lord, who later had a memorable career with the South African Air Force, was our course officer. We were also fortunate to have two F-104G pilots from the German navy during the flying phase. Believe me, it was quite exciting during two-v-two sorties when the F-104G pilots broke into excited German during the ensuing manoeuvres (took one back 40-odd years).

So, armed with lots of information regarding dive angle, lead angle, briefings and leading four-ship sorties against two bounce aircraft, I re-joined 809.

The squadron was still ashore awaiting *Ark Royal* to complete her refit, which would allow her, amongst other updates, to operate the F-4K Phantom. At this time, *Eagle* was still deployed with 800 Squadron. Dave Howard was in command, undoubtedly the best boss never to have had the opportunity to take his squadron to sea. However, undaunted, the squadron continued to evolve its operating tactics, the most adventurous of which was firing the Bullpup missile at night under a Lepus flare. Three aircraft running in at 400 feet in line astern; the Lepus carrier leading and tossing the flare, number two launching the Bullpup under the flare and breaking off while number three controlled the missile onto the target, in this case Gralis Sgeir off north-west Scotland. You would have been impressed.

I was fortunate enough to be appointed to the US Navy flying the A-6A/E Intruder from

Top: A Hunter T7 of 237 OCU.
Above: 237 OCU aircraft with a Sidewinder.
Right: A 111 Squadron Phantom takes on fuel, 1987.

Above: 237 OCU over North Scotland.
Left: Lossiemouth Wing on parade,
30 April 1988, for the aircraft's thirtieth
anniversary.
Below: Lossiemouth Maritime Wing pair
with full load of Sea Eagle anti-ship missiles

Above: 208 Squadron over Egypt in 1990.
Right: En route to a target during Operation Granby.
Below: Over the Iraqi desert, Operation Granby, during Desert Storm.

Above: Glen Mason and Norman Browne DFC man their aircraft at RAF Muharraq, Bahrain.
Left: Buccaneer squadrons always left their mark, here at Decimomannu.
Below: Queen's Birthday Flypast.

Above: Over North Scotland.
Right: Benny Benson displays over Mildenhall.
Below: Rick Phillips and Nigel Maddox with the Queen's Birthday Flypast team at Manston.

Above: Nigel Huckings leads the final team.
Left: Farewell signatures.
Below: Airfield 'attack' by 12 Squadron during the final flypast (*Malcolm Irving*).

Farewell to the Buccaneer

ROYAL AIR FORCE STATION
LOSSIEMOUTH
THOIR AN AIRE

RAF LOSSIEMOUTH
25 - 27 MARCH 1994

Above: The former XW 586 at Thunder City, Cape Town.
Below: The Buccaneer Aircrew Association roll out XX 901 at the Yorkshire Air Museum on 25 April 1998.

Above: The 'Buccaneer Boys' at Duxford in September 2005 after the restoration of XV 865.
Left: XW 544 at Bruntingthorpe in 16 Squadron markings.
Below: South African and British 'Buccaneer Boys' reunion at Pretoria in November 2008.

NAS Oceana in Virginia for the next two years. Apart from fantasising that a combination of the Buccaneer airframe and engine combination and the A-6 weapons system would have been a world-beater, I missed one of the major events proving the valuable contribution that long-range carrier-borne aircraft could make.

Well documented by Roland White in his book *Phoenix Squadron,* it recounts the deployment of a dash across the Atlantic by *Ark Royal* to be in position to launch two Buccaneers manned by the boss Carl Davis, with Steve Park as his looker, and 'Boots' Walkinshaw with Mike Lucas in the back. They launched some 700 miles north east of Bermuda and, with AAR support, flew a highly-successful 1,500-mile mission to show an impressive military presence over British Honduras (later Belize) which was under threat from Guatemala during January 1972. It was ironic that during the same month *Eagle* paid off for the final time. Had the fixed-wing carriers and their Air Groups still been around some ten years later, one wonders whether Argentina would have taken the gamble to invade the Falkland Islands.

So by the time I returned to the Buccaneer world in March 1973 we had seen the loss of three fixed-wing carriers and were reduced to just one Buccaneer squadron, 809, operating from the only carrier, *Ark Royal*. Of particular significance for the Fleet Air Arm, Lossiemouth, the spiritual home of the Buccaneer, had been handed over to the RAF and we moved to Honington in Suffolk to consolidate the whole Buccaneer force together. From an operational perspective, it seemed somewhat bizarre. The north of Scotland could have been designed specifically for Buccaneer operations. Fabulous flying weather, clear air space, weapons ranges to hand and unenviable scope for low-level flying, lots of empty sea and inviting dummy targets.

In contrast to the freedom we enjoyed in the north of Scotland, the airspace in East Anglia was full of RAF and USAF aircraft, the weapons ranges always seemed over-booked, the southern North Sea was full of gas rigs and their supporting helicopters and we were miles away from a decent low-flying area. Often it seemed a more worthwhile exercise to fly high level back to northern Scotland, complete a sortie, refuel at what was now RAF Lossiemouth, and complete a second sortie before returning to Honington.

However, for good or ill, by 1973 809 Squadron was well integrated into the way and pace of life at Honington. The Mineval and Taceval alert exercises took some getting used to and it came as a shock when the squadron was incorporated into Strike Command's Strike Plan whilst *Ark Royal* was in refit. However, with Roger Dimmock and then Johnny Johnstone as the senior naval officer, and with the help and understanding of our light blue brethren, many with experience of the way a naval squadron operated, we rubbed along pretty well. At this time, major aircraft upgrades were forthcoming in the shape of the RWR and the introduction of the Martel missile systems. It was sad that installation of a radio altimeter readout for the back seat was not forthcoming (but that's a very personal point of view).

Although our time operating from Honington during 1973 was relatively limited, a large portion of 1974 was spent operating from the Suffolk base as we waited for the carrier to complete her mini-refit. We finally re-embarked in September to participate in the annual NATO exercise. During the previous eighteen months I had flown with Ted Hackett and although I joked that he was the only pilot who could rattle my head on both sides of the canopy during the approach, I was extremely sad to see him depart as he was a really good guy.

I spent the first half of 1975 recuperating from a tragic accident, which my pilot, Steve Kershaw, did not survive. After enduring some time at sea on the cruiser *Blake*, learning how to be a real seaman, I headed for 237 OCU before taking over as the senior observer of 809 Squadron, undoubtedly the best looker's job going. By that time I had been a regular visitor to the OCU (three times) and I was always impressed at their professionalism and no-nonsense approach to operating the aircraft and qualifying the aircrew who were passing through.

I think it is important to emphasise the difference in philosophy in the way a naval squadron operated. Whilst ashore, our primary task was to prepare to be at the highest operational capability before embarking to be a key part of the carrier's Operational Readiness Inspection, which qualified the Air Group to be deployed operationally wherever and whenever required. We did not enjoy the permanence of an RAF squadron with the support of a well-equipped and manned engineering wing. Our maintenance requirements once ashore were very different and included deep aircraft maintenance, aircraft modifications, system updates, and the interminable anti-corrosion battle, all issues impossible whilst at sea. Time was also needed for aircrew and ground crew changeovers and training. This cyclical pattern of operations had to be heavily geared to the ship's refit schedule, so there was enormous pressure to complete a seemingly endless maintenance programme while at the same time continuing to work-up the air and ground crews.

Back at sea, maintaining the aircraft presented a completely different challenge. Working in confined spaces, often in intense heat, to maintain complex, and potentially dangerous equipment, tested the resolve of everyone. This essential maintenance had to be achieved alongside the intense flying schedule and this created additional pressure. Many pieces of equipment dated from the 1950s and aircraft launches and recoveries in particular, combined with unbearable heat and humidity, were all major obstacles threatening the success of squadron operations. However, to their lasting credit, there was little that the squadron maintainers could not achieve in those cramped and unpleasant conditions.

On deck, when the squadron engineer gave a 'thumbs-up' for launch on the catapult, I always had 100 per cent confidence that the aircraft was, in all respects, serviceable. Instant decisions were needed to turn round an aircraft for the next sortie, strike unserviceable aircraft below for fault rectification or squeeze an aircraft into a limited deck space so that some work could be carried out on deck ready for the next launch. Teamwork was everything, along with a good sense of humour and a flexibility and confidence in decision making. The series of aircraft moves seemed almost as complex as a ballet routine, while using slightly larger objects.

The other great boon to the squadron was the quality and attitude of the RAF officers who had volunteered or been selected to serve on 809 Squadron. The decision to draw down the fixed-wing carrier force meant that the RN pipeline producing pilots and observers rapidly shut down. As a result, light blue aircrew were needed to serve on 809 in addition to training the last throughput of naval aircrew. Since 1965, naval Buccaneer squadrons always had one RAF crew but by the time 809 Squadron deployed for *Ark Royal*'s final commission, around half the aircrew were light blue along with one US Navy crew. Incorporating a single crew from a different service into the squadron's way of doing business and imparting the squadron's empathy was a relatively easy operation and both sides undoubtedly benefited from the exchange of ideas. Incorporating larger numbers needed to be handled carefully to avoid any factionalism or 'them and us' feelings.

By 1976, pilots including Brian Mahaffey, Mike Rudd, Bob Joy, Ed Wyer and Rick Phillips among others were either already or would become integral members of the squadron. This is not in any way to discount the light blue looker contribution with the likes of Pete Huett, Dick 'Baker Street' Aitkin, and Mike Kennedy. To the greatest credit of the light blue aircrew who embarked, they pitched in enthusiastically and, as a result, the squadron remained very much 'all of one company' and were certainly a stronger and more cohesive and professional unit as a result. Moreover, the experience of newly arrived light blue aircrew being rushed below deck directly to the sick-bay after their first land on, told to strip for a medical examination and then led one by one into the wardroom to be greeted with a pint of beer and the odd chorus of 'Auntie Mary' was something to remember.

I also appreciated their adaptability and flexibility. As an example, we were deployed to the German naval air base at Schleswig Holstein in March 1977 operating against German FPBs. A day on board three FPBs was organised for the squadron and it was decided that we would send two Buccaneers to provide a bit of a show. Ed Wyer and I led with Keith Somerville-Jones, the boss, as number two with the CO of the German F-104G squadron in the back. We launched, made it up through the clag to 30,000 feet then let down over the sea to run in on the FPBs. So far, so good, except the cloud base was around 800 feet with about five kilometres visibility. This hampered setting up a bombing circuit, at least one that was by the book! However, undeterred, I briefed Ed on the 'Bravo Starboard' manoeuvre, which consisted of running in low over the target, breaking hard starboard and then pulling as hard as possible in the opposite direction to end up on the target's port bow whence we could commence a bombing run. Ed followed the instructions admirably and we made four pretty good runs from about ten miles out breaking over the targets and ending up with a modified bunt/laydown attack. Then it was back up through the clag and a pair's GCA back to base. Ed and I were pretty pleased with ourselves as we walked away from the aircraft only to come face to face with Keith S-J. He had spent the whole sortie hanging onto our wing for grim death lest he should lose us and find himself swanning about the Baltic with a passenger in the back seat! He was not best pleased but at least it showed just how 'can do' we could be. Perhaps the very good thrash that we'd had the night before also played a part in Keith's displeasure...

So, when the squadron embarked in April of 1978 for *Ark Royal*'s final deployment, it could not have been in better shape. The remaining dark blue aircrew had been 'around the buoy' on a number of occasions and had gained a wealth of experience in embarked Buccaneer operations. This included four lookers who had amassed over 2,000 hours each on the aircraft (Pete Huett, Mike Callaghan, Tony Francis and myself). Rosy Tyberg had also reached the 2,000 hours mark but he didn't make the photograph. The light

The 9,000-hour observers of 809 Squadron 1978.
L-R: Peter Huett, David Thompson, Tony Francis, Mike Callaghan.

blue and US Navy squadron members were also highly experienced and extremely well motivated and we had a well-trained and knowledgeable group of engineers who had seen most, if not all, the faults that the Buccaneer could throw at them. We also had a boss in Tony Morton who commanded with a light touch, which was much appreciated, and the senior pilot and senior observer's relationships with both the aircrew and engineering staff sought to follow suite. I was fortunate enough to fly with Tony for the final eighteen months of 809 Squadron. Relaxed and extremely affable on the ground, he was a bit of a 'tiger' once airborne. Totally competent around the ship (I don't think we bolted once in our time together), he led from the front and by example. Flying as his looker was a great way of completing my operational Buccaneer time.

The 'bread and butter' daily flying schedule focused on operating four attack aircraft, plus a supporting tanker, for each launch cycle with a stand-by tanker ready on deck. Given an average flight cycle of an hour-and-a-half, this normally achieved four or five cycles per day with two cycles at night. This generated some thirty sorties and represented a huge maintenance effort given the deck and hangar restrictions. The aim of each sortie was for every aircraft, as far as possible, to drop a weapon on a designated target. Thus, sortie content by day always involved AAR, normally straight after join-up to ensure the viability of the tanker's refuelling pod, before the four-ship opened out to prepare for a practice co-ordinated TV/AR Martel/medium toss attack (using the dreaded TV air trainer) either against the ship or some other unsuspecting target. We might also be bounced by

809 Squadron officers' final commission Ark Royal *(CO Lt Cdr Tony Morton).*

a nosy F-4 and the Gannet would stand-off and play both sides – vectoring in the F-4 and directing the strike towards the ship. The four-ship would then attack the splash target towed well behind the ship on a 'long stay'. Often, the designated ship was our accompanying tanker or frigate but even HMS *Britannia* had been used on occasions. The tanker meanwhile was available to refuel the F-4Ks and to carry out low-level bombing on the splash target using a profile 'just' within the flying limits of the refuelling pod.

One of the major advances as the Buccaneer force matured was the acceptance that an effective night ship-borne capability could be achieved and sustained. With experienced crews and maintainers and a well-worked ship, night flying became the 'norm' and this was maintained throughout the 1970s. We flew in pairs armed with Lepus flares and two-inch RP or 25lb practice bombs and an airborne tanker with the pair attacking a ship-towed splash target. With a well-directed Lepus, the number two could complete three runs at the target while the leader, having recovered sufficiently from the ensuing 'unusual attitude' after tossing the flare, could achieve two attacks, a good return from two aircraft.

Sorties were obviously less flexible at night as sufficient time and reserve fuel was needed for a CCA (carrier controlled approach) recovery. Fuel was the key to carrier-borne operations and 'conserve' the watchword. This was particularly true at night with an increased chance of having to make more than one pass or being held off while someone who had bolted ahead was fed in for a second approach before needing flight refuelling.

The ship often organised air defence exercises (ADEXs), which pitted the carrier, her escorts and the air defence asset (F-4Ks and Gannet AEW3s) against Buccaneer co-ordinated attacks. This gave both sides unique opportunities of testing attack profiles, navigation accuracy, and target identification in a realistic and often lively environment. Whenever possible these exercises were also conducted against units of other navies often as part of a larger, major NATO exercise.

Thus, although this was to be *Ark Royal's* final deployment, the well-tried pattern of operations continued apace. Ten days after embarking, the squadron was operating in the Caribbean using the range at Vieques. 1,000lb bombs were delivered either in the laydown or 20-degree dive-bombing mode while using two-inch RP under Lepus at night.

Launch of the Honington piano.

During a carrier against carrier exercise with USS *Kennedy*, it was decided that we needed to take the advantage so launched a recce aircraft as soon as the exercise started. Keith Oliver, with Ken Mackenzie in the back, were tasked to take off at dawn, so far so good. However, when we briefed the sortie the following morning it seemed very, very dark outside. We were then told that the ship had made her way westwards during the night so it was still about a couple of hours to first light. No real problem except that Keith was not night qualified. There was no time to find a replacement so Keith was given a rapid brief on night marshalling signals and sent on his way...All went well and the recce was a success. The only downside was that Keith was unable to log a night launch as he shouldn't have been doing it in the first place!

During a disembarkation to the A-7 Corsair base at NAS Cecil Field we were made to feel very welcome by Cdre Bert Chase who had flown on exchange with 800 Squadron embarked in *Eagle* in the mid-1960s. The highlight of this period ashore was to take two flights of four aircraft across to the A-6 Intruder base at NAS Whidbey Island in

Washington State to discuss stand-off missile attacks against shipping. The low-level portion of the flight to Whidbey Island was a great experience.

Once re-embarked, a carrier's flexibility was again highlighted when *Ark Royal* headed for the Mediterranean where the squadron participated in a coordinated strike on the ships of STANAVFORMED operating north of Crete while *Ark* was operating off Sicily.

As the *Ark* approached the end of its final commission, it was decided to mark the occasion by giving the 'last rights' to the wardroom piano. Having found its way on board from the officers' mess at Honington somehow when the squadron departed for the last time, it was considered only fitting that it should be launched and committed to the deep. After due ceremony, with the Royal Marine band in attendance, the piano was launched by the ship's captain, Ted Anson (later Vice-Admiral, Sir Ted). This was entirely appropriate as Captain Ted had been the first naval pilot to fly the NA39 and had led a distinguished career as a Buccaneer pilot. By the way, the piano gave a good account of itself making 104 knots off the end of the catapult when its aerodynamic qualities were found wanting.

Finally, on 27 November 1978, the squadron launched for the last time and delivered its fourteen Buccaneers to St Athan and parked them on the peri-track. There was to be no flypast either then or when *Ark Royal* entered Devonport to 'pay off' for the last time. This was considered by the powers that be to be a 'turning of the page' when anyone with any experience in the business knew that an important chapter in naval aviation had closed, perhaps never to be re-opened.

All I can add is that it was a privilege to have been a part of the Buccaneer history. The people involved and the aircraft will always hold a special place for me leaving great memories, some of which seem undimmed by the passing years and could have happened only yesterday. Life was never dull and nothing that I have done since even comes close to the years that I was associated with the Buccaneer; an unforgettable aircraft.

CHAPTER TWENTY
SAAF BUCCANEERS AT WAR

Peter Kirkpatrick (right) with his pilot Giel van der Berg.

PETER KIRKPATRICK

On my arrival at 24 Squadron in late 1985 the SAAF was at war again and the squadron was up at Grootfontein in Namibia. The MPLA (People's Movement for the Liberation of Angola) had started to push south east towards Mavinga in an attempt to defeat UNITA (National Union for the Total Independence of Angola) and the 'Boere' would have none of it. Army units and SAAF fighter and bomber squadrons were sent to the bush in support of UNITA. After a short sharp engagement that lasted a few weeks, the MPLA lost the heart for the fight and withdrew from the Mavinga area to avoid getting caught by the rainy season. The squadrons returned to their respective bases and were acutely aware that it was only a matter of time before they were back in the thick of the conflict.

By the end of 1985 there were in excess of 30,000 Cuban troops and 3,200 East German and Soviet advisors in Angola. In addition, the opposition's air force could muster over 120 combat aircraft including thirty MiG 23 fighters equipped with AA-7 air-to-air missiles. The SAAF struggled to get more than sixty front-line aircraft together at this stage and these included the aged Canberra, Buccaneer and Mirage III.

General Konstantin Shaganovitch had been appointed as overall commander of all the MPLA forces. He was the most senior Soviet officer to command forces outside Europe and Afghanistan. This was a clear indication that the Soviets and Cubans were deadly serious about winning this conflict and confirmed that the USSR's intentions for Southern Africa were very imperialist and not merely some benign benefactor supporting the oppressed African nations as some would like to have believed.

During 1986 the Soviets continued to pour in large quantities of ground equipment

168

including T-55 main battle tanks and modern air defence systems including SA-8, SA-9, SA-13, and ZSU 23-4 radar-controlled guns. By 1986 Angola had 350 T-55 combat-ready main battle tanks, South Africa had thirty-two operational Oliphant (modernised Centurion) tanks.

In September 1987 Angolan forces (FAPLA) attacked UNITA in the south east of Angola. In response the South African Defence Force (SADF) mounted a counter offensive to help bolster the UNITA defence along the Lomba river where FAPLA had positioned four brigades, all defended by a formidable array of anti-aircraft missile and artillery systems.

As part of the effort to protect the UNITA forces, the SAAF committed five air defence and ground-attack squadrons including 24 Squadron's Buccaneers.

By October 1987 the conflict had escalated into a full-blooded conventional war with tank battles ensuing in the bush. Most people do not realise that this was one of the major tank battles in Africa, post World War II, with FAPLA losing some 100 T54/55 main battle tanks in this conflict as the army pushed the enemy brigades back north west. Together with 1 Squadron's Mirage F1-AZs, 24 Squadron had been carrying out daily strikes against the FAPLA ground forces. We were always aware of the threat from a SA-8 on the run-in to the target.

We were fitted with a very effective radar-warning receiver (RWR), which provided early warning and the aircraft had been modified to carry active jamming (ACS) pods designed to counter the various radar-guided SAMs, especially the SA-8. We also carried a full complement of chaff and flares. Chaff was deployed from prior to the pitch until we returned to low level after the attack. We would deploy the flares at the apex of the release to deal with the infra-red missiles. This is where I learnt that SA-7 and SA-9 love flares! Giel van der Berg and I were normally No.4 in the formation, which meant that we were always last off the target. It would always fascinate me to watch the multiple SA-7 tracking our aircraft and then going for the flares as soon as they were deployed. Thank the Lord that they always worked.

During this phase we were tasked to carry out a strike against a convoy that was re-supplying one of the retreating FAPLA brigades on 13 October 1987. This must have been about our tenth combat sortie so we were over our initial nervousness of operating in such a hostile environment (not that we were ever calm during an attack). We were flying in Buccaneer 422 and were No.3 of a three-ship and as we pitched up to commence the bomb release I noted that the RWR was making a lot more noise than usual. By the time we had commenced the break off, the RWR was screaming and the jamming pod was lit up like a Christmas tree. The SA-8 had locked on to us. It was directly in our six and I screamed at Giel to break. Like an idiot I omitted to tell him which way, which he immediately queried. My response was to get him to break downwards to low level and get the trees between the SA-8 radar's line of sight and us. We were safely back at low level very quickly. Fortunately a combination of our attack profile, the chaff, the flares, RWR, jamming pod and some very hard manoeuvring allowed us to survive to fight another day.

Giel and I would normally chat on the way back (forty-five-minute transit at low level) after a strike. On that day we did not say too much to each other until we landed. We had both realised how lucky we had been to survive the sortie. We subsequently found out that some kind SAAF intelligence man had mis-plotted the position of the SA-8 to the north by some two miles. This meant that we had virtually pitched over it, which explained why it had managed to acquire the aircraft so early. Needless to say that particular intelligence officer was not very popular with the two of us.

One week later, on 20 October 1987, we had our opportunity to settle the score. We were tasked as part of a four-ship to go and destroy the SA-8, which was located on top of a ridge and was becoming a serious threat to operations in the area. We were flying in Buccaneer 414 and used the same initial point (IP) as the rest of the formation but separated from them on the run-in. We pitched, released our bombs and broke back to low level where I watched the string of ten Mk 82s start to detonate (as air-burst) short of the ridge. The SA-8 was starting to go into acquisition and I could clearly hear it getting louder on the RWR audio. The stick continued to the top of the ridge and then the audio disappeared, a sure sign that the SA-8 was not working anymore. The ground forces confirmed a few days later that it had been destroyed. Not quite a HARM (high-speed anti-radar missile), but just as effective.

On 9 October 1987 Giel and I had been tasked to do a photo-recce sortie on the Cuito Cuanavale river bridge. The sortie was scheduled for 11 October during a busy time in the conflict when the Buccaneers flew fourteen strikes in a nine-day period.

The plan was to fly the sortie at the same time other Buccaneers, and some Mirage F 1s, were operating against FAPLA in the area between the Lomba River and SE of Cuito Cuanavale.

Given that operations were in full swing, and the Angolan MiG 23s were also operating over the whole of the area (see below), we were cautious with our planning.

Considering that most of south-eastern Angola was completely without friendly radar coverage at low level, we were well and truly in 'Indian' territory. Fortunately we had plenty of fuel and were fitted with full chaff and flare as well as ACS pods.

I planned the run so that we could skirt the combat area by transiting to the east of

Mavinga and running up the Cuando river, staying in the river valley and then approaching Cuito Cuanavale from the north east. This allowed us to use the terrain to remain masked from the radars at Cuito until the last minute, pitch for the photo run and then break off to the south at low level to return back to Grootfontein without transiting through the combat area.

On the 11th we took off in Bucc 416 at 0900 and headed to the east of Mavinga to set up for the run. At the same time three other 24 Squadron Buccs were conducting strikes in the main combat area. The camera pack (a Vinten LOROP pod) was fitted in the bomb bay and was primarily used to take oblique photos at relatively low angles. This reduced the risk to the aircraft by not having to overfly the target and minimised the time the aircraft was exposed to missiles and fighters. The pilot used a graduated mechanical sight and roll control.

The initial transit was to the east of Rundu and we cruised at low level 100-200 feet AGL at 420 knots. While still over friendly territory we conducted our normal checks on the system. After rolling the bomb door open I conducted a check-out on the camera. Giel deployed the starboard sight for the camera and set up the sight angle to coincide with the camera setting. In this case the angle setting would have been about ten degrees to the starboard. Everything checked out, so we closed the bomb door and stowed the sight.

We accelerated to 480 knots, 'descended' to 100 feet and transited to the north and joined up with the Cuando river and turned north west. Having been used to over-flying many rivers in South Africa it really amazed me to see that this river was about four to five kilometres wide (in the flood plain) and, despite being the dry season, the actual river was twice the size of the Orange river in full flood (the Orange river is the largest river in South Africa). The Cuando is only one of a dozen similar-sized rivers in SE Angola.

Along the river we reached our IP and turned west to start our run-in. Although the Buccaneer was fitted with a good (for its day) navigation system, it was still effectively a dead reckoning system that required regular and accurate updates to ensure optimal performance.

We remained in the valley of the tributary and then accelerated to 580 knots at 100 feet. The RWR was still quiet. We hit the pitch point and Giel pulled at 5g and climbed to 10,000 feet, rolled inverted and pulled down at 5g to stop the rate of climb before rolling back to restore straight and level flight. By now we were at 12,900 feet (15,900 feet altitude) and Giel rolled the bomb door open. This manoeuvre took about thirty seconds, which was not bad for our old bus.

By now the RWR was very lively, with several SA-8s and SA-3s making themselves heard. The stand-off range from the target was seven miles, which kept us outside the range of most of the missiles in the Cuito area, but left us very exposed to any MiG 23s that were operating in the area. Once we were detected, the MiG 23s would have to be vectored to intercept us via the long-range search radars, which would take at least twenty seconds to establish a track on us once we had pitched from low level. By now the search radars were coming through loud and clear on the RWR. Although they did not pose a direct threat towards us, the clock was ticking and it was time to get the job done and back to the relative safety of low level as quickly as possible.

I switched on the camera and checked that it was running while Giel lined up the camera sight with the bridge. So far the sortie had worked out well. We had come through undetected and the bridge was where it should have been. The run was completed, I switched the camera off and Giel closed the bomb door and plunged back to low level using the barn doors (airbrake!) to get down fast. By now the RWR was screaming its head off with all the radar activity from Cuito and Menongue.

We hit low level at 580 knots and headed south, only to hear over the radio: "We are in your seven o'clock!" Giel and I gave the compulsory response of "Huh?!?!" It took us about fifteen seconds to realise that we had heard Pikkie Siebrits talking to Mike Bowyer on their way out from their own strike to the south east of our position. That was a long fifteen seconds while we scanned the world around us for bogeys.

The rest of the journey was uneventful and we landed back at Grootfontein.

The film was removed for developing and analysis and we felt that this was a job well done, or so we thought.

Two days later, we got the message from Rundu that they were not happy at all with the photo run. Instead of the bridge lying in the lower third of the photo, it was two thirds up in the frame. Although usable, the intelligence people wanted better photos for later operations. After the usual ribbing by all parties, Giel and I were tasked to repeat the run, 'mutter, mutter'. We triple checked the previous run and could not fault it at all.

On 14 October 1986, we climbed back into Bucc 416 and got airborne at 1,000 to repeat the exercise, determined to make up for the previous sortie.

After the system checkout before Rundu we were convinced that all was well, but could still not work out what went wrong on the previous sortie. As we passed north of Mavinga, Giel decided to check the camera sight again. It was then that he realised that the starboard graduated sight was in fact slightly loose and had vibrated itself to eight degrees instead of the ten initially selected. After some choice words he corrected the problem. The rest of the sortie was completed uneventfully apart from the RWR making a lot of noise as usual. This time the intelligence guys were happy with the photos and left us in peace without too many chirps.

By late October 1987 the FAPLA brigades were being pushed back from the Lomba river by the SADF and UNITA forces. The SADF wanted to create as large a buffer between Mavinga and Cuito as possible before the rainy season started and all fighting stopped. We were carrying out strikes virtually on a daily basis in support of the ground forces.

Our aircraft had been modified to carry eight Mk 81s or Mk 82s internally and eight Mk 82s or twelve Mk 81s externally. As an aside, we used to fly an air show routine with one 'clean' Bucc and one Bucc flying in this configuration doing some hard manoeuvring giving the message to the rest of the SAAF: 'see if you can top this!' Operationally these bombs could be conventional iron bombs or pre-fragmented bombs with up to 26,000 ball bearings and fused with airburst fuses. This inherently made the use of toss attacks a seriously viable option. The combined sticks from four aircraft would cover an effective area of one square kilometre.

To increase our chances of survival we made extensive use of toss bombing. We had modified the standard medium toss profile to release the bombs at a much higher angle

24 Squadron low over the bush.

(38-42 degrees). This increased the stand-off range at bomb release keeping us out of the SA-8's range for long enough to carry out an attack and break off in reasonable safety.

We had initially made sole use of the pre-fragmented Mk 82 bombs with air-burst fuses. These were extremely effective on any troops that were exposed at the time of the strike, but were less effective against troops dug into foxholes. According to the intelligence reports, FAPLA learnt this lesson quite quickly. The pre-fragmented Mk 82s were also very effective against trucks and light armour, especially radiators and tyres. Reports were being received of FAPLA resupply convoys coming from Menongue and Cuito Cuanavale being heavily laden with replacement tyres and radiators. This reduced the space available for food and ammunition, which meant that the tactic was working.

At times a specific brigade would get bogged down and the SADF and UNITA ground forces would be battling to dislodge them. At these times we switched to conventional 'iron' Mk 82 bombs with delay fuses. The time delay set would vary from two to forty-eight hours and we would toss up to forty-eight of these bombs into the area where a FAPLA brigade had dug in. These bombs would penetrate the soft ground and remain there until the delay times expired. This meant that we effectively mined the area with a bomb going off every hour for the next two days. After twenty-four hours the brigade would be so frazzled that they would up-sticks and continue withdrawing. The SADF troop could move into the area forty-eight hours after the strike, knowing that there would be no more bombs left to explode.

On 20 October 1987 Giel and I took part in a three-ship formation of Buccs on a strike south east of Cuito Cuanavale. The planned route was to approach along the Cuito river past Villa Nova Del Armada, find the pre-IP navigation point, route to the east to get there, which was a strange shaped pan, and then turn to the north to the target. The break off was to starboard and to return to the south at low level. The reason for this was fourfold:

- The FAPLA brigade that we were attacking was defended by SA-9s and SA-8s spread out around the brigade. Army intelligence had reported that there was a defensive gap to the south and south east of the brigade.

- We were part of a combined strike with a formation of four Mirage F1-AZs attacking from the south east thirty seconds before our intended strike time.

- We were getting too close to Cuito Cuanavale to risk approaching from the north.

- The pan to the south of the target was the only usable IP in the area.

We were airborne at 1520 in Buccaneer 422 and as usual, Giel and I were No.3 in the formation. As mentioned previously it was critical to keep the navigation system accurately updated but this was not easy in wide battle formation 3,000-6,000 feet on the beam of the lead aircraft. Giel and I had developed a technique of lagging the lead pair during the crossover in formation to ensure that we positioned ourselves over the fix point to ensure an accurate update of the navigation system. This was especially important just before the IP, particularly when it was a pan in the middle of an otherwise featureless area and we were flying at 480 knots at 100 feet.

As we came up to the navigation fix point on the river, we were expecting to turn eighty degrees to the right and as usual we ensured that the navigation system was accurately updated in the crossover in formation.

The lead aircraft turned thirty degrees right and no further. We were now heading directly for the target, via the SA-8 defences, with the IP moving to the right and Mirages still in the area.

Keeping in mind that we always operated in full radio silence (particularly before the attack), I immediately told Giel that we were heading for a disaster. He concurred and agreed that I break radio silence. I called the lead navigator and politely asked if he needed help and indicated that the IP was sixty degrees to starboard. It is important to note that we were moving off track very quickly at eight miles a minute.

Cmdt Lappies Labuschagné (OC 24 Squadron) was the formation leader and realised that things were going horribly wrong. We either had to correct matters quickly or return home. He told us to take over formation leadership. I called a 270 degree turn left to close in on the IP from the west.

I must admit that my heart was in my mouth because I realised that if I was wrong, I would never live it down. Thanks to the accurate navigation system update prior to the IP we ended up right on top (albeit forty seconds late) and marked it, starting the weapons system run in to the pitch point. We turned hard left to the target and went 'buster' (full power) accelerating to 540 knots with the rest of the formation lined up behind us for the attack.

Giel rolled the bomb door open and I started the chaff running just before the pitch. By now the RWR confirmed that the SA-8s were indeed to our left which agreed with the intelligence reports. Giel was now flying the aircraft using the weapons system commands in the HUD (head-up display) and we were flying at about eighty feet and 550 knots. The beauty of a two-man crew in these conditions is that the pilot just has to worry about flying the aircraft and the navigator sorts out the weapons system, arming, chaff, flares, active jammer and look-out. We hit the pitch point at 4.7 miles from the target and Giel followed the commands in the HUD pulling up at 4g. After six seconds the bombs released automatically in sequence at a pitch angle of about thirty-five degrees. We felt the 'thump' of the ERUs (ejector release units) ejecting the bombs from the aircraft. Once the bombs were all released Giel commenced the escape manoeuvre hard right as I visually confirmed that the bombs were released and started the release of the flares to deal with any infra-red missiles. By now the chirp of the SA-8 was becoming very loud, but it had not locked on for launch yet. Thirty seconds after the pitch-up we were back in the relative safety of low level and 580 knots heading south. At this stage it was the navigator's job to check the tail was clear from missiles and other bogeys. We would also try to assess if the bombs were on target – not easy in such featureless terrain and at six miles range.

It always amazed me how well the Buccaneer handled under those conditions. The aircraft had a reputation of turning like a brick. This was true at 500 knots, but was not true at 380 knots, which was the typical speed at the top of the apex after weapon release for toss bombing. At this speed the pilots could safely turn the aircraft at 5g without risking a nasty flick-in that the aircraft had a reputation for doing. The pilots on the squadron actually made use of the onset of buffet (the buffet occurs when the aircraft is approaching the stall and is very predictable if you know what to look for) to be able to control the aircraft during these conditions.

A testimony to the handling of the aircraft was that no Buccaneers were lost during these operations in Angola. Once or twice we ended up (inadvertently) in the same airspace as the Mirages when we struck the same brigade and from similar directions due to operational limitations. In this case the timing of the strikes was only separated by thirty seconds to avoid giving early earning to FAPLA. If the timing was slightly out by one or both parties we could end up pitching simultaneously. The Mirages would pitch from six miles and we would pitch from four-and-a-half, giving us some separation, although as far as I could remember this only occurred twice in the campaign. During one such case Mike Bowyer ended up in formation with a Mirage at the apex of the escape manoeuvre.

It also helped enormously that the Bucc pilots did not have to worry about anything other than flying. In contrast the poor F1-AZ pilot was very busy in his office at this stage of the sortie. With very few of the onboard systems being integrated, he had a massive workload. I can still clearly remember one of the F1-AZ pilots (Reg van Eeden) telling a story of how he nearly flew into the ground during an escape manoeuvre. During the early phase of the operations the Bucc navigators were continually reporting on the amount of SAM and AAA activity at the debriefings and some of the F1-AZ pilots were sceptical about our reporting, due to the fact that they had not seen as much activity as we had. By their own admission, however, the F1-AZ pilots agreed that they really did not have much time to look around. After flying about five strikes, Reg felt that he could sneak a peek at the RWR during the escape manoeuvre. In his own words, he nearly 'cr***ed himself' when he saw the number of SA-8s on the RWR as he took a handful of stick to get back to low level ASAP. In the process he ended up heading for the ground in a near vertical dive and only just managed to stop himself from becoming a permanent feature of the Lomba river landscape. When he returned from the flight he was really shaken up by what he had seen and what he nearly did to himself. His account made me even more thankful for the fact that I was operating in a two-man crew with a good weapons system and a damn good EW system.

The operation lasted from September 1987 until April 1988. The Mirage F1-AZs flew over 1,000 combat sorties in this period (with just ten aircraft) and the Buccaneers flew 150 combat sorties (with just four aircraft). All of these sorties were into areas that were heavily defended and we were always met with a barrage of anti-aircraft fire and missiles. On several occasions 1 Squadron did run into a few MiG 23s at low level but, for most of the time, the Cuban pilots were loath to operate outside radar coverage. Amazingly, during this period only one ground-attack aircraft, a Mirage F1-AZ, was lost to enemy fire.

Our extremely low loss rate was due to a number of factors. Excellent passive and active ECM kit, tossing bombs from a few miles out and the aircraft's outstanding performance at very low level when it was quite normal for us to fly at 540 knots at eighty feet on the run-in to a target – the only place to be in a Buccaneer.

CHAPTER TWENTY-ONE

OPERATION GRANBY – PRECISION BOMBING

BILL COPE

Following Saddam Hussein's invasion of Kuwait, the RAF rapidly built up a powerful air force in the region as part of the Allied Coalition. The AOC of 18 Group, Air Marshal Sir Michael Stear, reminded the Joint HQ that the Buccaneer force with its Pavespike laser-designator pods was the only RAF asset with a precision-bombing capability. He was told we would not be needed. However, our station commander, Gp Capt Jon Ford, a very experienced Buccaneer pilot and former squadron commander, consulted OC 12 Squadron and myself and we decided it would be prudent to review the capabilities and investigate high level 'spiking' in addition to carrying on with the low-level method. The AOC agreed and the two squadrons carried out the work and were soon able to report that the technique worked well.

Shortly afterwards, the shooting war started and Tornados commenced low-level airfield attacks during which several aircraft were lost. Once it was apparent that the Iraqi air force was effectively grounded, the Tornados commenced bombing from medium level with Second World War vintage, unguided 1,000lb bombs. The AOC again approached the HQ to offer the Buccaneers but the response was the same as it had been for the preceding weeks, an emphatic No!

Meanwhile, the Royal Navy was working up ships to deploy to the Gulf and our sister squadron, No. 12, was deployed to Gibraltar and I had taken my outfit, 208 Squadron, to St Mawgan to assist in this programme. I had watched the opening shots of 'The Gulf War' on television along, no doubt, with a significant proportion of our nation.

Many weeks previously I had booked leave to go skiing with my wife and, on the evening of 22 January 1991 I was on the dispersal at St Mawgan having handed over command of the squadron to my very capable deputy, Sqn Ldr Tony Lunnon-Wood. I was waiting for a Hunter from Lossiemouth, bringing the AOC to visit the squadron, and flown by Jon Ford, it would take me home to pack for my holiday. *En passant* I jokingly asked the AOC if he was going to spoil my skiing by sending us to the Gulf. He replied, "I am sorry Bill, they do not want us. Have a good holiday."

On arrival back at Lossiemouth I went home for dinner. Unknown to me Jon Ford was not so lucky; he was called to the secure telephone in the Wing Operations Centre later that evening and was asked: "How long will it take you to deploy Buccaneers to the Gulf?" Without any previous hint of the Buccaneers being involved, or any justification for detailed preparation, he gulped and said, "three days".

So, after thirty years of continuous service, one of the most outstanding low-level bombers was finally going to war – at high level! When asked why such an old aircraft was being sent to the Gulf, the Secretary of State for Defence was quoted as saying: "Because we need to improve the standard of precision bombing." Some accolade.

In three days, the aircraft had chaff and flare equipment installed and armed, a desert camouflage paint scheme, an AIM 9L Sidewinder procured, loaded and armed, Havequick secure radio obtained and fitted, bomb-bay fuel tanks fitted, and one under-wing fuel tank on one wing with the all-important Pavespike laser-designator pod on the other wing. In addition, some 140 personnel (later to grow to about 180) had to be inoculated (against almost everything), kitted out with real anti-chemical warfare personal equipment, encouraged to make wills and arrangements for families, and issued with personal weapons.

At 0400 on 26 January the station commander bade us farewell and we took off from Lossiemouth with the paint in some places still wet. My navigator was Carl Wilson and the second aircraft was crewed by Glen Mason and Dick Aitken and we set off to rendezvous with a TriStar tanker over southern England, and then flew together non-stop to Muharraq airport in Bahrain. Another four aircraft followed us over the next few days. The initial detachment consisted of the most experienced aircrews of 208 and 12 Squadrons and also 237 OCU.

Our arrival in Muharraq was uneventful, indeed, it was underwhelming. I was quite surprised when no one from the base came out to meet us, just our own ground crew. If we had expected a welcome for bringing a much-needed additional capability to the RAF element in-theatre, we were to be disappointed.

On our first evening in Bahrain I met Wg Cdr Bill Pixton, the Jaguar squadron commander, in the top floor bar of our hotel and during our conversation I asked him what the drill was for a Scud missile alert. Did we all go down to some designated shelter in the basement? His reply was "Not much point really, if a Scud hits the hotel it will be coming vertically downwards at about Mach 5 and will probably pass through all floors

Gp Capt Jon Ford, OC Lossiemouth, bids farewell to Bill Cope and his navigator Carl Wilson.

before ending up in the basement! So most people rush up here and have a beer while watching the Patriots (missiles) launching from Dhahran across the causeway." After about two seconds reflection that seemed very realistic advice.

We were required to operate with RAF Tornados from three bases; Muharraq in Bahrain, and Tabuk and Dhahran in Saudi Arabia. I assigned one squadron leader to liaise with each base, to ensure standardisation of Buccaneer/Tornado procedures, and to effect prompt dissemination of good ideas.

We were accommodated in hotels in Manama, and had our self-drive (hired) transport to move between the hotels and Muharraq airport. Life took on a bizarre nature for what was a war theatre. We were not permitted to travel to and from the airport in flying kit. So I drove my hire car to 'work', we changed from civvies to a desert-coloured flying suit, drew our automatic pistols and bullets from the armoury and the necessary survival equipment from the Intelligence Section, planned the mission, bombed our targets, debriefed and drove back to the hotel where most of the aircrew not engaged in that day's programme would be lounging by the swimming pool. A polite "how did it go?" from those nearest to your sun-lounger was all the interest shown in your exploits.

The Buccaneer had no electronic interface between the aircraft's navigation system and the Pavespike laser. Consequently we had no electronic means of directing the laser onto

Training over the desert with Tornados.

the target. We had to rely on the aircrew harmonising the navigator's laser bore-sight with the pilot's strike-sight aiming mark on an object in the foreground prior to taxiing. When airborne the pilot had to acquire the target visually, aim his sight at it, and then call "sight on" to the navigator, who then opened his viewfinder, hopefully to see the target. This is what passed as modern technology! Nevertheless, it worked most of the time. However, any alignment errors made on the ground, (at short range, typically 100-200 yards), could turn into significant differences in the air, when the visibility was sometimes twenty miles or more, and particularly so when there were several examples of the same type of target clustered together. This caused problems on more than one occasion.

Virtually all logistic support for the Iraqi forces in Kuwait came through Iraq by road. In order to isolate them from resupply our first targets were to be the many bridges in Iraq where main routes crossed the major rivers. We operated a standard 'package' consisting of two Buccaneer laser designators (in case one Pavespike failed) and four Tornado bombers. We were protected by two US F-15 Eagle fighters, two Wild Weasel SAM suppression aircraft (usually F-16 Fighting Falcons), one F-111 E Raven jammer, and all this under the very comforting overview of an AWACS radar/surveillance aircraft which periodically transmitted a much appreciated 'only friendlys airborne'. In the event, we met no Iraqi aircraft in the air at all.

I believe most squadron commanders have a mental image of how they think they will go into battle for the first time. Typically it would be to lead the crews we have trained with for months, or even years. On my first mission, with Glen Mason and Norman Browne as my No.2, reality was rather different. As we transited over Iraq, heading for the bridge at Al Suwaira I wasn't leading at all – the Tornados were. We were at high level, not low level, and over land, not over the sea. Visitors always assume that the Middle East is in burning sunshine. Not so. I was in cloud, staring at a Tornado's wingtip. I was listening to lots of Soviet radar systems, just as I had in the simulator at home, but these were real signals coming from enemy radars. The thought running through my mind was, 'It's not supposed to be like this!'

We came out of cloud, as forecast, but still under cloud cover, into a flat, brown landscape in a flat grey light. The roads were brown, the rivers (lots of them) were murky and there was no colour contrast at all so both Buccaneers were late acquiring the target. However, direct hits from both salvos of six LGBs demolished the bridge completely: "Strike One!" This instance of bad weather was by no means unique. Over the following weeks we were to lose several days' operations due to cloud/rain and also sandstorms. So much for imagining the desert's endless bright sunshine!

Targets marked by Buccaneer crews.

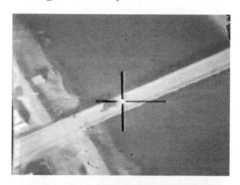

Iraq bridges were all on a large scale and included both motorway and suspension types. We initially had some misgivings about the effectiveness of our rather ancient 1,000lb bombs. In the event it transpired that their rapid, successive impacts and explosions produced a synergistically greater destructive effect and proved very effective at destroying bridges. However, not every mission went according to plan. The LGBs that we were using were guided by what was described as a 'bang bang' system, which meant that the fins were capable of only moving from zero to full deflection and back to zero again, there was nothing between the two. If they jammed at full or no deflection, there was no means of controlling the weapon. This happened on an attack against a bridge near the town of Fallujah causing large numbers of unintentional civilian casualties when some bombs malfunctioned and ended up in a busy market square.

On some suspension bridges, the bombs went right through the roadway before detonating in the river below the bridge; that was soon corrected by shortening the fuse time-delay. We also settled an old argument as to which was the best aiming point on suspension bridges; the abutments or the suspension towers? Bombs striking the thousands of tons of concrete that make the abutments did little apparent damage (surprise, surprise); when we hit the towers the bridges came down.

We were more effective than we knew. The Iraqis were using fibre-optic cables to communicate with their troops in Kuwait and these crossed the rivers on the bridges. So we cut not only the supply routes, but also the communication links giving us two for the price of one. The Iraqis tried to reinstate their supply routes by deploying pontoon bridges but they have very weak abutments and they were easily sent floating rapidly down river towards the Persian Gulf.

Although we saw frequent AAA shell bursts below, and sometimes around us, there was little SAM activity against us. Our Raven jammers and Wild Weasel support was normally sufficient to keep the enemy's heads down. But on the occasions we did see SAM trails I was very grateful for the advice given by our electronic warfare specialists to the effect that if the smoke plume appeared to be 'jerky', the missile was guiding and if straight it had lost target information. It was quite comforting to find that I could easily tell the difference. The nearest a missile got to me was an Allied HARM launched from above us against an Iraqi missile radar; I think it went past us about fifty feet to our left, on its way down. A rather strangled expletive to the effect of 'I am on your side' provoked an apologetic response of "sorry about that, but once we launch the HARM it takes its own course down to its target – it wasn't aimed at you".

As the time for our land forces to begin the ground offensive came closer, we were tasked to attack runways, taxiways and ammunition storage in order to prevent the Iraqi air force from getting airborne and intervening against our ground operations and this was a much more difficult task than it first appeared. The Iraqi airfields were vast (you could have fitted Lossiemouth several times inside them) and repeated attacks were necessary to deny them a viable take-off run. We were also tasked with attacking their hardened aircraft shelters (HAS), against which our LGBs again proved highly effective. The Iraqis tried to decoy us away from our assigned HAS targets by painting large black circles on intact shelters to try to fool us into believing that someone else had already hit them. It worked on some occasions.

With no enemy fighter threat, and the proven superiority of our fighter escorts, we were able to dispense with our Sidewinder missiles from early/mid-February. Instead, each Buccaneer carried two LGBs. All these precision bombs were delivered in a forty-degree dive attack, tipping in from around 27,000 feet and releasing at about 20,000 feet. During the steep dive-bombing there were instances of some of the navs, mainly the youngsters, inadvertently hitting the Pavespike 'park' button. Whilst tracking the target with a roller-ball control, under a 4g recovery from the dive, occasional such errors were hardly surprising, but this resulted in the bombs dropping unguided and so they were wasted.

Although most of our tasking was against airfield taxiways and runways and HAS sites, we also hit some weapons-storage facilities – usually with quite spectacular effect. We also caught two transport aircraft in the open at Shayka Mazar airfield on 27 February.

Two bombs, which did not explode, destroyed one and the other went up in an enormous explosion. They may have been the only two 'kills' recorded by the RAF in the conflict, but being on the ground I suspect they did not satisfy the definition. The ceasefire was announced the next day.

The press made much of the age of the Buccaneers allocating them the soubriquet 'The Golden Oldies'. That is very much what they proved to be, albeit we were not the oldest RAF aircraft in theatre; the Victor tanker had that honour. The Tornado aircrews were initially quite sceptical of our ability to keep up with them but they were very much mistaken. Although our navigation accuracy was clearly inferior to the Tornado (operating overland we could not use our maritime radar to update our inertial navigation system), the Buccaneer's aerodynamic performance was clearly superior. It out-climbed the Tornado, cruised faster and higher, could refuel at much higher altitudes and required less fuel from the tanker on all missions. Despite always being the last aircraft to leave the target area we invariably arrived home first. Newer is not always better.

We were very lucky regarding battle damage; the Buccaneers took no hits at all. Nevertheless I think it would have fared very well in this regard. By the time we reached the target area all remaining fuel was in the eight tanks, which made up the upper half of the fuselage. The wings of the Buccaneer carry no internal fuel and, apart from electrical and hydraulic lines, are virtually solid metal.

Most modern twin-engine fighter-bombers mount both engines side-by-side at the very back of the fuselage. If heat-seeking missiles destroy one then they are likely to destroy both. On the Buccaneer the engines were/are at the front of very long (about fifteen feet), separated jet-pipes; it was therefore highly unlikely that a heat-seeker could get either, let alone both engines. I doubt that battle-damage survival is given much priority in the design of our modern aircraft. I am sure it receives none from politicians or Treasury civil servants. Cost is usually the over-riding issue; it is a very false economy.

Our initial successes resulted in a doubling of our aircraft numbers with an additional six bringing the unit up to twelve aircraft, eighteen aircrews and commensurate extra ground crews. This resulted in the need for more of our first-tourist crews and a resultant dilution of experience. However, there were enough experienced leaders for each mission; riches indeed! I was concerned that the evident anxiety present amongst the Tornado detachment would be transmitted to my crews. Inevitably there was a degree of concern amongst them, but thankfully no hysteria. I am very proud of the Maritime Buccaneer Wing aircrews' performance. They quietly and efficiently got on with the task in hand.

The aircrews walking back from a mission were understandably much happier and relaxed than those walking out. Some of our youngsters on the way out were perplexed to meet Mike Scarffe walking in, looking quite dejected. On asking him why, he said "I was tasked with bombing a disused airfield". After a few seconds to let that sink in he broke into a mischievous grin and added: "Well it is now!"

Our ground crew played a blinder. Albeit we had more engineers than a squadron at home would have – and two SENGOs as well – but the results they achieved were still extremely impressive. So much so that, on at least one occasion at the HQ in Riyadh the general stopped his morning briefing on aircraft serviceability statistics to ask why his briefing staff always emphasised the availability of the Tornados when the statistics for the older Buccaneer and Jaguar were nearly always better. I am not sure how they replied. The Buccaneer serviceability rate in theatre was second only to the Jaguar. We never lacked a spare aircraft at crew-in and the ground crew stoically put up with stressed aircrews' foibles, errors and even rejection of serviceable aircraft when pilots sometimes failed to properly set up the Havequick radio – one being me.

The technical support from Lossiemouth was better than I could have hoped for, in fact it was exemplary. If we had fallen short in our task it would not have been RAF Lossiemouth's fault.

After the ceasefire I received a telephone call from a wing commander on the staff in Riyadh. "The Air Commander wants to know how all his detachment commanders had got on using RAF Germany's Air Staff Instructions – what is your opinion?" I replied that since no one had told me that I was to use any version of Air Staff Instructions I was unable to offer an opinion – I thought we were fighting a war.

The results achieved by the Buccaneer/Tornado cooperation are self-evident. We were responsible for the destruction of twenty-four bridges, fifteen airfields and one large fuel depot and two enemy aircraft were destroyed on the ground.

At our pre-deployment briefings I expressed a sincere wish that we would bring back everyone we took. I got my wish. All came home – that is a more pleasing definition of achievement.

Whilst I did not think that there were any particularly heroic achievements by our people, I believe they made one of the most significant contributions to the RAF's participation in Desert Storm. I was, therefore, very disappointed when our contributions were largely ignored when the post-war decorations were handed out.

That was somewhat remedied a few years after the war when I met General Sir Peter de la Billière at Bentley Priory. I had not previously met him, so I introduced myself as "the commander of the oldest front-line aircraft unit under your command in 1991". His response was: "Young man (I knew I was going to like him!), your aircraft saved the RAF's reputation." And, I have Sir Peter's permission to use that quote. The Buccaneer had more than justified its place in the history books as a 'warbird'.

We returned to a splendid welcome from our families and the local populace who had turned out to greet us – and a month's leave!

CHAPTER TWENTY-TWO

PUSHING THE BUCC
TO THE LIMITS

BENNY BENSON

The scene is 208 Squadron at Lossiemouth in the winter of 1992/93. Amidst the 'routine' maritime tactics sorties, occasional overland low levels, range details, medium and low-level Pavespike sorties, major exercises and the odd live weapon drop, the initial planning for the end of the Buccaneer era has commenced. The decision is made to run two display crews from the Buccaneer Maritime Wing for the final year of the aircraft and the shout goes round for volunteers for a display crew. I throw my name into the ring but, with only about 800 hours on type amidst a vast wealth of experience, I don't hold out much hope. Next thing I know, I'm programmed with the station commander (Jon Ford) for an 'assessment' in the Hunter. Nothing to lose really, so as quite a fan of both the Hunter and of aerobatics I rather enjoy popping up to a patch of clear sky over 'moon country' west of Wick and subjecting the group captain to my best off-the-cuff, and to be honest, fairly aggressive sequence of Hunter aeros using a good 7g for most of the vertical and max rate turn stuff. Quite happy with the overall effect but not sure if the man in the right-hand seat agrees. Still, nothing to lose…

A few weeks later, with my newly-selected display navigator Gary Davies in the back, I'm at 5,000 feet overhead the east coast just north of Montrose, with the 'official' Buccaneer display sequence written on my kneepad, giving it a try. (With HQ 18 Group as the authority there was little leeway – actually there was none – from the same sequence as in previous years. I don't think 18 Group were comfortable at all with the idea of a fast-jet aerobatic display so it was handled the same as the Nimrod display, i.e. the sequence was cast in stone and that was it.)

The whole sequence feels awkward; too big, too loose and, aileron rolls aside, not really that comfortable as I try to avoid any excursions beyond the 'steady note' AOA (angle of attack). We give it a few runs through; trying out some different speeds, angles and pitch attitudes but in the end it doesn't feel particularly great. OK, but just not great. Mind you, not an awful lot of guidance has been acquired beforehand; due to the 'healthy' rivalry between 208 and 12 Squadrons there was just no way that we were asking their experienced display crew (who had been given another season) for detailed advice. We're determined to do it our way and put up a better display than them. (Maybe somewhat foolhardy looking back, but that was just the way it was, as the majority of Buccaneer aircrew will understand only too clearly!)

An airframe (XV864) with sufficient fatigue life is selected for the display season and we get to know her. She flies well; not too much yaw at high speed and with the trims set correctly not excessive adverse aileron yaw/roll-yaw coupling. As the height reduces, it all starts to feel better, and when we're down to 500 feet for the aerobatic bits, and 100 feet for all the other bits, it really starts to make sense.

We make a few decisions on the way ahead; the arrival needs to be as fast and as low as possible within the rules, so that's 100 feet and 570-580 knots; we want a really snappy roll to transition from the low, slow dirty pass to the forty-five-degree angle for the high-angle climb-out, and our experiments show that for that we need 30-10-10 and not a blown 30-20-20 configuration; we want to hold an impressive pitch angle as long as possible, so that means a forty-degree pitch-up holding 30-10-10 until banked, unloaded and descending again; we want a sharp pull into the barrel-roll, so we need to start from as low as possible –100 feet – for the initial pitch; we need the 360-degree max-rate turn to appear level so will have to climb a bit on the outside (level turns apparently appear to descend from a crowd perspective); and we want the best chance of a visible vapour-covered upper wing as we pull up hard to the finishing vertical roll, requiring us to start the pull from crowd centre and accept that the vertical will be achieved to crowd left.

And that's just what we practised. The station commander and OC 208 Squadron supervised from the ATC tower as we smoothed out the rough bits. Apart from the groupie wanting us to use 30-20-20 (we managed to persuade him that 30-10-10 was the best – thanks Sir!) all was well and we settled into a sequence that flowed smoothly, looked pretty good, and took, with practise, about five minutes forty seconds. We could have trimmed it by another twenty seconds or so by reducing speed at various points of the sequence, but as we were permitted six minutes for every display we simply couldn't see the point. Besides, a few knots in the bag are no bad thing when it comes to high AOA low-level display flying. All progressed well, with a series of display practices early in the morning, again after the last wave had landed, in a variety of weathers, over the airfield and also over the bay. Our confidence in the aircraft built steadily – in routine squadron flying I think we all gave the Buccaneer tremendous respect when it came to handling, especially at low speed, and we soon built towards achieving the display aims mentioned above.

The 208 Squadron lineys (ground crew) always enjoyed a good view, especially as we used the disused short runway (the one that ran past the tower) at Lossie and the hard turn and pitch-up from slow speed and dirty happened right over the Squadron's HAS site. They were hard to please though, and weren't slow in giving us the unofficial debrief as soon as we unstrapped. Mind you, what they enjoyed even more was the morning we knocked the JEngO off his pushbike as he was pedalling serenely around the perimeter track on his way to work and we shot over his head at 580 knots and 100 feet on the run-in.

Once we'd cracked the routine, and the station commander and boss were happy, it was off to Kinloss in front of the AOC where a couple of runs through both the full and flat sequences were enough to get us our display authorisation (DA) for the year. That done, we headed straight for Decimomannu to join the rest of the squadron to hone our weaponry skills on Capa Frasca weapons range. Arriving later than the rest, and on a Friday afternoon, had its disadvantages as our DA celebrations, combined with 'first night madness', created scenes that made me cringe for years to come every time I opened the squadron diary. The next day just wasn't funny!

One month on...

......once more around the hold.......check timing with Fat Boy (Gary Davies)....... adjust as required on the outbound leg.....final check of cockpit – fuel quantity, FNA valves, engine instruments, artificial horizons, radalt bug and trims....last careful look at the distant display line, the weather and terrain features......roll out on heading..... final timing check.......1,500ft, 400kts........throttles forward..... locate the display line crowd centre....... 450kts.....steady descent......500kts...... trying to judge 100ft at the airfield boundary.........550kts.......fine tune descent.........570kts.........descend further......100ft radalt.......slight bank towards crowd area......hold the yaw......... 580kts........crowd centre NOW........hard roll left......idle......airbrake full......5g... squeeze 5.5g.....shallow climb......*'roll out THERE'* from Fat Boy.....unload......roll wings level.......pitch 5.5 g.........check.......hard roll left 270 deg......pull right........locate crowd line and centre......adjust the pull......check that speed.......280 kts......change hands on the stick.......aileron gearing to low speed........change hands again......select 15-10-10...... *'cheeses moving'*.....*'cheeses moving'*.........*'cheeses STOPPED'* ......hook down.......240 kts.... gear down.......select flaps 30.......descend.......3 greens...... hook confirmed down.......confirm 30-10-10........roll out.....100 ft again........hold it.......speed back......power coming up......steady note.......hold it there....

.......crowd centre.....NOW....hard roll right with a boot full right rudder.....full power & airbrake in.....hold steady note......don't descend.....*'roll out NOW'*......pause to correct for wind....steady pitch to forty degrees nose-up....check.....gear up.....3 reds......hook up......check lights out.......'1,500'....'2,000'.....roll left....don't pull...... stay unloaded....watch speed....150 kts.....speed increasing......select 0-0-0...*'cheeses moving'*....*'cheeses moving*.....*'cheeses STOPPED'*.... change hands on the stick ...... ailerons to high speed.....change hands again.......confirm clean with Fat Boy...... keep pulling..... still on steady note ....descending.......hold the steady note......hope I've judged this right as can't pull any harder.....for God's sake don't bust the crowd line........

'Dirty' configuration over Mildenhall, 1993.

made it......relax g.....roll out.....360kts.......400kts......100ft.......NOW.....steady pull up......nose above horizon....roll left.....keep it steady.........inverted......check height......check speed......keep rolling......keep pulling.......nicely aligned......... descend....watch for obstacles.......450kts....100ft......quick cockpit scan......*'rolling left'*.........5g.........slight climb..........look for crowd centre.......keep turning....... adjust g for spacing...adjust power a tad....point at crowd centre....420 kts......300 ft...... locate bomb-door switch...... roll door NOW ......check door open rolling in NOW...... hard turn right...... 5.5g.......here comes crowd centre.... ...... keep turning.......gentle climb to 500 ft.....adjust g for wind......padlock on crowd centre again........where's that bloody bomb-door switch.....got it......descend to 300ft......g coming on again to 5.5 ....full power......almost crowd centre....roll bomb door NOW....relax g a tad.... ....check door closed........g back on.......*'roll out THERE'*....

........pitch up...check.....270 deg turn right......pulllllllllllllll.........5.5g.....tight round.. .....lining up on the crowd line again.......500ft, 420kts........adjust power....hold it....... .....rolling NOW.......stick hard over left........anticipate and snap wings level..... let her yaw and settle...adjust heading......check speed....420kts......here comes crowd centre....rolling NOW.....hard right....anticipate 270 deg.....pulllllllllllllll......... power up......5.5g......*'roll out THERE'*......pitch up.......check.....hard roll left 270 deg.....pulllllllllllllllll........back off to 4g.........how's it looking.......squeeze more g to tighten up the turn........descend........450 kts........480 kts.....roll out along crowd line.......500 kts.......520 kts...here comes crowd centre.....check above....pulling NOW......wings level.....5.5g......hold it......transfer eyes to side.....check terrain

1993 display crew, Benny Benson and Gary Davies.

feature.......approaching vertical.....check.....hard roll left....... anticipate..... NOW.... stop roll..... bollocks, we're IMC......glued to IFIS......pullllllllll......roll wings level on horizon......scan cockpit..........breathe!

There you have it. Five minutes and forty seconds of legal hooliganism, in front of thousands, and with (almost) no threat of a bollocking afterwards!

Needless to say, we had a great season, although not without its controversial moments. No real problems for the first display, which, operating from Waddington, was a belter at Brough, the home of the Buccaneer. Apparently we set off all the car park car alarms on the run-in. It was a marvellous location though, surrounded by tall chimneys and buildings on one side and the Humber on the other.

Next up on the Sunday was Londonderry (Eglinton), and one we were very keen to do well for two reasons: firstly, we were opening the show in timed coordination with a celebrity actress, and secondly it had taken not inconsiderable persuasion from 18 Group to let us display in Northern Ireland. We only got the go-ahead after agreeing to carry pre-programmed flare packs due to intelligence of a Stinger SAM threat. Needless to say, a niggling sun-cream allergy (from the stuff the squadron doc gave me at Deci) flared up and made me look like a creature from outer-space, the aircraft hot-started due to a weak Palouste, we ended up in the spare aircraft with far too much fuel, and the VHF radio failed. Not to be outdone by such small obstacles, we did actually make it and open the display but it was an interesting day out. Pride stops me recalling the whole story here, but let's just say that the fuel dump was involved and that after a curtailed routine we popped in to see our Wessex friends in Aldergrove.

Whilst that was pretty much our (my) doing, Fat Boy and I did suffer more than our share of bad luck throughout the season. A very helpful USAF liney managed to blow the electrics up (literally; it took a ground team a week to fix it) with a ground power cart at Mildenhall; we suffered a TRU failure on start at Lossie for the Den Helder (Holland) display, and that after arranging a VC10 tanker bracket to refuel on the way home; the clag at St Mawgan limited us to a couple of 100-foot passes from an ILS approach, we never even saw St Athan after completing a low-level abort on the run-in over the Bristol Channel; and an airbrake structural problem at Lossie grounded the fleet just after we landed in Belgium for what was to be the last public Buccaneer display. We watched with long faces from the beer tent before being rescued by Hunter later that week. After staying current throughout the winter I even missed out on the display for the 'Farewell to the Buccaneer' bash at Lossie in early 1994 due to a dose of chicken pox, but at least recovered in time to make the Diamond Nine.

The positives outweighed the negatives by a long way though, highlights including waking the entire squadron (plus thoroughly cheesing-off the married patch and triggering a flood of complaints) in Akrotiri with a couple of early morning practices during the annual night tactics detachment. However, my abiding memory has to be of looking down on the Rock of Gibraltar after completing the vertical roll and roll off the top at the Air Day there. Bloody marvellous. And you know what, despite the gruelling punishment she took in every display, the old girl never let us down in the air one bit; I only recall one 'hairy-legs' on a practice at Lossie for the RCDS visit. I often think about the fact that although quite a few have flown the Bucc, including some valiantly in war and some fearlessly from a pitching deck, not many got to really experience her at the extremes of the handling envelope. I regard myself as bloody lucky. Here's to the Last of the Few.

CHAPTER TWENTY-THREE
FINAL YEARS

RICK PHILLIPS

From an early age I had always wanted to become a fighter pilot. My dream was subsequently refined when I decided that the most exciting way to accomplish the aim would be to join the Fleet Air Arm flying from our (then) fleet of aircraft carriers. Sadly, politics hindered my plans; in the late 1960s, the future of FAA fixed-wing aviation looked bleak when the proposed new aircraft carrier, CVA-01, was cancelled by the Labour government of the day and RN flying training became rotary wing only. Not wishing to become a helicopter pilot, I decided to join the RAF, and assumed that my ambition of becoming a carrier pilot would have to remain a childhood dream.

Having joined the RAF in April 1968 with the hope of flying the TSR2, the politicians once more upset my plans as this too was cancelled, and so I set my sights on its replacement, the F-111K. This was also axed, but this time the political cloud had a silver lining – the RAF was to receive the Buccaneer Mark 2, already much loved by FAA crews who flew it. I reset my sights, and was fortunate to be posted to the Buccaneer, serving in its early Cold War days in RAF Germany. During this tour on XV Squadron, our existing aircraft carriers received an extension of service and the FAA needed more fixed-wing aircrew to man their Phantoms, Buccaneers and Gannets. I volunteered for secondment at the earliest opportunity. After some pre-carrier familiarisation training, I joined 809 NAS, the FAA's last Buccaneer squadron, in May 1977.

After a very exciting eighteen months afloat, I returned to the RAF and a tour with 12 Squadron, initially at Honington until we 'disbanded' for a few weeks in November 1980, and then reformed again at Lossiemouth, which could have been purpose built for the Buccaneer. Flying on a front-line maritime squadron from such a magnificent location could not be bettered in my opinion. I therefore had mixed feelings when my appointer suddenly announced out of the blue that I was posted to fly the F-111, as I feared such a move could signal the end of my Buccaneer flying, a hard decision for sure. He was shocked when I replied that I would have to think abut it, such was the professional pleasure of being on 'Shiny 12', a really great team who certainly led the field. There then followed a very happy tour in the USA before returning in mid-1986 to be a flight commander on 208 Squadron back at Lossiemouth.

In recent years, tactics had been based on the anti-radar and TV versions of the Martel anti-shipping missile, which provided a stand-off capability. However both missiles had their limitations and were coming to the end of their operational life, particularly the TV version.

Another significant limitation in developing more effective tactics was the antiquated nav/attack system that the navigators had to handle. Over the years, it had become increasingly obvious that it was the weak link in the otherwise outstanding capability of the aircraft. All this changed in the mid-1980s when MOD finally found enough money to modify the fleet with a new nav/attack system based around an inertial navigation platform. With the impending introduction of a new stand-off anti-shipping missile, the Sea Eagle, such an update to the navigator's kit was essential.

This new capability sent the back-seat QWIs into ecstasy and they beavered away at how best to optimise their new toys as the rest of us started devising co-ordinated attack tactics. These were based on the requirement to destroy the Soviet navy's Kirov class battle-cruiser, the largest (non-aircraft carrier) warship afloat. The probability of kill (PK) derived by the Air Warfare Centre staffs dictated that a total of twenty-four Sea Eagle missiles were required to ensure penetration of the defence systems and to destroy the high-value target. Thereafter we embarked upon a period of work-up training with Sea Eagle, culminating in declaring each squadron operational by day with two six-ship teams.

Soon after this declaration, I was tasked with putting together, training and leading a constituted six-ship team to carry out deep-water attacks at night. Initially, I had a great deal of trouble finding willing volunteers for this task, not surprising really, when you consider that each sortie was to be two hours plus of close formation in the dark at 300 feet, with night tanking thrown in to spice things up. Mike Scarffe was my trusted navigator for this period, and together we worked up a sound team, with Tony Lunnon-Wood and Pete Binham as our deputy lead. Some of the debriefs were almost as tiring as the sorties themselves, but the 'youngsters' finally appreciated the professional satisfaction of success in September 1988 when, on Exercise Teamwork, the culmination of our efforts was a copybook night attack which we finished by flying through on the missile profile onto the target. We were totally undetected until a visual sighting by the target ship. The whole sortie had been ZIPLIP (radio silence) until that point, including the air refuelling with the Victor tankers. It felt good to have done it and I doubt this was ever repeated. Tony Lunnon-Wood summed it up when he commented, "the age of the silent ship killer had well and truly arrived. We had the ability to project our personality over vast distances in total silence and deliver weapons with devastating accuracy." I could not sum it up any better.

Pavespike laser-designator pod and Paveway bomb.

Over the next few months we perfected our techniques at very low level over the sea and were confident that we could do serious damage to an enemy surface action group. Then, one night in a bar whilst on detachment in Gibraltar, we witnessed on TV the start of the first Gulf War. I well recall the swift walk back to the officers' mess at North Front, where we had received the signal 'White Cliffs', our coded instruction to return immediately to Lossiemouth.

Just a few weeks earlier, the AOC had told us it was unlikely that we would be needed. Now we had got the call to fly out to the Gulf and operate at medium level and overland. This, surely, must be one of the most classic examples of the old adage of 'the flexibility of air power'.

I had often said that if I ever had to go to war, then the Buccaneer would be my first choice aircraft. I was not wrong. I had total faith in our magnificent aeroplane. One particularly satisfying sortie for me and my navigator Harry Hyslop, was the demolition of a primary target which had been missed by one of our Tornados. (They seemed to have trouble at times getting their LGBs into the laser 'basket' and their bombs often fell short.) The night before this particular attack, being very conscious of the criticality of this forty-five degree basket (an imaginary inverted cone into which the bomb had to be released in order for it to reach the target before it ran out of energy), Harry and I invited our staff QWI advisor, Terry Yarrow, to our hotel room for a wee dram. We then asked him to do some 'back of a fag packet' calculations, to see if we could go for a steeper dive angle, nearer sixty degrees, in order to guarantee getting our own bombs in the basket. This of course was outside the aircraft's Release to Service limits, but we were not going to get that changed overnight. We concluded over the next dram that the reason could only be due to the test pilots at Boscombe Down not having trialled it. After a third dram, Terry assured us that the bomb would release with no problems, so we carried out our own 'trial' the next day. It was a resounding success, which we subsequently went on to repeat every sortie thereafter. One undesirable aspect of the steep dive was seeing the flak from below as well as from above. After that, I realised that dropping a 28lb practice bomb at Tain would never be quite the same.

One very 'unreal' aspect of this war was that at Bahrain, where all Buccaneers were based together with Jaguars and some Tornados, we were accommodated in luxury hotels, with the Diplomat Hotel used exclusively for Buccaneer and Jaguar aircrew. This bizarre arrangement created a magnificent camaraderie between us; a distinct internal 'attitude switch' within the brain had to be thrown each time we left the hotel in casual planters attire for the short transit to the airfield where we would don our operational desert flying gear. At that time there were no government issue hot-weather flying suits, so we had all trooped off to a bespoke tailor on arrival in theatre to have the best of flying suits tailor made for us overnight. Many of us had a couple of civilian suits tailored to Saville Row standard and fitted in our spare time too.

Going back to the hotel after a successful bombing sortie over Iraq seemed almost improper, especially having witnessed from above the spectacle of swathes of our British armour advancing towards Kuwait city, trailing plumes of dust clearly visible from above, a sight I shall never forget and which stirred deep patriotic pride. However, being Buccaneer aircrew, each night we drank to our valiant 'pongos' with a few drams after dinner in our rooms. I had taken the wise precaution to put three cases of malt whisky up the back hatch of my aircraft when stowing our kit at Lossiemouth, such was the excellent luggage-carrying capability of our mighty steed (I even included water bottled from my own spring on the hill at home!). The Air Staff certainly got the basing option for Buccaneers and Jaguars correct; Saudi Arabia being 'dry' would have been totally unsuitable.

Of interest, the medics had prescribed sleeping pills to assist us, with express instructions NOT to take with alcohol owing to the danger of not waking up. I am pleased to report they were wrong – the mixture worked admirably on all occasions, and we always flew afterwards with great success.

Throughout the period that is now referred to as Gulf War 1 the risks were very real, as we were forcibly reminded by the tragic losses of some of our fellow Tornado crews. It was a pleasure to join them in their hotel after flying, especially I recall on a Tuesday night when a seafood special in the Sheraton surpassed our own excellent cuisine. However, that all changed once Saddam Hussein opened the oil wells at Basra directly into the Gulf. Local seafood was 'off' for the rest of the war, but soon returned a year later despite the pessimistic forecasts of the environmental marine biologists.

I was so proud of the service and reliability of the Buccaneer whilst in the Gulf, that I decided to write a letter between sorties to Roy Boot, the designer of the aircraft and who, over a very long period of time, had shown the greatest interest in the aircrew and how we operated the aircraft. I wanted to thank him most sincerely on behalf of all of us for his sterling design efforts, and to make sure he was in no doubt whatsoever as to our profound love of the aeroplane we flew and of its success. For some reason, perhaps political, we were rarely mentioned on the press releases on TV at the time, as the Tornado had to have the limelight, on occasion by using our video films without mention of the origin. By complete coincidence, my letter was delivered to his home before breakfast on his seventy-fifth birthday; he would later tell me over a glass of beer with a tear in his eye that my letter was the finest birthday present he had ever received.

Having returned from the Gulf another exciting challenge came my way when I was tasked to lead the Buccaneer contingent in the 1993 Queens' Birthday Flypast over London. This would also coincide with the Buccaneer's last major appearance on the public stage before the draw down of the force.

Initially I was surprised that the choice of lead pilot had fallen to me; I had assumed that it would be 'grabbed' by someone of greater seniority with career enhancement prospects. However, having led flypasts at a number of recent major anniversaries I suppose the choice should not have been totally unexpected. I had always taken such leadership tasks very seriously, but I am compelled to record that the burden was always a professional pleasure. With such a great team of aircrew behind me I could always rely on them to get it right. Thankfully, the Buccaneer force had always been totally ruthless during the selection and training of aircrew and those unable to meet our exacting standards were weeded out at the earliest opportunity. We never accepted 'training risk candidates', unlike some other aircraft types in later years, where some aircrew were 'carried' in the hope they might improve – a huge distraction for those in the other cockpit as well as the leaders and supervisors.

The first major hurdle was the briefing I was tasked to give to the AOC. This had to be a maximum length of twenty minutes including question time. My first attempt was interrupted by the AOC after just twenty seconds when he said: "Rick, you are going to brief me on the ENTIRE flypast, and not just the Buccaneer element, aren't you?" This I was not prepared for. I was then given just four hours at Northwood to prepare another brief, this time with me as the overall leader of the entire formation including the Victors and the '75' Hawk formation bringing up the rear. I soon realised why my navigator (Nigel Maddox) had declined to attend this initial brief with me.

Fortunately, my 'old' nav from the Gulf, Harry Hyslop, was on the staff at group HQ and we spent the remaining time drawing up holding patterns, timing legs and, of course, new slides to suit the revised brief. (No computers or Power Point in those days!) The other element leaders were all unavailable on the phone for advice, save one Victor navigator, who we located on a golf course in Lincolnshire and he alone gave us the essentials of the Victor holding speeds etc. The brief went well and there were no questions from the AOC. There was one however from his chief of staff, which was slightly complex. I was putting the relevant slide up when, to my surprise, the AOC stood up and answered the question perfectly on my behalf. He had clearly not only listened but more importantly, had fully understood my brief. He was to supervise my performance from the roof of Admiralty Arch, so no additional pressure.

Veteran Buccaneer observer, Steve Park, retires from the Royal Navy.
L-R: Nigel Yeldham, Steve Park, Bill Cope, Rick Phillips.

I decided to mount the Buccaneer formation from RAF Manston, to give us the close proximity to the city and cut transits to a minimum for the practices. One essential event for me was a helicopter trip down the route a week before the flypast. This was invaluable, and to this day all the key checkpoints I selected are glued into the brain. Thereafter, all the practices went well, including an exercise to replace one of the aircraft in the formation, chosen by me at random, with one of the airborne spares to make sure the plan worked. It was a wonderful sight to see all twenty Buccaneers (we flew four airborne spares) with wings folded plus a Hunter as 'whipper in' as they followed me off the ramp at Manston.

Come the great day, before the briefing, which would be attended by some of the media, I wanted to be sure of the weather. I had been the victim of other people's decisions on these big flypasts before. I had written into the operation order that the lead crew was to do this check, consequently when I briefed, I had only just left the route and had a firm feel for the situation. We checked in and taxied out on time with all aircraft serviceable. A huge crowd of well-wishers waved us off as we taxied to the runway, and we gave them a flypast in diamond sixteen before departing.

Thereafter it was on track and on time the whole way, with Nigel Maddox doing an outstanding job whilst I concentrated on smooth flying and, most importantly, the lookout for 'puddle jumpers'. Sure enough, one pitched up right on the nose some twenty miles

Rick Phillips completes 6,000 hours 'fast-jet' time. L-R: Mike Scarffe, Harry Hyslop, Rick Phillips, Ed Golden (acting OC Ops), Tim Courton.

out from the palace, with a cameraman filming us out of the side door as we flew straight at him – just what you do not need when leading a large unwieldy formation. The palace was overflown on time, and the formation (call-sign Blackburn) turned for Coningsby, where a station open day was being held. Unfortunately, a combination of bad weather and air traffic control meant that we had to turn away and recover to Lossiemouth for a final sixteen-ship flypast. Only then did I realise what an enormous strain I had been under; to have made any errors at all on such a sortie was unthinkable. I was relieved that it had all gone so well, which was the result of sound planning, training, excellent aircrew and of course a fantastic aeroplane.

Soon after this memorable event, I was again fortunate and was tasked to deliver a Buccaneer to British Aerospace's airfield at Brough, the birthplace of our aircraft. Previously Buccaneers had only flown out of nearby Holme-on-Spalding-Moor after major parts of the aircraft had been moved by road before re-assembly at Holme. Again, Nigel Maddox accompanied me on this rewarding and significant task. There was intense opposition to the flight on safety grounds (the runway is extremely short with an office block at the far end) so I was pleased to deliver an example of their finest product for display and dedicated as a memorial to those who had sadly lost their lives in the early development years – we owed them so much for our years of professional pleasure and satisfaction.

By now the end of the Buccaneer in RAF service was in sight and preparations were made for the final 'Buccaneer Bash'. I had personally decided to leave the squadron just before the very end. I had flown a few dignitaries in the back seat already (it was no surprise at all to see so many wanting to experience such a unique aircraft as we prepared to disband) but I found a perfect way to have my last flight and so bring to an end my long association with an aircraft of such fine qualities. I was determined to finish with a fitting sortie that would be fun, memorable, but more importantly benefit our heritage and style.

The FAA Museum had asked me to ferry a Buccaneer to RNAS Yeovilton. I was only too pleased to help out with such a worthy cause until I discovered that the airframe they had already 'bought' was not only in storage at Shawbury, but it had a maintenance serial number. Despite being flyable, it could not be flown as a military aircraft. I did some rapid talking with some faceless wonders in the Disposals Branch of MOD, and was fortunate enough to 'acquire' a current flying airframe chosen from the list of those soon to be scrapped.

Thus it was that I flew XV333 on a most memorable last sortie with my navigator Phil Walters from Lossiemouth to Yeovilton on a clear day in March 1994. I doubt much of the two-hour sortie was spent above fifty feet, apart from a selection of our old air display sequence for the (traditional for us!) benefit of the lightship keeper and crew of the Inner Dowsing, and a visit to a farm airstrip in Norfolk just for old times sake. A subsequent (wrongly filed) air miss by a cross-Channel hovercraft out of Ramsgate and a close encounter with some huge seagulls under the cliffs at Beachy Head completed the scene, prior to our customary low-level flypast, break and landing at Yeovilton.

As I write these closing words I realise that this magnificent aircraft has become a huge part of my life. That said, I am of course no different from all those other Buccaneer aircrew who have been equally fortunate to have had this unique aircraft create a bond between us and an enduring friendship that remains to this day and will continue. I know of no other aircraft that has formed such a band of brothers who are always ready to recall with such lively passion the joy of having been incredibly privileged to fly the Buccaneer.

CHAPTER TWENTY-FOUR
REFLECTIONS

GRAHAM SMART AND GRAHAM PITCHFORK

To bring the story of the Buccaneer Boys to a close, Graham Smart and Graham Pitchfork, with a combined total of thirty-six years and 4,000 flying hours on the aircraft, offer a few observations.

GRAHAM SMART

Whilst fighting my way back to fitness after an argument with a parachute, I was enjoying myself as an OCTU flight commander at RAF South Cerney pondering what flying lay ahead for me and how I could avoid the threat of heading for the V-Force.

A notice appeared asking for volunteers to fly Buccaneers with the Royal Navy and pilots were to be QFIs and Canberra experienced. As I qualified on both counts, and this seemed about as far away from the V-Force as one could get, my name went in. The plot, as I understood it, was that after the Buccaneer tour the TSR2 would be coming into service and that was where the initial RAF Buccaneer crews would be heading – all good news.

So that was how, after parking my young family in Malta, Graham Pitchfork and I were the first of the many to arrive at Lossiemouth not quite knowing what to expect. Little could I foresee then that there would be no TSR2 or F-111 and that the Buccaneer would be an integral part of my life for the next eighteen years or so, nor that I would have the enduring delight, pleasure and honour to fly operationally and instruct with the navy, be the Buccaneer member of the Central Tactics and Trials Organisation, be the chief flying instructor at the RAF Buccaneer OCU, command 12 Squadron flying in the maritime role

Graham Pitchfork and Graham Smart.

that the aircraft was designed to fulfil and finally to command RAF Laarbruch in Germany – home to two Buccaneer strike/attack squadrons (XV and 16) and a Jaguar recce squadron (2 Sqn).

But all that was way ahead, first the small task of coming to grips with the Buccaneer Mark 1 and its Gyron Junior engines. My first impression of the Fleet Air Arm was of an apparently rather care-free approach to life, particularly in contrast to the RAF where on occasions we tended to take ourselves rather too seriously. I'm sure that this in part was what made the operational bond between the two services very straightforward and made the initial volunteers for exchange duty with the RN feel very much at home.

Much has been written about the aircraft in previous chapters; suffice to say that whilst the Mark 1 was a joy to fly, the engines made life very interesting during the stages of flight when they were working at their hardest, i.e. take-off and landing. Of my five familiarisation flights I experienced enforced single-engine landings on Fams 1, 3 and 5, events almost inexorably leading to a day a year later when I had to abandon one during the Beira Patrol whilst serving with 800 Squadron on board *Eagle*. As recorded earlier, the introduction of the Mark 2 with Rolls-Royce Spey engines ended all that nonsense.

Carrier flying was generally a joy – day deck operations in reasonable weather with a diversion handy if required were akin to licensed hooliganism. Night ops with no diversion and a moving deck were a different matter and very sweaty! Deck flying, plus the demanding maritime environment that was 12 Squadron's domain and the rigours of overland operations (very low, very fast and very close together by day and by night) give some clue as to why the Buccaneer Boys are a bit different.

The aircraft itself was all British and ideally suited for the task that it was designed for, both marks were a joy to fly and operationally very effective. It engendered in its crews a fierce loyalty and affection – more so than the normal aircrew bonding with other types. I have been lucky enough to have flown a number of aircraft in similar roles, the F-111, Phantom, Jaguar and Tornado among them – none flew as well as the Buccaneer and in my experience none produce the misty-eyed look among its aircrew that the Buccaneer does.

The roles the aircraft operated in were another factor be it over the sea or overland in Germany, Norway, the Middle East or South Africa. They were all onerous ones, demanding of the crews involved total concentration and reliance on each other in an aircraft fitted with navigation aids and electronic equipment that are best described as 'steam driven'. The crew were therefore totally reliant on their skills and complete trust of each other to get the job done. There was nowhere to hide as a Buccaneer pilot or observer/navigator. Everyone knew the worth of everyone else and any not up to the job for whatever reason, were necessarily weeded out and quite a few were.

Of course, this almost 'band of brothers' feeling was enhanced by the limited size of the force and we all knew each other. This exclusiveness was enhanced by many lengthy detachments by all the squadrons – no wife or OC Admin to watch over you! The result was a great number of escapades best not gone into here but some that gave the odd squadron or station commander a slight headache – I never did discover how twelve of my blokes together with all their kit managed to break a hotel lift in Denmark built for four.

So there it is – what a marvellous scenario. A really wonderful aircraft, a small force operating in very demanding roles and environments, a two-man crew totally reliant on each other, some exciting and sometimes exotic detachments and above all a demand for complete professional competence. Is it any wonder that the Buccaneer Boys are a bit different?

––––––––––

GRAHAM PITCHFORK

Heading north out of Elgin on the familiar road to Lossiemouth my mind was full of many great memories of the four years of life spent at this northern outpost. However, this time my pleasure at seeing the familiar lighthouse and the fantastic panorama stretching across and beyond the Moray Firth was tinged with sadness.

It was 25 March 1994 and the Buccaneer fraternity was drawn to the RAF station to join in the ceremonies to bid a fond farewell to our cherished aircraft. A few hundred colleagues and their families were gathering to ensure that we said good-bye in an appropriate manner. An amazing weekend that will live in the memory forever was about to unfold.

After appropriate greetings with countless chums and an evening of reminiscing in the familiar surroundings of the mess bar, we gathered the following morning at the dispersal

The last of the Buccaneer Boys (CO Wg Cdr Nigel Huckings).

area to be met by the sight of eight Buccaneers in an immaculate line up. It was the first of many stirring sights and events that day and it was clear that the last generation of Buccaneer Boys were determined to go out in style.

OC 208 Squadron, Wg Cdr Nigel Huckins, had the brilliant idea of painting the eight aircraft in the markings of all the RAF squadrons but his masterstroke was to, secretly, have one aircraft finished in the full 809 Naval Air Squadron livery. This did not go down well with the C-in-C once he discovered the plot but it was too late.

Nigel's brief to his crews was simple, "lots of panache and style and an immaculate formation flypast, then we break up for the airfield attack when we will make lots of noise and stay low. Any questions?" He taxied out at the head in the 809 Squadron aircraft, another masterstroke which drew huge applause from the large gathering as the eight aircraft taxied to the end of Runway 23.

After a series of immaculate flypasts, the rules appeared to go out of the window for what was the very last official flight of the mighty Buccaneer. A series of 'airfield attacks' from every direction then followed. Having witnessed, and participated in, countless other 'attacks' over the years, this final show was spectacular beyond words and will live long in the memory. After forming up again for a final flypast followed by a perfect run-in and break, the aircraft taxied in through the crowds, turned into line, folded wings on the leader's command and then sixteen Spey engines wound down in unison. The silence was deafening and even the Buccaneer hard men in the large gathering were observed with a tear in their eye.

Standing on the airfield it was a moment for reflection when countless memories flooded back. One's thoughts turned to the colleagues we had lost in all three services, to the comradeship, the professionalism and the excitement of operating the Buccaneer.

There had been setbacks and I could think of numerous examples of how the Buccaneer fraternity had responded to them and quickly regained our operational capability. To me, this was never more apparent than the reaction after the tragic accident at Nellis AFB in February 1980 in which we lost two of the best, Ken Tait and 'Rusty' Ruston. The indestructible Buccaneer had suffered a fatigue failure in the wing and the whole force was grounded. The unthinkable had happened and there was much speculation that we might have seen the last of our aircraft.

The British Aerospace team at Brough conducted exhaustive tests and discovered the problem and identified a remedy. In the meantime, with our future still in doubt, additional Hunter aircraft were obtained and each of the squadrons were allocated a number, including some Hunter 6s for the UK-based units. For 208 Squadron and my two (ex Hunter) flight commanders, this was an enjoyable return to the Hunter days of old but this time a navigator was their boss! For almost four months, the squadron ground crew had a focus and we operated normally and, with the exception of dropping weapons, we flew the same Buccaneer profiles with the two-seaters, which were invaluable for keeping the navigators up to speed.

So, when the Buccaneer was cleared to fly again in August, all the squadrons were ready and soon regained full operational capability. This was an immense tribute to the air and ground crews and also to our masters at 1 Group and the engineers at Brough who provided essential support. For those who doubted that the Buccaneer would ever be the same again, they underestimated the determination, skill and dedication of all those who were part of the Buccaneer family and their achievements over the next fourteen years speak volumes for all those privileged to be a Buccaneer Boy.

After this moment of reflection, the weekend continued. We enjoyed the company of our faithful and highly-skilled ground crew with some, like many of the aircrew, having served with the Buccaneer force for most of their careers. The evening functions reminded us of the comradeship and immense fun that had enriched our times together and, amongst the immense enjoyment of the occasion, there was a deep inner feeling that a massive chapter in our lives was closing. And it was a very reflective, and sad, crowd that headed south a couple of days later.

The events had left such an indelible mark on most of us; we vowed that we must stay in touch. A few weeks later I received a telephone call from David Herriot indicating that he was planning to set up a Buccaneer Aircrew Association with the question, "how about it?" Within a few weeks we had mustered a membership of a few hundred from all elements of the Buccaneer world, including the aircrew from Blackburns and British Aerospace who had done so much to develop the aircraft. We persuaded our two most senior 'boys' to be our president and vice-president. Air Chief Marshal Sir Michael Knight, a former station commander at Laarbruch, took on the mantle of president with Vice-Admiral Sir Ted Anson, 'Mr Buccaneer' to all of us, becoming our vice-president. A Buccaneer (XX 901, a Gulf War veteran) was saved from the scrap man, for a mere five grand, and was safely housed pending identifying a final home for it. Two years later it left by road for the Yorkshire Air Museum where it is on permanent display resplendent in its Gulf War colours and with a wide range of armament 'acquired' from some unsuspecting donors, including MOD.

The seeds of staying in touch had, in fact, already been sown. During the 1980s, under the ebullient stewardship of David Wilby, a number of us had been meeting up in early December at a London hostelry for the 'Buccaneer Blitz' and by 1994 this annual event was well established and a must for all those who could find an excuse for a 'meeting' in London. Potential gate crashers had to run the gauntlet of volunteer off-duty RAF policemen patrolling the adjoining street. Soon the Nag's Head in Belgravia was bursting at the seams and we moved to more spacious London accommodation, courtesy of the Royal Navy. Over the years, attendance has grown and the Blitz is a permanent feature in the lives of the Buccaneer Boys. To that we have now added a biennial 'Ladies Night' at one of our old haunts. Nostalgia, banter, rising voices and the old spirit, which appears not to have declined despite the advancing years, all abound.

The solidarity of the Buccaneer fraternity is amply illustrated by the venues and attendance as we make regular pilgrimages back to Yeovilton, Honington and Lossiemouth. After a memorable occasion dining under the wing of Concorde at Yeovilton in April 2010 to celebrate the fiftieth anniversary of the Buccaneer's first flight, seventy of us with wives and partners headed for South Africa to join our colleagues of the SAAF to participate in joint celebrations of the aircraft's milestone.

The emotional, exciting and stimulating weekend in Pretoria matched anything that had gone before and graphically illustrated why we in the Buccaneer world think we are special. The mixture of informality, fun and the formal, spread over four days, captured everything that is so dear to all of us. General Jan van Loggerenberg, a former CO of 24 Squadron and chief of the SAAF echoed all our feelings when, in his formal address, he spoke of "the brotherhood of the Buccaneer world".

As we get a little greyer and conversations now include topics such as hip replacements, by-pass operations etc, the spirit that brought us all together still burns bright. Our twice-yearly newsletter, attendance at the Blitz, annual golf meetings and various other informal gatherings in the UK and in South Africa, merely cement the comradeship that was shaped by the biggest influence in all our lives.

The Buccaneer – the last All-British Bomber

SENIOR BUCCANEER BOYS REMEMBER

"It was not so much the Buccaneer itself but the way of life that went with it. Big squadrons, a lot of aircrew, splendid engineering people, a challenging task by day and night, plenty of low flying and weaponry – a big honest brute of an aircraft that never let us down."

Rear Admiral Roger Dimmock, CO 801 Squadron, SNO RAF Honington

"Whilst it was always a thrill to fly the new Tornado, the Buccaneer in those days flew further, faster and lower than any other strike/attack aircraft. Six years of magical flying."

Air Vice-Marshal Peter Harding, OC 12 Squadron,
Station Commander RAF Honington

"It is more years than I care to remember since my last flight in a Buccaneer, yet there are still times when my thoughts turn to the thrill of so many flights in that great aircraft. What a privileged lot we were!"

Lieutenant General Jan van Loggerenberg,
OC 24 (SAAF) Squadron and Chief of the SAAF

"I was associated with the Buccaneer for over twelve years. I look back with the happiest of memories of all the outstanding aviators with whom I was privileged to fly, both navy and air force. The loyalty the Buccaneer generated was unique in my experience."

Rear Admiral Mike Cole, 700Z Flight, 801 and 736 Squadrons

"On retirement, I spent more than a few hours in misty-eyed reflection on my career's noteworthy memories. My thoughts kept centering back to the three fantastic years I spent at Honington on exchange flying as a Buccaneer navigator."

Major General Scott Bergren USAF, 237 OCU

"In my view the two-man team reigns supreme and the quality of crew co-operation developed in the Buccaneer world became the 'gold standard' to be copied elsewhere. Why was my tour on XV Squadron so special? It was the people."

Air Vice-Marshal Bob O'Brien, XV Squadron

"The Buccaneer spirit lives on in South Africa. The spirit encountered amongst former Buccaneer aircrew appears to be stronger than that associated with any other aircraft type. Well, this is what we believe and who is going to challenge us?"

Colonel Neil Napier, 24 (SAAF) Squadron

"I am deeply grateful to all those observers who have contributed to make my assignment with the Fleet Air Arm the most rewarding period of my aeronautical life."

Rear Admiral Jean-Claude Blanvillain, French Navy, 800 Squadron

"Work hard, play hard is an enduring motto for most air forces, and there is no doubt in my mind that the Buccaneer force exemplified this in full measure whether ashore or afloat. But it did so with a feeling of affection for the aircraft that I have not sensed to the same degree elsewhere."

Air Marshal Sir Peter Norriss, XV Squadron, 237 OCU, OC 16 Squadron

THE BUCCANEER BOYS

IN ORDER OF APPEARANCE

Sir Michael Knight
Sir 'Mike' Knight started his RAF career as a National Service pilot and later commanded a Canberra squadron in Cyprus. He was OC Strike Wing at RAF Tengah, Singapore before converting to the Buccaneer prior to his appointment as the station commander at RAF Laarbruch in December 1973. Later he was the AOC 1 Group when RAF Honington came under his command and his involvement with the Buccaneer continued when he was appointed as the senior air staff officer at HQ Strike Command before serving on the Air Force Board as the Air Member for Supply and Organisation. After serving as the UKMILREP to NATO in Brussels, he retired in 1989. Throughout the eighteen-year existence of the Buccaneer Aircrew Association, he has been its dynamic president.

Graham Pitchfork
Graham Pitchfork trained as a navigator at the RAF College Cranwell before serving on a Canberra photographic reconnaissance squadron in Germany. In April 1965 he started a three-year exchange tour with the Fleet Air Arm and spent a year with 800 Squadron embarked in *Eagle* before becoming an instructor on 736 Squadron. Back in the RAF, he served two tours on Buccaneers at Honington before being appointed as OC 208 Squadron in July 1979. After tours at MOD and as Director of the Department of Air Warfare at RAF Cranwell, he was the station commander at RAF Finningley. His final appointment was as Director of Intelligence (Commitments) in the MOD. He retired in 1994 and is chairman of the Buccaneer Aircrew Association.

Bill Ryce
Bill Ryce flew Seahawks and Scimitars, including operations during the Suez crisis, before becoming one of the first Royal Navy pilots to fly the Buccaneer. He served with 700Z Flight (the Intensive Flying Trials Unit) before embarked service with 801 Squadron in *Victorious*. His final appointment was as an instructor with 736 Squadron. He left the Royal Navy in 1966 to pursue a career in civil aviation, initially on the Vickers Viscount with BEA (later part of BA), but thereafter mostly on Boeing aircraft. He spent twenty-two years with Britannia Airways and most of that as a training captain. He finished his

flying career with Air Seychelles, once again as a training captain and retired just before his sixty-second birthday.

David Howard

After six years seaman service, David Howard was commissioned and trained as a pilot. He flew Seahawks, including operations over Suez, and then converted to the Scimitar. He qualified as an air warfare instructor (AWI) before becoming an instructor on the AWI training squadron. In 1965 he trained on the Buccaneer before becoming senior pilot of 800 Squadron. He was the CO of 736 Squadron followed by command of 809 Squadron both at Lossiemouth. After serving as captain of HMS *Lincoln* during the Second Icelandic Cod War, he was commander (air) at RNAS Yeovilton. He served with SACLANT before retiring in 1984 after thirty-seven years service.

Theo de Munnink

Theo de Munnink joined the SAAF in 1957 and trained as a navigator serving on Canberras and Venturas before becoming one of the first two SAAF navigators to train on the Buccaneer at Lossiemouth and a founder member of 24 Squadron. He later served on Shackletons and was an instructor at the Air Navigation School. Amongst his staff appointments he served at Maritime Command and was the Director of Intelligence at Air Force Headquarters. His final appointment was as OC Southern Air Command in the Cape. He retired in 1992.

Anton de Klerk

Anton de Klerk joined the SAAF in 1960 and trained as a navigator. After attending the Military Academy he served on Canberras with 12 Squadron before travelling to Lossiemouth in 1965 to be one of the first SAAF crews to convert to the Buccaneer. After service with 24 Squadron he was second-in-command of the SAAF Air Navigation School. He served in military intelligence and was the officer commanding the SAAF College. He was the personal assistant to the Secretary of Defence before retiring in 2006.

Tom Eeles

After training as a pilot at the RAF College, Cranwell, Tom Eeles served on a Canberra bomber squadron in Germany. He was one of the first RAF pilots to serve on exchange with the Fleet Air Arm converting to the Buccaneer in 1966. He joined 801 Squadron and was embarked in *Victorious* and *Hermes* before becoming an instructor on 736 Squadron. He attended CFS and trained as a QFI before returning to the Buccaneer world to complete a tour on 12 Squadron and three on 237 OCU, culminating in 1984 when he was appointed as the chief instructor. He later served at the Central Flying School and was the station commander at RAF Linton-on-Ouse. He retired in 1997 and then served as a reservist on Cambridge University Air Squadron for ten years. He is vice-chairman of the Buccaneer Aircrew Association.

David Mulinder
David Mulinder joined the RAF in 1964 after flying night fighters and a tour as a flying instructor in the RCAF. He was a QFI at Acklington and then left for Cyprus to fly Canberra bombers with 32 Squadron. He was a founder member when 12 Squadron reformed at Honington with Buccaneers in October 1969. He completed two tours on 237 OCU, first as the chief flying instructor and then as its chief instructor. He later served on the air staff in RAF Germany and in NATO before retiring in 1988. For almost ten years he was an instructor on the RN Grading Flight at Plymouth.

Al Beaton
Alasdair Beaton joined the RAF in 1966 and after completing flying training he was posted to No. 4 RAF Buccaneer Course on 736 Squadron as one of the first two RAF first-tourist pilots. He joined 12 Squadron at Honington followed by a second tour at Laarbruch on 16 Squadron. In 1976 he was posted as a QFI at Valley instructing on the Hunter and the Hawk. He had a third tour on the Buccaneer, initially on 12 Squadron then as a flight commander on 208 Squadron. With over 2,000 hours flying the Buccaneer he served at the Maritime Tactics School, HMS Dryad before retiring from the RAF in 1984 to become the CO of 11 Squadron, Qatar Emiri Air Force, and eventually a second career in the airlines.

Sir David Cousins
After graduating from the RAF College, Cranwell, David Cousins flew Lightnings before embarking on his long career on Buccaneers, which was almost all spent at Laarbruch. A founder member of XV Squadron, he trained as a QWI and in 1977 was appointed OC 16 Squadron. In 1984 he returned to Laarbruch as the station commander as the Tornado started to replace the two Buccaneer squadrons. After tours in the Operations Division in MOD, he was the commandant at Cranwell before being the senior air staff officer at HQ Strike Command. His final appointment was as Air Member for Personnel and AOC-in-C Personnel and Training Command. He was the controller of the RAF Benevolent Fund for five years.

David Herriot
After completing his training as a navigator, David Herriot started his 'Buccaneer Life' in 1971 as the first RAF-trained first-tour navigator to join the force. He completed four tours, all on different RAF squadrons (XV, 12, 237 OCU and 16) and flew almost 2,500 hours on the aircraft. He completed the QWI course and subsequently became the weapons leader on 16 Squadron. He later flew with 17 Squadron on Tornados and, later,

was the weapons standards and evaluation officer at RAF Brüggen. Apart from a tour as wing commander cadets at the RAF College, all his ground appointments were associated with air warfare training and operational requirements. He served as a RAF detachment commander in Italy during the Kosovo War. Before retiring in 2007 he held command of the Training Wing of the RAF's Air Warfare Centre at Cranwell. He is the founding member and honorary secretary of the Buccaneer Aircrew Association.

Bruce Chapple

After a tour as a flying instructor teaching Royal Naval students and a second on Canberra B(I)8s, Bruce Chapple joined the Buccaneer world in 1972 for a tour on 12 Squadron. In 1975 he was posted to 237 OCU where he became re-acquainted with some of the naval pilots he trained at No. 1 FTS! He served on 12, 208, and 216 Squadrons and 237 OCU, variously as weapons instructor, flying instructor, instrument rating instructor and display pilot until 1981. After three years on Tornados as weapons leader on 9 Squadron, he served on the Tornado Operational Evaluation Unit at Boscombe Down and as a unit test pilot at St Athan. When they discovered his age, and despite passing the annual medical for a twenty-five year old, he was asked to retire after nearly forty years of flying.

Mick Whybro

After navigator training Mick Whybro served on a Canberra ground-attack squadron, based in Cyprus from 1963-1966. He was one of the first RAF navigators to be attached to the Fleet Air Arm to fly the Buccaneer. His first tour was with 801 Squadron embarked in *Hermes* before becoming an instructor with 736 Squadron. After five years with the FAA, he returned to RAF service as a founder member of the newly-formed Buccaneer OCU as an instructor. He completed his five years of RAF Buccaneer flying with 12 Squadron as a squadron QWI, before moving to group headquarters as a Buccaneer exercise planner. Before leaving the RAF in 1994, he spent twelve years as a weapons leader on ground-attack Tornado squadrons in UK and Germany. After leaving the RAF he flew with FR Aviation as an electronic warfare officer for ten years.

Ted Hackett

Ted Hackett trained as a seaman officer at BRNC Dartmouth and was the navigation officer of a minesweeper during the Indonesian Confrontation. After training as a pilot he joined 801 Squadron in *Hermes* in 1969 and was later the AWI in 809 NAS before becoming the squadron's senior pilot in 1974 embarked in *Ark Royal*. Flying the Buccaneer, he accumulated 512 deck landings. He served in the Directorate of Naval Air Warfare in MOD before being appointed the first commander (air) of the light aircraft carrier *Illustrious* in 1982. He commanded the Type 22 destroyer HMS *Coventry* on her first commission in 1988 and was later captain of the Port of Portsmouth. After retiring in 1994 he was appointed an admiralty trials master in 1996, a post he held until 2007.

David Wilby

After training as a navigator and a tour on 16 Squadron at Laarbruch flying the Canberra B(I)8, David Wilby started an exchange tour with the Fleet Air Arm in August 1969 and served with 809 Squadron on the Buccaneer embarked in *Ark Royal*. At Honington he served on 12 Squadron, 237 OCU and 208 Squadron. He qualified as an electronic warfare officer (EWO) and as a QWI. Staff tours in Operational Requirements, MOD and HQ Strike Command were followed by a conversion to the Tornado and a tour as OC Operations Wing at Laarbruch. He was the station commander of RAF Finningley before completing a tour with the United Nations in Bosnia. He was the Director of Intelligence (Commitments) in MOD and, finally, Chief of Special Weapons in SHAPE; he retired in 2000. He is a founder member of the Buccaneer Blitz.

Gert Havenga

Gert Havenga qualified as a pilot in the SAAF in 1963 and flew Vampires, Impalas and Sabres before he converted to the Buccaneer in January 1975 when he joined 24 Squadron. He was appointed as the CO in December 1978 and flew operations over north South West Africa and southern Angola. Having just completed his 1,000th hour on the Buccaneer he left in January 1982 on promotion to take up a post as the senior operations officer at SAAF Strike Command. He was appointed as Director Operational Plans in the SAAF in the rank of brigadier general in 1990 and then seconded to the Secretary of Defence as Director Defence Policy in 1993. He retired in 1995.

Phil Wilkinson

After a National Service commission, served underground as a fighter controller, and a modern languages degree from Oxford, Phil Wilkinson was posted to a Canberra strike squadron in Germany. An exchange slot in Paris, Chipmunk instructing, and more Canberra time were the lead-in to his single exposure to the Buccaneer, from 1977 to 1981, as chief instructor at the OCU. After that it was both West and East – exchange duties at the USAF Air War College in Alabama, command of RAF Gatow as the Berlin Wall came down, and finally as the defence and air attaché in Moscow. After 1996 retirement, he has been active in ex-service welfare.

Sir Rob Wright

Rob Wright joined the RAF in 1966 and after a tour on Hunters in the Middle East he converted to the Phantom for a tour in Germany. He spent three years on exchange with the US Navy as a fighter weapons instructor on the Phantom. In 1979 he trained on the Buccaneer and was the deputy squadron commander on 208 Squadron at Honington for almost three years. After commanding 9 Squadron with Tornados he was the station commander of RAF Brüggen in Germany. He served in senior appointments at Strike Command and Personnel and Training Command followed by three years in a senior post on the Policy Staff at SHAPE in Mons before becoming the UKMILREP to NATO and the European Union in Brussels. He retired in 2006 when he became the controller of the RAF Benevolent Fund.

Gary Goebel

The son of a World War 2 fighter ace, Gary Goebel joined the USAF in 1966. He flew the F-105 with the 355th Tactical Fighter Wing completing fifty missions over North Vietnam and ninety over Laos. He converted to the F-111 in 1971 and returned to Vietnam and flew a further twenty missions. In 1973 he started an exchange tour with the RAF and spent almost three years on 12 Squadron. On return to the USAF, he became an instructor on the A-10. He left the USAF in 1986 and worked for the Boeing Aircraft Company as an industrial engineer. He now flies a RV-4 with the Blackjacks, a group of fellow enthusiasts.

Ken Alley

Ken Alley completed his pilot training in 1971 and was assigned to an F-111 squadron. He flew seventy-two missions over Vietnam, the majority in the north and was three times awarded the DFC. He spent three years on exchange with the RAF flying the Buccaneer, initially with 12 Squadron, before becoming an instructor on 237 OCU. On return to the USA in 1981 he was a flight commander on an F-16 squadron before being appointed the squadron commander of an OV-10 squadron seeing service in Panama, the Gulf War and in Korea. His final appointment was as the vice-wing commander at Shaw AFB, South Carolina equipped with the F-16. He retired in 1997.

Mike Rudd

Mike Rudd joined the RAF in 1969 and after receiving his wings was posted as a QFI on Jet Provosts. He joined the Buccaneer fraternity in 1975 and served with 809 NAS embarked in *Ark Royal*. He then joined 12 Squadron in June 1977 before a short tour with XV Squadron at Laarbruch. In 1982 he returned to 12 Squadron as a flight commander and flew over Beirut during the Lebanon crisis. He returned to XV Squadron in 1985 as the officer commanding on the Tornado GR 1 and later was the station commander of Valley. After serving with UNPROFOR in the Former Yugoslavia and as Air Commodore Flying Training at RAF Innsworth, he took up employment in 1997 with British Aerospace as the Director of Eurofighter Export.

Jerry Witts

Jerry Witts entered the RAF College Cranwell in 1968. Having flown the Vulcan B2 in Cyprus and the UK he completed crossover training to the Buccaneer serving two consecutive tours on 16 Squadron at Laarbruch, latterly as deputy squadron commander.

Staff appointments followed and, in 1989, he took command of 31 Squadron flying the Tornado GR1 at Brüggen. During the Gulf War he commanded the Tornado GR1/1A detachment at Dhahran, Saudi Arabia. He led many attack missions and was awarded the DSO. On promotion to group captain, he was the executive officer to the USAF NATO commander at Ramstein, Germany. He then commanded RAF Northolt. His final appointment was as the UK air attaché to the USA. He retired in 2005.

David Thompson
After completing his observer training, David Thompson's association with the Buccaneer began in 1964 and came to an end in December 1978 when he was serving as senior observer with 809 Squadron during *Ark Royal*'s final commission. He served on six Buccaneer squadrons operating from three carriers: *Eagle, Hermes* and *Ark Royal* (three times) amassing almost 2,500 hours on the Buccaneer including over 600 carrier arrests. He also completed the AWI course. He served on the staff of the Maritime Tactical School at HMS Dryad and at SACLANT in Norfolk, Virginia. Later he served in MOD as an assistant director in the Nuclear Policy Directorate. His final naval appointment was as the naval attaché in Paris. On retirement in 1999, he served for five years on the staff of the United Nations Headquarters in New York.

Peter Kirkpatrick
Peter Kirkpatrick trained as a navigator in 1980 and initially served with the SAAF transport force when he flew on fifty-seven combat sorties in the C-130 of 28 Squadron before converting to the Buccaneer in 1985 and joining 24 Squadron. He later became the squadron's weapons and tactical officer. During the late 1980s he completed twenty-seven combat sorties over South West Africa (later Namibia) and Angola. After completing an engineering degree he served on 2 Squadron as a navigation officer and systems engineer on the squadron's Cheetah D aircraft. Since leaving the SAAF in 1996, he has been the project and programme manager for various military radar systems.

Bill Cope
Bill Cope followed the RAF's fast-jet training route and was one of the first two RAF first-tour pilots to be posted to the Buccaneer. He flew with 12 Squadron in the maritime-attack role, and then with 16 Squadron in Germany in the overland strike/attack role. He served as a QFI at 4 FTS instructing on the Gnat and later the Hawk before returning to RAF Germany, and the Buccaneer, with XV and 16 Squadrons. Following Staff College he commanded 208 Squadron and was the Buccaneer detachment commander in the 1991 Gulf War when he flew twelve operations over Iraq. He was one of the most experienced Buccaneer pilots with 2,500 hours on the aircraft. He later served as chief of staff of the European Air Group and then deputy inspector of Flight Safety, RAF. He retired in 2002.

Benny Benson

After completing his pilot training in October 1986, Neil 'Benny' Benson's first tour was as a QFI on the Jet Provost at Cranwell. This was followed by a move to Lossiemouth to fly the Buccaneer and he joined 208 Squadron in October 1990. He was selected as the Buccaneer display pilot for the 1993 season and became the last of a long era of Buccaneer pilots to qualify as a Hunter captain. Following the retirement of the Buccaneer in 1994 he served as a Hawk QFI, tactics instructor and QWI on 74(F) Squadron at Valley before taking command of 19(F) Squadron training instructors on the Hawk. He left the RAF in 1999 and, after a successful civil flying career as an airline captain and manager, he joined the Civil Aviation Authority in 2012.

Rick Phillips

On completion of his first tour on the Canberra, Rick Phillips joined the Buccaneer world in 1973 and completed a three-year tour on XV Squadron at Laarbruch. This was followed by a tour with the FAA serving on 809 Squadron embarked in *Ark Royal* for her final commission. In 1979 he completed a short tour on 12 Squadron at Honington prior to the move to Lossiemouth, initially on 216 Squadron, and then back to 12 Squadron. After an exchange tour on the F-111 in the USA he returned to Lossiemouth in 1986 as a flight commander on 208 Squadron and he remained on the Maritime Buccaneer Wing at Lossiemouth until the Buccaneer was retired in 1994. He then spent seven years flying the Canberra PR9 prior to retiring from front-line service in 2002. He is still flying cadets in the RAF Tutor with 12 AEF at Leuchars.

Graham Smart

An experienced Canberra bomber pilot and QFI, Graham Smart began his long association with the Buccaneer in April 1965 on an exchange appointment with the FAA. He served on 800 Squadron and was embarked in *Eagle* before becoming an instructor on 736 Squadron. Returning to the RAF he was the Buccaneer staff officer at the Central Trials and Tactics Organisation before becoming the chief flying instructor on 237 OCU. Later he commanded 12 Squadron and, after serving on the British Defence Liaison Staff in Washington, he was the station commander at RAF Laarbruch. His final appointment was Director of Air Armament in the MOD and he retired from the RAF in April 1989.

ABBREVIATIONS

AAA	Anti-Aircraft Artillery	DFGA	Day Fighter Ground Attack
AAR	Air-to-Air Refuelling		
ADC	Aide de Camp	DH	Direct Hit
ADD	Airflow Direction Detector	DLP	Deck Landing Practice
		ECM	Electronic Counter Measure
ADSL	Auto Depressed Sight Line		
		EW	Electronic Warfare
AEO	Air Engineering Officer	FAA	Fleet Air Arm
AFB	Air Force Base	FAPLA	Angolan Forces
AFNORTH	Allied Forces Northern Europe	FONAC	Flag Officer Naval Air Command
AOA	Angle of Attack	FPB	Fast Patrol Boat
AOC	Air Officer Commanding	GCA	Ground Control Approach
APC	Armament Practice Camp	GIB	Guy in the Back
		GIF	Guy in the Front
ASI	Air Speed Indicator	GPI	Ground Position Indicator
ATAF	Allied Tactical Air Force		
ATC	Air Traffic Control	GPS	Global Positioning System
AWI	Air Warfare Instructor		
BAA	Buccaneer Aircrew Association	HARM	High-Speed Anti-Radar Missile
BAI	Buccaneer Attack Instructor	HAS	Hardened Aircraft Shelter
BLC	Boundary Layer Control	HE	High Explosive
CAG	Carrier Air Group	HF	High Frequency
CAP	Combat Air Patrol	ICAO	International Civil Aviation Organisation
CBU	Cluster Bomb Unit		
CCA	Carrier Controlled Approach	IFIS	Integrated Flight Instrumentation System
CFB	Canadian Forces Base		
CFI	Chief Flying Instructor	IFTU	Intensive Flying Trials Unit
CFS	Central Flying School		
CHAG	Chain Arrestor Gear	IGV	Inlet Guide Vanes
CTTO	Central Trials and Tactics Organisation	INS	Inertial Navigation System
DA	Display Authorisation	IRE	Instrument Rating Instructor

LGB	Laser-Guided Bomb	SADF	South African Defence Force
LOPRO	Low-level Probe		
LSO	Landing Sight Officer	SAM	Surface-to-Air Missile
MARTEL	Missile Anti-Radar Television	SARAH	Search and Rescue and Homing
MNF	Multi National Force	SENGO	Senior Engineering Officer
MPLA	People's Movement for the Liberation of Angola	SID	Standard Instrument Departure
MRR	Maritime Radar Reconnaissance	SOP	Standard Operating Procedure
MU	Maintenance Unit	SWAPO	South West Africa People's Organisation
NAS	Naval Air Squadron		
NOTAM	Notice to Airmen	SWP	Standard Warning Panel
OCU	Operational Conversion Unit	TBC	Tactical Bombing Competition
QFI	Qualified Flying Instructor	TFM	Tactical Fighter Meet
		TLP	Tactical Leadership Programme
QRA	Quick Reaction Alert		
QWI	Qualified Weapons Instructor	TOT	Time on Target
		TVAT	TV Airborne Trainer
RAAF	Royal Australian Air Force	TWU	Tactical Weapons Unit
		ULL	Ultra Low Level
RADALT	Radio Altimeter	UNITA	National Union for Total Independence of Angola
RAFG	RAF Germany		
RNAS	Royal Naval Air Station		
RP	Rocket Projectile	USAFE	United States Air Force Europe
RSA	Republic of South Africa		
RWR	Radar Warning Receiver	VFR	Visual Flight Rules
SAAF	South African Air Force	WP	Warsaw Pact

Index

RAF St Athan 53, 153, 158, 167, 190, 210
RAF St Mawgan 178, 190
RAF Valley 50, 63, 138, 143, 151, 212, 214
RAF Waddington 140, 150, 189
Rhodesia 28, 116
Riemvasmaak 118
RNAS Brawdy 32, 33, 98, 125, 133, 138, 143
RNAS Yeovilton 21, 27, 31, 40, 42, 46, 58, 150, 159, 160, 198, 204, 208
Roosie Roads 101
Rundu 171, 172
Sal 43, 44, 46
Scarborough Sholes 30
Schleswig Holstein 122, 163
Scilly Isles 32
Senanga 116
Shayka Mazar 182
Singapore 28, 30, 48, 69, 94, 98, 207
Skagerrak 93
Solva 98
South Africa 8, 11, 13, 40, 41, 103, 114, 169, 171, 201, 204, 206
St Omer 153
Stanley 145-147
Stranraer 153
Tain 13, 36, 54, 64, 66, 194
Theddlethorpe 68
Tsumeb 119
Vieques 101, 166
Wainfleet 68
Waterkloof 41, 44, 46, 114-117
Whale Island 26
Whidbey Island 166
Wideawake 44, 146

Personnel
Aaron, Tim 126
Ager, Stu 107, 110, 113
Aitken, Dick 145, 148, 178
Alley, Ken 121, 122, 125, 127, 133, 138, 141, 212

Allison, Sandy 114
Alsop, Andy 10
Anson, Ted 167, 203
Bairsto, Peter 85
Beaton, Al 63, 151, 209
Beaton, Harry 37, 38
Becker, Ken 55
Beddoe, Dave 159
Bee, Martin 150
Benson, Benny 185, 189, 214
Bergren, Scott 122, 125, 140, 141, 206
Berryman, Nick 153
Bickley, Mike 99
Binham, Pete 145, 192
Blissett, Mike 100
Botha, Koos 116
Bowerman, Graham 151
Bowyer, Mike 172, 175
Bradley, Tom 70
Brittain, David 99
Browne, Norman 149, 153, 180
Bucke, Peter 59
Burtenshaw, Tony 145
Bush, Mike 105, 110
Butler, Bill 91, 92
Buxton, Colin 153
Caldwell, Dennis 151
Callaghan, Mike 163, 164
Capewell, Cas 145
Carr, Roger 144
Chapple, Bruce 89-93, 121, 122, 210
Chase, Bert 166
Chown, Barry 85
Cleland-Smith, Dave 126
Cockerell, Tim 8, 47, 51, 59, 61
Coleman, John 17, 18
Collins, David 70, 74
Cope, Bill 63, 177-184, 213
Cosgrove, John 145
Cousins, David 70-79
Cox, Eddie 157
Cox, Frank 158
Cox, Robin 159, 160